SHADOW ON THE CHURCH

SHADOW ON THE CHURCH

Southwestern Evangelical Religion

and the Issue of Slavery,

1783–1860

DAVID T. BAILEY

CORNELL UNIVERSITY PRESS

ITHACA AND LONDON

Copyright © 1985 by Cornell University

All rights reserved. Except for brief quotations in a review, this book,
or parts thereof, must not be reproduced in any form without permission
in writing from the publisher. For information, address
Cornell University Press, 124 Roberts Place, Ithaca, New York 14850.

First published 1985 by Cornell University Press.
Published in the United Kingdom by
Cornell University Press Ltd., London.

International Standard Book Number 0-8014-1763-5
Library of Congress Catalog Card Number 84-45795
Printed in the United States of America
Librarians: Library of Congress cataloging information
appears on the last page of the book.

The paper in this book is acid-free and meets the guidelines for permanence
and durability of the Committee on Production Guidelines for
Book Longevity of the Council on Library Resources.

For Mary Cookingham

Contents

Preface

This book began (as so many do) in research on a slightly different topic. I wanted to try to understand the nature of the southern religious accommodation to slavery, and I planned to look at everything that churches and their clergymen had to say about the subject over two centuries. The more I read, the more I understood that the subject had twists and turns I had not imagined. And the final years, after the first northern states began to abolish slavery, became less and less clear to me the more I knew. As the subject began to break apart into time periods, it also began to separate geographically as I played with my notes and wondered what to make of them.

The following chapters in the history of religion and slavery, the product of my intellectual travels from one subject to another, focus on the postrevolutionary southern frontier as it gradually transformed itself into a region, the Old Southwest. Although many excellent historians have written about the region, it remains something of a mystery to the majority of American historians. I have attempted to make sense of the region as a developing culture, as rich and complex in its way as the Southeast or New England were in theirs. It is only in the context of this unique culture that the interplay between church and race makes sense. At its deepest level, this book is cultural history.

It is also necessarily the history of a changing religious mind. The Old Southwest is perhaps best known for the outburst of religious feeling known as the Great Revival. Ministers leading this revival were in fact the second important clerical generation, after the initial pioneer preachers. Following the awakening, a generation tried to cope with real or imagined declension, only to find itself replaced by another group, intent upon spreading benevolent reform west.

Against this background, I have attempted to portray one central story: the relation between churches in Kentucky, Tennessee, Mississippi, and Alabama and the enslaved black population everywhere around them. Some ministers, especially early in the history of the region, fought slavery with passion. Others gradually moved toward a proslavery stance. Some looked to reform slavery through evangelism, and still others avoided the subject as much as possible. This rich mixture of views ultimately yields some understanding about the matrix of society, religion, politics, ideas, and race.

Books are collaborative activities. This book would not have been written without the legion of librarians and archivists upon whom I have depended. Among these are the staffs at the Dargan-Carver Library, Baptist Sunday School Board of the Southern Baptist Convention, Nashville; Disciples of Christ Historical Society, Nashville; Library of Congress; Presbyterian Historical Society, Philadelphia; Tennessee State Library and Archives, Nashville; United Methodist Church, Commission on Archives, Lake Junaluska, North Carolina; and William Perkins Library, Duke University. In particular, I thank the staff of the Historical Foundation of the Presbyterian and Reform Churches, Montreat, North Carolina, and its remarkable librarian, Mary Lane, and the staff of the American Baptist Historical Society, Rochester, New York. I had the pleasure of dealing with the long-term director of the American Baptist Historical Society, Edward C. Starr, just before his retirement, and I treasure his sound advice. I want to make a special point of thanking the entire staff of the interlibrary loan office at the University of California, Berkeley. Each of these librarians made my work a great deal easier, and their skill is rare indeed. A diverse group of people gave help and inspiration in writing this book. Among these are David Gerber, Mark Goldsman, Samuel Haber, David Hollinger, Winthrop Jordan, Douglas Loeser, William McNeill, Lewis Perry, Edward Pitts, Dorothy Shannon,

Ida Spirawk, Mark Summers, and Konrad Von Moltke. Several scholars read portions of the manuscript at various stages. Kenneth M. Stampp and Albert J. Raboteau gave the early manuscript close and thoughtful readings. At Michigan State University, William Hixson read a more recent version and provided me with excellent general comments. Steven Botein also helped me rethink several aspects of my work. John Boles gave me some of his usual perceptive criticism, almost all of which went to improve the work. An anonymous reader for Cornell University Press may have given me the most thoughtful, most demanding criticism of all, always with high professional courtesy.

Quotations taken from the sources listed in the Bibliography are by permission of the Historical Commission of the Southern Baptist Convention, Nashville, Tennessee; the Historical Foundation of the Presbyterian and Reformed Churches, Inc., Montreat; the Disciples of Christ Historical Society, Nashville; and the Presbyterian Historical Society, Philadelphia.

I cannot easily explain how deep and lasting my debt is to Henry F. May. There is no part of my work which is not touched by his intelligence and his kindness. I trust he understands how important he was to this project and to me. I know of no other teacher who so powerfully influenced his students, both as scholars and as people. Finally, and of ultimate importance to me, I thank those closest. My parents have helped me every way they could, often at great sacrifice. My daughter, Elizabeth, has changed my life. My wife, Mary, has sustained it.

DAVID T. BAILEY

East Lansing, Michigan

SHADOW ON THE CHURCH

Introduction

American cultural historians have viewed the past as somehow unified, or at least dominated by one or two sets of cultural values. David B. Davis recently published an anthology of sources entitled *Antebellum American Culture*, which seems to portray an American culture dominated by New Englanders and slaveholding southerners. A few glimpses of life across the Appalachians intrude into Davis's vision, but he finds mostly rustic, unsophisticated folk, certainly no contenders for the high culture of the East. If one is concerned with high culture as might be understood in Europe, this vision is absolutely on target. It does, however, undervalue somewhat the little-known culture of the West.[1]

Indeed, ever since Perry Miller rescued the American mind from the Parringtonian model, intellectual historians who have worried about the development of American culture have tended to stress the importance of New England. Those with less genius than Miller often simply identified that region with the nation. Conferences on such subjects as the nature of midwestern literature and the definition of an "Old Southwest" have made few dents in this oversimplified view of our past. Of course, many intellectual historians have been employed or trained in New England, so it is little wonder that this distortion has developed.

1. See Davis, ed., *Antebellum American Culture* (Indianapolis, 1979). These comments are not intended to dismiss what is an excellent collection of sources.

Nevertheless, it is time, I think, to consider more of the parts that make up the puzzle of nineteenth-century American culture.[2]

In addition to New England, at least six other regional cultures existed in the period this book examines (1783–1860): New York City, Long Island, and the Hudson Valley; Philadelphia and the Delaware Valley; the eastern, relatively urban South; the New England West, including western New York, Vermont, and most of Ohio; the Old Northwest, the area settled mostly by northern European immigrants; and the Old Southwest. Each of these regions had special intellectual, social, and political characteristics that distinguished it from the others. More important, each region had its own style. The lines between the regions, however, were hardly clear. The towns and villages along the Ohio drew some elements from north and south of the river; the state of Delaware looked at once to Philadelphia and Baltimore for self-definition. Yet these imprecise divisions of the nation mattered. Inhabitants of the different regions saw America in separable ways. They represented divergent interests in Congress, and they also wrote occasional chauvinistic manifestos, such as Daniel Drake's *Remarks*

2. Among the most obvious of these works see Rush Walter, *The Mind of America, 1820-1860* (New York, 1975). Welter seems to assume that "Americanism" as a creed was the central fact of antebellum thought. For a more general argument along similar lines, see Robert Bellah, *Beyond Belief: Essays on Religion in a Post-traditional World* (New York, 1970), pp. 168-169; other seminal works of nineteenth-century intellectual history which downplay regional variation include John William Ward, *Andrew Jackson, Symbol for an Age* (New York 1955); Marvin Meyers, *The Jacksonian Persuasion* (Stanford, 1957); and Leo Marx, *The Machine in the Garden* (New York, 1964). A recent work on southern religion, Donald G. Mathews, *Religion in the Old South* (Chicago, 1977), although clearly intended to be a social rather than an intellectual history, ignores the distinction between the Southeast and the Southwest. Instead, almost all of the sources are drawn from the seaboard states. Mathews's work comes to conclusions which vary from mine on numerous issues, at least in part because his focus is on the Southeast. Two powerful works by intellectual historians have looked at the importance of regional *mentalité* in antebellum America. Perry Miller, *The Raven and the Whale* (New York, 1956), is an often ignored, occasionally inaccurate, but characteristically brilliant attempt to understand the life of the mind in New York and Baltimore. William R. Taylor, *Cavalier and Yankee: The Old South and American National Character* (New York, 1961), argues for the importance of mutual misunderstanding among American regions.

on the Importance of Promoting Literary and Social Concert in the Valley of the Mississippi.[3] The regions had their own literatures, their own newspapers and periodicals, and often their own religions. Just as the Disciples of Christ had a unique place in the history of the Old Southwest, so the Adventists and Mormons belong to the history of the New England West and Transcendentalism belongs to New England. Certainly, institutions crossed regional boundaries. The Democratic party of the Northwest, however, differed remarkably from the party in Philadelphia. Colleges in the Southwest had little in common with those in New England. Architecture, food, accents, customs, and much more differed so much from region to region that a full understanding of their variety remains well beyond our reach. As American historians increasingly appreciate the work of the *Annales* school, a better understanding of this diverse culture will surely emerge.[4]

Of course, the sum of regional cultures does not produce the complete picture of nineteenth-century American culture. Migration, still little understood today, tended to blur these distinctions. The legal system and the Constitution bound Americans together in countless ways. The American economic system, with the rise of new transportation network, interregional trade, and the complex and often interdependent monetary system, forced Americans together. Abolitionists and other reformers, enemies or advocates of Andrew Jackson, clergymen, developers, and numerous other groups crossed sectional lines to promote their causes. The story of American culture, then, is in large part the balance between parochialism and nationalism, between Americanism and regionalism.

3. Henry D. Shapiro and Zane L. Miller, eds., *Physician to the West: Selected Writings of Daniel Drake on Science and Society* (Lexington, 1970), pp. 230-247. Consider also, for example, the arguments traced out in Jesse T. Carpenter, *The South as a Conscious Minority, 1789-1861: A Study in Political Thought* (New York, 1930).

4. I thank James Kettner for pointing out Bernard Bailyn's amusing attack on some aspects of *annaliste* theorizing: Bailyn, "Review Article of Traian Stoianovich, "French Historical Method: The Annales Paradigm," *Journal of Economic History* 27 (1977); 1028-1034; for one interesting attempt at using the *mentalité* approach, see James A. Henretta, "Families and Farms: *Mentalité* in Pre-Industrial America," *William and Mary Quarterly* 35 (1978): 3-32.

Introduction

This book can only modestly begin to fill in some of the gaps in the historical record by looking closely at one region, the Old Southwest. This term seems to be relatively recent in origin, arising from regional historians' attempts to distinguish an early frontier from a more recent one. As is the case with all regions in America, the boundaries are far from rigid. For most of the period between the opening of the frontier after the Revolution until the beginning of the Civil War, however, the territories or states of Kentucky, Tennessee, Mississippi, and Alabama tended to identify themselves as part of a unit—the slaveholding West, the lower Mississippi West, the land of the revivals, the land of Jackson. It was a region with many internal differences, to be sure, the mountain folk often despising Tennessee Valley people with more passion than they could summon against northerners or easterners. The region also included at least some inhabitants of bordering states: western Virginians, Carolinians, Georgians, northeastern Louisianians, various settlers just across the Mississippi. A precise census of southwesterners, in short, would probably be impossible.

Because of this problem of definition, I am forced to reduce the implications of the term "culture" somewhat. Culture is one of a long list of virtually undefinable terms that historians insist upon using. It clearly encompasses more than the institutions and accomplishments of a given group of people. Anthropologists have stressed structure, ritual, custom, or psychological interdependence in their definitions, often at the expense of other elements. Any full analysis of a modern culture must include politics, social life, art, science and technology, religion, folklore, and economics. Unfortunately, only a few historians have attempted to include every one of these elements in analyzing a particular culture; most must confess ignorance, lack of patience, lack of time, or lack of interest. Instead of following the higher but more hazardous road toward complete cultural history, I intend to use a much less broad definition of culture in this book. The culture of a society can be seen as the way in which it perceives itself, the general themes it stresses, the mood or atmosphere that dominates life. For example, although slavery underwent some changes as an institution in the nineteenth century, of greater importance in this book is how attitudes toward slavery changed in the Old Southwest.

Though institutional changes did occur throughout the period I am investigating, these will receive less attention than the changes in the way major figures in the culture responded to them. In short, by "culture" I mean a complex of attitudes and beliefs rather than institutions and actions. In particular, this book examines some of the leaders of southwestern society, a group of self-conscious and frequently troubled ministers, who attempted to understand their place in a culture fundamentally at odds with many of their own most basic beliefs.

The Time

The great mistake made by historians of slavery is to assume that time made little difference to the institution and to attitudes toward it in the first half of the nineteenth century.[5] A few intellectual historians are drawn into the same trap. Perhaps this is but another effect of the increasing homogenization of our society. In the attempt to understand the relation of southwestern ministers to their culture and especially to slavery, such an assumption would produce serious misconceptions. The attitude of these clergymen toward religion, toward southwestern culture, and toward slavery underwent dramatic and often painful changes over the three-quarters of a century between the first permanent settlements and the Civil War. The ways in which succeeding generations of ministers developed their beliefs deserve close study.

Sociologists, demographers, and other social scientists have taken to discussing the nature and characteristics of "cohort groups," made up of people who experienced the same formative events and who therefore tended to take on similar, or at least comparable, traits. Historians, however, find the term "generations" more to their liking for it includes the defining element of cohort groups—a shared, shaping experience in the past—and it also

5. See Kenneth M. Stampp, *The Peculiar Institution: Slavery in the Antebellum South* (New York, 1956); and Eugene D. Genovese, *Roll, Jordan, Roll: The World the Slaveholders Made* (New York, 1974). Winthrop D. Jordan, *White over Black* (Chapel Hill, 1967), influenced this study in countless ways, and is much more conscious of the distinctions in slavery over time than were other historians.

assumes a relation to preceding and succeeding groups. Generations, that is, are *in* history in a way that cohort groups are not. For intellectual historians, the term "generations" usually has little to do with fathers and sons, at least biological ones. Rather, the crucial element is the succession of ideas, of world views, of *mentalités*. So a generation of philosophers, a generation of writers, or a generation of ministers could last for five years or thirty years as the dominant force in a culture. The same person could be a member of two or three generations of thinkers, changing ideas to fit the new flow of events. Two or three generations might overlap, or one might supersede the previous one. As we shall see, in the intellectual life of ministers in the Old Southwest, each of these traits of historical generations was exhibited.

In the churches of the Old Southwest, four intellectual generations of ministers appeared over the pre–Civil War years. The first, the ministers of the frontier, dominated religious life from the founding of settlements in Kentucky and Tennessee until most of the region became more or less "civilized." In Mississippi and Alabama, because of the later settlement of both territories, ministers who behaved much like the eighteenth-century clergy of Tennessee and Kentucky survived well into the second decade of the nineteenth century. Indeed, in pockets throughout the region, frontier ministers probably exist today. Such clergymen frequently preached their own brand of theology, related to a certain extent to the views of their denomination, but with the flexibility necessary in an uncertain and difficult situation. Almost all led demanding and often dangerous lives, threatened by the environment and by the frequently unruly frontiersmen they were trying to convert.

With the Great Revival of the early 1800s, a second generation of ministers succeeded the frontier clergy in dominating the life of southwestern churches. Such preachers remained in control of church governments until about the War of 1812, when the revival lost much of its energy and motivating spirit. This generation is particularly important because of its many bitter internal disputes about the meaning, importance, and control of the revival and, by implication, the future of the regional culture; the outcome of these debates would have critical importance for succeeding generations of ministers.

The third group, a silent generation, held sway from the end of the revival until about 1830 and in some areas remained in control until the Civil War. These ministers had little enthusiasm for any but the blandest and most perfunctory church activities, and many fought any and all innovations with great vigor. In a period of retrenchment and reevaluation for southwestern culture as a whole, these clergymen reflected their culture as much as they shaped it. And because of their conviction that debate and introspection had to be avoided at all costs, they remain the most difficult generation to define precisely.

In about 1830, a fourth generation of ministers began to dominate religious life in the Old Southwest. Often led by recent migrants from the East, these clergymen felt that modernization was a critical task of their ministries. Specifically, such clergy brought benevolent reform west, and in the years before the Civil War the southwestern churches began to bubble over with enthusiasm for temperance, missions, Bible societies, sabbatarianism, and all the other trappings of conservative reform that had been so popular in New England since the turn of the century. At the same time young and enthusiastic ministers tried to rebuild the prestige of southwestern churches through the creation of effective institutional structure, the publication of denominational journals, the reinstitution of interdenominational quarrels, and, occasionally, purges of old-style clergy.

This periodization is hardly revolutionary. It follows closely the traditional periods of postrevolutionary America: the Federalist period; the Jeffersonian era; the Era of Good Feelings; the Age of Jackson. Moreover, several intellectual historians have found at least comparable periods in the regions they studied, especially Whitney Cross in his work on New England West and Daniel Howe in his analysis of the Unitarian mind in New England. I have argued elsewhere that an analogous periodization helps in understanding the development of religion in the Southeast.[6] It is surprising and puzzling that historians of culture in the antebel-

6. Whitney Cross, *The Burned-Over District* (New York, 1950); Daniel W. Howe, *The Unitarian Conscience* (Cambridge, Mass., 1970); David Bailey, "From Frontier Pulpit to Regional Church: The Development of a Religious Mind in the Old Southwest," paper presented at the Chancellor's Symposium on Southern History, University of Mississippi, October 1979.

lum South have defined an unusually simple process of development, or more precisely, one of decline. Part of the historian's problem is, of course, that historical actors are seldom aware of their own place in intellectual and cultural generations. Moreover, southerners, with their concentration on the one subject that separated them most clearly from the rest of the nation, may seem upon cursory examination easier to understand than other contemporary Americans.

The Issue of Slavery

No other problem so troubled, confused, and damaged the United States in the nineteenth century as slavery. In half the nation it dominated life; in the other half it produced passionate reform movements and political arguments. Because slavery was a national problem, churches with a national structure attempted to establish rules regulating Christian interaction with the peculiar institution. The effect of those rules, and more important, the failure of the national churches to maintain consistent rules, meant that ministers in the Southwestern states of Kentucky, Tennessee, Mississippi, and Alabama, where slavery thrived, had somehow to confront the dilemma it posed within their own congregations. To be sure, it was not for most ministers a day-to-day obsession. Relatively few owned slaves, many preached in counties with small slave populations, and during periods of great religious upheaval, they could forget slavery for a while. Nevertheless, the issue always reappeared and forced ministers of the various generations to deal with this great anomaly in their lives.

Members of the first generation, the frontier ministers, appear mostly to have opposed slavery, but their disorganization and distance from political affairs impeded the emergence of any nascent antislavery movement. During the Great Revival, the second generation of ministers followed the lines of theological division in dealing with the growing institution. By avoiding direct confrontation with this as well as most other issues, the quietistic third generation allowed a hardening of implicitly pro-slavery beliefs to take place, and this attitude was reflected in the changed position of black members within individual churches. The fourth generation, in bringing benevolence west, soon discovered suspicion among many of their parishioners that an integral part of such reform was opposition to slavery. In what must be seen as a somewhat cynical decision, these benevolent reformers sacrificed the slaves for the sake of their other preoccupations, assuaging their consciences with missionary work among the slaves.[7]

The special characteristics of religion in the Old Southwest throughout the period 1783–1860 meant that attitudes concerning slavery differed dramatically from those held by ministers in the Southeast. First, because the West had far less formal learning, fewer traditions, and a less structured group of churches than did Virginia, the Carolinas, and Georgia, a variety (or confusion) of voices could be heard on the issue of slavery throughout the history of the region. Second, the liveliness and confusion of the frontier continued to characterize the Old Southwest in the antebellum period and consequently affected the tone of religious life. Revivals and controversies punctuated the life of southwestern churches with a regularity and intensity seldom known in the Southeast. As a result, discussions of slavery were, at certain points, far more extensive, more obviously divisive, and occasionally far more personal in style in the Southwest. Third, many of the leading southwestern ministers, especially before 1800 and after 1830, had migrated from the East; they therefore changed the western churches to mirror the religious life they had left.

---

7. On the guilt thesis, see Charles D. Sellers, ed., *The Southerner as American* (Chapel Hill, 1960); Kenneth M. Stampp. *The Imperiled Union* (New York, 1980), pp. 246-269. For an interpretation of the mission to the slaves which takes a much more sympathetic view of its proponents' arguments, see Mathews, *Religion in the Old South*, p. 149. The guilt thesis has been attacked in two general ways; one, put forth in Genovese, *Roll, Jordan, Roll*, argues that slaveholders were fundamentally unapologetic about their institution because of their unique, preindustrial culture. A second, more disturbing interpretation is the psychological one presented by Winthrop Jordan, *White over Black*, pp. 581-582. Jordan suggests that sexuality, race pride, and other social and psychological factors were transformed by southerners into a positive justification of slavery. Jordan's view approaches a sense of original sin, and it is reminiscent of the feelings of those abolitionists analyzed in Lewis Perry, *Radical Abolition: Anarchy and the Government of God in Antislavery Thought* (Ithaca, 1973).

While the nature of the churches in the seaboard South continued to change, the Southwest began to model its religious life on discarded or unfashionable eastern concepts, so the antislavery elements of eighteenth-century southern thought lingered longer in the West than in the East. Moreover, the later migrants, feeling a need to appeal to as broad a constituency as possible, may have fought more vigorously in favor of slavery than was necessary in the region. Fourth, for a variety of reasons, including the distance between settlements, the difficulty of western life, and the remarkable ministers such a life attracted, religion seems to have mattered more in the Southwest than in the seaboard South. The relatively complaisant Episcopal church, for example, never made many inroads in the Old Southwest. Instead, the story of southwestern religion is that of the evangelical denominations at their most enthusiastic and powerful. It was, in part, this influence that made them concentrate so frequently and so intensely upon the great issue troubling their region, slavery.

This story is ultimately painful and occasionally tragic. Most of the ministers I will discuss were, by any standards, basically decent, thoughtful, and deeply committed men. Faced with a deep and pervasive problem in their society, they, as many ministers before and since, failed to find a solution which they felt was morally proper, mutually satisfying, and politically shrewd.[8] Their tragedy was their inability to deal with the peculiar institution consistently in any of these ways. Characterized by compromise and indecision, the story of the relationship between these churches and slavery is occasionally ugly and always very sad.

---

8. Consider the ministers analyzed in John R. Bodo, *The Protestant Clergy and Public Issues, 1812-1848* (Princeton, 1954); Henry F. May, *Protestant Churches in Industrial America* (New York, 1949); Donald B. Meyer, *The Protestant Search of Political Realism, 1919-1941* (Berkeley, 1960). See also Anne Loveland, *Southern Evangelicals and the Social Order, 1800-1860* (Baton Rouge, 1980). Two recent studies of early antislavery in the churches suggest some of the roots of southwestern thought on the subject: James D. Essig, *The Bonds of Wickedness: American Evangelicals against Slavery, 1700–1808* (Philadelphia, 1982) especially pp. 140-157; and Lester B. Sherer, *Slavery and the Churches in Early America, 1619-1819* (Grand Rapids, 1975).

PART ONE

THE PIONEER
GENERATION

Daniel and Squire Boone typified the contrasting interests, desires, and dreams of immigrants to the eighteenth-century Southwest. Daniel was boisterous and destructive, but he was also adventurous and, no doubt, courageous in his battles over the "dark and bloody ground." The West was his playground, and his intimacy with nature would help fuel, in a way he probably would not have understood, the American romantic vision half a century later. His brother Squire was a man of less commanding presence, whose central concern was not to learn from the West but to build a successful colony in the transappalachian southern frontier. He was orderly, careful, and when necessary ruthless. He was also a Baptist preacher.[1]

White settlers with characteristics of both the Boones came to Kentucky and Tennessee in the eighteenth century. The more rambunctious ones became legendary. Visitors to the West reported

---

1. There are countless works about Daniel Boone. I found the most helpful to be S. H. Bogart, *Daniel Boone and the Hunters of Kentucky* (Auburn, N.Y., 1854); Timothy Flint, *Biographical Memoir of Daniel Boone, the First Settler of Kentucky, Interspersed with Incidents in the Early Annals of the Country* (1835; reprint, New Haven, 1967); the single best work on Squire Boone is in Hazel Spraker, *The Boone Family* (Rutland, Vt., 1922), pp. 72-82; on another member of Boone's group, see Charles G. Talbert, *Benjamin Logan: Kentucky Frontiersman* (Lexington, 1962).

numerous knife fights, wild, drunken brawls, and general rowdyism. Many of the citizens paid no regard to the Sabbath or churchly affairs; indeed, some sections of the West became havens for criminals and renegades. One minister remembered that "murderers, horse thieves, highway robbers, and counterfeiters fled" to Logan County, Kentucky, "until they combined and actually formed a majority."[2]

Other settlers concerned themselves with creating a structured society in the West. Among these, a few gentlemen from Maryland and Virginia, such as John Breckinridge, read Thomas Paine, professed deism, and wanted to bring a genteel culture to the frontier. This "enlightened" elite never expanded far outside Lexington, but it served to remind more conservative evangelical members of southwestern society of the dangers of culture and deism.

The southwestern settlers contrasted sharply with migrants from New England who settled the frontier in New York, Pennsylvania, and eastern Ohio. Whereas the Southwest began and remained primarily rural, the future "burned-over district" settlers established town-centered communities, strong churches, newspapers, and a much more orderly, secure society. The difference between the two frontiers reflects the vast gap in culture between New England, with its complex social structure and institutions, and the Southeast, which depended more on individuals.

The mode of settlement in the Southwest explains, to some extent, the failure of the small elite in the few towns of the region to establish a genteel culture. To be sure, they tried. John Bradford's bookstore offered for sale works by David Hume, Constantine Volney, and Jonathan Edwards. Although historians have overstated his western audience, Thomas Paine had many readers in Kentucky. In Lexington, the late eighteenth-century mania for clubs expressed itself in the organization of a Democratic society, which enthusiastically supported the French Revolution. The gentlemen of the West even founded a proindustrial organization,

2. Peter Cartwright, *Autobiography* (New York, 1856), p. 24; see also Alexander Finley, *The History of Russellville and Logan County, Kentucky*, 2 vols. (Russellville, 1878), 1:44-45 and 2:8; George M. Chinn, *Kentucky Settlement and Statehood, 1750-1800* (Frankfort, 1875), p. 355.

the Kentucky Society for the Encouragement of Manufacturers."[3] Yet these gentlemen proved much less influential than men of humbler backgrounds: Protestant clergymen. This frontier needed local figures of moral authority who could speak for the hardworking, peaceful settlers. Few people lived in towns, so the meetings held by ministers served as central features of what traditional culture the frontier could muster. Clergy, in short, provided a moral center for western culture.

The clergymen of eighteenth-century Kentucky and Tennessee varied enormously in age, health, training, piety, and enthusiasm. John Lythe, an Anglican, probably conducted the first service in the region, yet his church was never influential in the religious life of the region. Instead, the Southwest was fallow ground for the three evangelical denominations: Baptists, Methodists, and Presbyterians. Ministers of these denominations served as the first generation of southwestern clergymen, the pioneers. As a group, they shared several demographic characteristics.[4]

Of the southwestern ministers who served churches there between the beginning of settlement and the turn of the century 97.7 percent were migrants from the East. A majority (56.9 percent) came from Virginia, and 80.1 percent came from southern states. Of the northerners, 9.4 percent moved to the Southwest from Pennsylvania, 0.6 percent from New York, 2.9 percent from New Jersey, and 1.3 percent from New England; 5.9 percent came from foreign countries, mostly Great Britain. The first generation of ministers, then, was primarily southern in origin, with a smattering of Scotch-Irish from Pennsylvania.

An even more specific sense of the migration pattern of Virginia-born ministers can be gleaned from the various biographical dictionaries of the clergy. Of the Virginia ministers who moved west before 1800, 25 percent came from coastal or tidewater counties, 25 percent from the piedmont, 40 percent from the Blue Ridge or Shenandoah Valley, 7.5 percent from southern counties

3. See Niels Sonne, *Liberal Kentucky, 1780-1828* (New York, 1939); Arthur K. Moore, *The Frontier Mind: A Cultural Analysis of the Kentucky Frontiersman* (Lexington, 1957).

4. For demographic characteristics and other statistics on ministers, see the Appendix for an explanation of sources and methodology.

bordering on North Carolina, and the remaining 2.5 percent from the Appalachians. Thus the majority came from parts of Virginia which were more recently and more sparsely settled and, importantly, from parts of Virginia with relatively few slaves.

Once in the West, the pioneer generation of ministers was somewhat less mobile than all ministers who moved west before the Civil War (see Table 1).

Table 1. Mobility of pioneer ministers and all migrant ministers, 1783–1860 (in percent)

	Pioneer ministers	All ministers
Stayed in one state	68	58.7
Lived in two states	28	29
Lived in three states	4	12.3

This relative lack of mobility once in the West certainly reflects the pioneer conditions, both in the remarkable and well-chronicled difficulties of frontier transportation and in the shortage of ministers who could move from one pulpit to another.

Part of the reason for the relative lack of mobility of these ministers once they reached the west may well have been their age (see Table 2).

Table 2. Age ministers began careers (in percent)

	Age pioneers began western ministry	Age all western ministers began careers
Under 25	27.4	36.2
25–30	28.6	27.8
Over 30	44	36

These ministers were substantially more mature than later western ministers in part because almost all were migrants who had established their careers in the East. They also appear to have been relatively robust and healthy; fully 92 percent lived past the age of fifty, and a majority (57 percent) were over seventh when they died.

Western ministers of the pioneer generation had received much less education than had the entire group of ministers who preached in the region before 1860. Of the pioneer ministers 8.8 percent had attended college, as opposed to 15.9 percent of all southwestern ministers. Only 3.4 percent enthusiastically supported education, as teachers of fund-raisers, as opposed to 9.6 percent of all southwestern preachers. In this way they reflected their origins in sections of the country without many colleges.

As a group, then, the pioneers came primarily from the South, particularly its less densely settled parts. They were on average older and lived longer than all western ministers. They were less educated than later western ministers would be. In short, they stood as a demographically unique cohort in the history of religion in the region.

CHAPTER 1

Pioneers and Slavery

The census of 1790 placed the number of slaves in Kentucky and Tennessee at 15,847. Not surprisingly, they made up only about 15 percent of the population, for the area had not yet developed much beyond a subsistence economy, and the need for slaves was consequently limited. In the more densely settled central area, the percentage of slaves was somewhat higher.[1] The experience of slaves in the early West will probably never be known, for even material comparable to that written by slaves in the nineteenth century is missing in the literature of the eighteenth-century Southwest. A few scattered accounts by whites mention slaves, often citing some heroic act of a black man to save or protect his master. In one such story, a black man and his owner had been attacked by Indians while on a hunting trip; together they wandered for twenty hours until they found a way back to the settlement.[2]

Certainly slaves had a different life on the frontier than in Virginia and North Carolina. Few plantations existed in the eighteenth-century Southwest, and of these few masters owned farms with fifteen to twenty slaves, such as predominated in Virginia. Most often, master and slave worked together clearing land and planting, building houses, barns, fences, and furniture.

1. U.S. Bureau of the Census, *Negro Population, 1790-1915* (Washington, 1918), pp. 45, 47.
2. W. W. Clayton, *History of Davidson County, Tennessee, with Illustrations and Biographical Sketches of Its Prominent Men and Pioneers* (Nashville, 1971), p. 26; see also J. Winston Coleman, *Slavery Times in Kentucky* (Chapel Hill, 1940), pp. 6-12.

Sometimes a family of slaves lived with the master's family in a primitive home; a separate quarter for slaves was considered a wasteful luxury in this rough environment. Of course, any hardships suffered by whites were more than passed on to their chattel. Although rarely sadistic, masters in this period often had little for themselves and spared only meager supplies for their slaves. The treatment, one man recalled, "was severe, as to food, clothing, punishment and required service," compared to the situation fifty years later.[3]

Only a very few slaveholding ministers came west before 1800. Among these, Baptists predominated. The "Travelling Church," an entire community of Virginia Baptists who traveled west en masse, included several slaves among its six hundred members; one of these, Pastor Lewis Craig's slave "Uncle Peter," later took the name "Old Captain" and became the leading black preacher in the West.[4] Few Presbyterian ministers owned slaves. One, John Rankin, had earned a great deal of money in the East, and a friend had pressed him for a loan. He "at length offered me a colored boy in security of money." Rankin reluctantly accepted, and when the friend needed more capital, Rankin "became a slaveholder; the idea did not sit well on my mind, the more lightly while he was a minor, but insupportable when he arose to maturity."[5] I have found no evidence linking a Methodist clergyman of this period to slavery, hardly surprising in that most Methodist preachers were itinerants, and lacking wife, children, or home, they were unlikely to have a slave.

Indeed, it is no coincidence that Baptists more frequently owned slaves than did members of the other churches. Their finances were somewhat more secure than those of Methodist preachers, and they settled whereas Methodists rode the circuits. Presbyterians, who were better educated, were likely to be aware of the arguments concerning the evils of slavery and thus to

3. Daniel Drake, *Pioneer Life in Kentucky* (Cincinnati, 1870), p. 206,

4. George Ranck, *The Travelling Church: An Account of the Baptist Exodus from Virginia to Kentucky in 1871 under the Leadership of Rev. Lewis Craig and Capt. William Ellis* (Louisville, 1891), pp. 13, 22.

5. John Rankin, "Autobiography" (typed copy), p. 7, Historical Foundation of the Presbyterian Church, Montreat, N.C. (hereafter cited as HFPC).

eschew slaveholding. Baptists, moreover, shared more of the typical migrant experience than did the Presbyterians, and the settlers in the Southwest showed no particular animosity to the peculiar institution. Presbyterian ministers were much more town-oriented, with most of their churches in such settlements as Danville or Nashville, where "modern" ideas were heard regularly. In contrast, Baptists usually moved from a eastern rural community to a similar settlement across the mountains. It was somewhat easier, therefore, for Presbyterians to condemn slavery; for the Baptists, who lived and worked in the backwoods, sometimes in counties with large numbers of slaves, such proclamations against slavery required remarkable courage.

Pioneer Baptists and Slavery

Baptist attitudes toward slavery deserve primary emphasis because they formed the largest denomination in the Southwest during the eighteenth century, with eighty-eight ministers in the area by 1792 and a claimed membership of 4,373, or somewhat less than 5 percent of the total population. With eighty-four churches, the Southwest contained more than 8 percent of the Baptist congregations in the United States.[6]

Among southwestern Baptists, attitudes on slavery revealed little direct, formal influence by Enlightenment ideas. The Enlightenment, with all its controversies and confusions, rarely appears in the records of these eighteenth-century Baptists, except for their occasional attacks upon the deistical menace.[7] Most

6. *American Baptist Register* (New York, 1856), p. 24; see also Clayton, *History of Davidson County*, p. 317; William Frederick Kendall, A History of the Tennessee Baptist Convention (Brentwood, Tenn., 1974), p. 22; Henry Clay Smith, *Outline History of the Wilderness of Kentucky and Religious Movements of the Early Settlers of Our Country and the Church History of the North Middletown Community* (Paris, Ky., [1923], pp. 43-44.

7. James Garrard is an exception to this statement. An early leader of the Baptist in Kentucky, Garrard became governor of the state of 1796. He soon shocked his fellow ministers by becoming a Unitarian. Not enough has been written about this fascinating character.

moved from the rustic life of western Virginia, Maryland, or North Carolina to the often brutal existence of the frontier. Many Baptist preachers, lacking even the most rudimentary formal education, found reading their Bibles a struggle. Those who could be considered at all well-educated invariably began their careers in a different denomination. John Gano, for example, was raised in a respectable New Jersey household and until his twenties expected to go to Princeton and become a Presbyterian clergyman. He took his education but then joined the Baptist church, for which he became an important preacher in New York. Only in his sixties did he head west, and he stayed close to what cultural and intellectual life of an eastern nature he could find, at that point pretty much restricted to Lexington and Frankfort.

The career of William Hickman reflected more closely the usual experience of southwestern Baptist clergymen. Raised by his grandmother in King and Queen County, Virginia, he later recalled that his "chance of learning was very small, having little time to go to school; I could read but little, and barely write any." At age fourteen he was sent out to a trade, and he began to preach only after a long and difficult conversion. When Hickman moved to Kentucky in 1784 at the age of thirty-seven, he founded churches in barely settled regions and worked the land alongside members of his congregations. He led the building of the South Elkhorn church "the first that was built on the north side of the Kentucky River."[8] Although articulate and intelligent, Hickman was, along with most of his brother clergy in the Baptist church, more a man of action than a scholar or theologian.

In many ways, the most resolute of the Baptist opponents of slavery represented in his thought the general characteristics of his fellow Baptist ministers. David Barrow, born in Brunswick County, Virginia, in 1753, just on the edge of settled Virginia of the day, was the son of a poor farmer who could afford little education for his children. By age 19, Barrow had joined the Baptist church and almost immediately became an itinerant preacher, traveling through Virginia and North Carolina preaching the

8. William Hickman, "A Short Account of My Life and Travels" (typed copy), pp. 3, 15, Southern Baptist Theological Seminary, Louisville, Ky.

Regular Baptist doctrines and attempting to promote mild and controlled revivals in contrast to the more experimental revivals of the Separates. Barrow married well, and gradually he acquired slaves and some wealth. After the Revolution, he even entered politics, becoming the magistrate for his county. Gradually, however, Barrow began to believe that slaveholding was incompatible with the ideas of liberty he had learned during the war, and he finally freed his own slaves. Without clearly recognizing their origins, he had been influenced by vague Enlightenment notions. On Barrow's first journey to Kentucky, he often discussed slavery in his journal, from which one can deduce some of his thought processes. He felt that slavery "degraded the human race and is fraught with evils of almost every description; whether political, natural or moral; absolutely inconsistent with every idea of republicanism as well as humanity and Christianity." This passage is most interesting for its failure to clarify Barrow's theological judgments. The passing reference to Christianity seems an afterthought. Instead, the stress upon the ideas of republicanism suggests that Barrow, like most of his western Baptist brethren, hoped to make moral points through practical connections. The passage contains at least a dim echo of the commonwealthmen's reservations about slavery, reaching Barrow either directly or indirectly through a process of diffusion.[9]

Emphasizing the concrete rather than strictly theological destructiveness of slavery, Barrow provided a striking argument by way of analogy in his discussion of Indian attacks upon white settlements. Unlike most other early westerners, Barrow was impressed by the few Indians he had met, especially "that these very heathen profess as good principles and exhibit in their general conduct, as much honesty and humanity as those very good Christians who deride them." He concluded that the fabled cruelty of Indians had in large measure been produced by the expansion of white society into the frontier: "Many advantages have been taken of them repeatedly in the purchase of lands. And if they have scalped and . . . tortured prisoners they have been hired and encouraged thereto by the Christian party or another."

9. David Barrow, "Diary" (typed copy), p. 3, Southern Baptist Theological Seminary.

The worst cruelties committed by the Indians, Barrow believed, resulted from imitation of the ordinary relations between masters and their slaves: "If the Indians whip and cruelly treat the whites, it is no more than the whites serve the blacks. If the Indians force people who fall into their hands, to break the bonds of wedlock, it is no worse than our people serve the negroes." At the center of the problem, Barrow later wrote, was thoroughgoing hypocrisy; he found many in the West who were "extremely clever and orthodox, very clear in theory concerning the rights of man, and what are commonly called good republicans; but what is worse than all this, they mostly miss it in practice, for few have freed their slaves."[10] Again, a concentration upon practice, or works, has crept into the thought of an otherwise orthodox, theologically conservative Baptist.

Barrow's concentration throughout his journal remained firmly fixed upon the practices rather than the beliefs of his western Christians. He discussed the treatment of slaves, for example, which would continue to trouble western ministers up to the Civil War. He attacked the failure of masters to protect marriage and the family, a shortcoming of the peculiar institution which would appear in the writing of ministers time and again. But Barrow failed to investigate the underlying religious issues, even in a journal filled with religious meditations and concerns. It appears that the Baptists, living and working side by side with members of their congregations, wished to compartmentalize their theology, separating it from practical Christianity and proper behavior. In this sense, Barrow most clearly reflects the need of frontier ministers to maintain the interests of their church, avoiding the falling away of members so prevalent in the West, by stressing practice over theory.

Eighteenth-century southwestern Baptists in general maintained a simplified form of orthodoxy, especially stressing its determinism. They mostly tended to follow the orderly Regular Baptist program rather than the looser, wilder practices of the Separates, but careful explications of dogma were extremely rare. Lewis Craig, who had been indicted in prerevolutionary Virginia for "preaching

10. Ibid., pp. 10, 11, 20.

35

the gospel contrary to law," took over the South Elkhorn church from William Hickman. A perceptive colleague noted that Craig seldom pursued complex doctrinal argument; rather, his "orthodoxy mainly lay in salvation through Christ by unmerited grace."[11] These Baptist ministers also emphasized a Calvinist doctrine of original sin. Related to their Calvinism was their emphasis upon baptizing only the converted. Beyond those three cornerstones, however, pioneer Baptists forced little doctrine upon their congregations. Diverging from the tendency in Virginia and the Carolinas, few Baptist churches required evidence of conversion experiences from their communicants, perhaps from fear that such a mandate would deplete even further the scant membership of the frontier churches.

Their lack of formal education and their failure to write detailed theological tracts did not mean that these Baptist ministers were fools or yokels. On the contrary, a great many had impressive minds, and ministers invariably debated theological matters at their annual meetings. All surviving association records report debates on the validity of the Philadelphia Confession of Faith; differences in emphasis on a number of issues continued to arise between Separates and Regulars. As in their sermons, however, western ministers tended to discuss among one another issues of practical religion rather than arcane theological matters. In part this concentration was a result of the nature of the congregations, among which ministers could expect little patience with complex theological hairsplitting. Moreover, few preachers commanded the knowledge required to analyze many of the most abstruse aspects of Calvinist/orthodox theology, nor did they have the books that raised such matters. As a consequence, professional discussion tended to focus upon questions that most clearly pressed upon the nerves and consciousness of western preachers. In 1793, for example, the Elkhorn Association issued a circular letter on "the subject of practical religion." The author insisted that although Baptist ministers must base all their sermons on a faith in election

11. See John Taylor, *A History of Ten Baptist Churches, of which the Author Has Been Alternatively a Member* (Frankfort, 1823), p. 44; see also Drake, *Pioneer Life,* p. 194.

and in free grace, they must give most of their attention to providing an example of proper Christian living toward which all western laymen might aspire: "By your humble walk and pious conversation, you may recommend the Gospel of Christ and the religion of Jesus to all your acquaintance." The author of the letter ended with the hope that such piety would result in a revival of religious sentiment, which would allow a greater concentration upon doctrinal detail. His message for the present came through clearly, however; the nature of proper religious conduct was, in the short run, the most important subject for weekly sermons.[12]

If the general disinterest in theology among pioneer Baptists helps explain Barrow's practical antislavery, he may also have been influenced by his experiences in Virginia's struggle for freedom of religion. Because evangelicals had demanded complete freedom of activity in the new state, many, including Barrow, entered politics. Unable to tolerate state interference in religious affairs, they entered into an alliance with the often deistic intellectual leadership of the state in order to protect their rights to proselytize. Yet the evangelicals did not feel that the sword cut both ways. Restrictions upon government interference in church matters did not imply restrictions upon church interference in government matters. So Baptists appealed to the Virginia government for "laws of Morality," allying themselves with the other evangelical denominations.[13]

The alliance obviously restricted the use of specific denominational dogma in the promotion of "Christian" legislation. Instead, defense of moral legislation had to be made on relatively bland and general principles, all of which tended to limit infighting among the evangelical denominations. When they moved west, Barrow and other Baptists retained some of the same sense of a united front, especially in opposition, ironically, to deists, who had helped bring about religious freedom in Virginia. In fact, the

12. Minutes, Elkhorn Baptist Association, Tennessee (1793), Baptist Historical Society, Rochester, N.Y. (hereafter cited as BHS).

13. Thomas E. Buckley, *Church and State in Revolutionary Virginia*, 1776-1789 (Charlottesville, 1977), pp. 180-182. For a broad, if somewhat overstated, interpretation of the Separates, see Rhys Isaac, *The Transformation of Virginia*, *1740-1790* (Chapel Hill, 1982), pp. 161-177.

Southwest in the eighteenth century was relatively free of religious bickering. Tensions between denominations flared into mean accusations at times; one pioneer recalled that the arrival of the first Methodists into Kentucky led some "of the old Baptists and Presbyterians [to] say, 'the false prophets are come.' "[14] Yet Green Hill, a Methodist circuit rider, recorded in his journal that he preached to a congregation at a Mr. Winters's and that there were "three Baptist and one Presbyterian preacher present, who all spoke in turn, after I had preached, but without controversy and parted very affectionately."[15]

Such a united front meant that Barrow tended to stress general ethics, morality, and Christianity in his attack upon the great social and moral problem of the West, and he avoided specific theological matters almost by second nature. Moreover, the special status of the Baptist minister strongly encouraged the retention of the eastern view of a united front. Methodists, traveling upon circuits, and Presbyterians, found mostly in the more urban centers, saw less of the specific life of the backwoods Southwest. Baptists, living amid the settlers, had to maintain the united front because they realized that citizens of their county might not agree with the specifics of Christian practice they wished to promote. Presbyterians and Methodists could restrict their dealings in life to members of their own churches; Baptist ministers had no such luxury.

Pioneer Methodists and Slavery

Second to Baptists in membership and influence, Methodists were much more carefully regimented by the hierarchy in expressing their views on social issues. The new denomination had begun its work in the United States precisely at the time when the western territories became available for settlement. Francis Clack, an unordained preacher known more for his farming than his learning, organized the first Methodist society in Kentucky in 1783, the

14. Lewis Garrett, *Recollections of the West*, 2 vols. (Nashville, 1834), 1:307.
15. John McFerrin, *History of Methodism in Tennessee*, 3 vols. (Nashville, 1869-73), 1:307.

year before the Christmas Conference oficially created the new denomination. In 1786, the Baltimore Conference established the Kentucky circuit, with two preachers appointed to ride through the wilderness. Not until 1790, when Francis Asbury, the spiritual leader of the new Methodist Episcopal church, came to organize the Western Conference at Masterson's Station, Kentucky, did Methodism become an important feature of southwestern religion; Asbury provided the church with a measure of respectability, a sense of mission, and, most important, clergymen.[16]

Bishop Asbury's position on slavery had become increasingly complicated during the Revolution as he had learned more about the needs of the untended flock in the new nation. He had become particularly careful in his public statements about social issues after his virtual exile to Delaware during the early fighting, and the first antislavery rule passed by a conference of Methodist preachers, held in Baltimore in 1780, called for religious instruction of the slaves and for the use of moral pressure by ministers to produce gradual emancipation. Many of Asbury's ministers were more enthusiastic in pressing antislavery demands than he, and probably at the urging of Thomas Coke, one of John Wesley's ambassadors to the American church, the Christmas Conference called for no-participation in the institution of slavery by all members of the church. Asbury's moral qualms about slavery should never be understated, but his practical concerns (and perhaps his struggle for control of the new denomination) made him somewhat more cautious in practice. His journals and letters are replete with condemnations of the peculiar institution, but at the same time he expressed doubts as to whether abolition could be effected in the seaboard states. Significantly, he appears to have relaxed his guard somewhat in his journeys to the Southwest, where he exercised virtually full control over the denomination. When in Tennessee, for example, Asbury spoke freely against slaveholding, often to an unreceptive audience. Even in the transappalachian South, however, his antislavery pronouncements remained infrequent; for Asbury, building a base of support for the denomination remained the primary task, and moral rejuvenation

16. W. E. Arnold, *A History of Methodism in Kentucky* (n.p., 1935), p. 24.

would follow, not precede, the secure establishment of Methodism throughout the new nation.[17]

Asbury's caution did not produce precisely the result he might have hoped for; his few antislavery comments gave Methodists in the Southwest a reputation of opposing slavery, however accurate that reputation might have been. The ministers Asbury sent west left few records, however, and their precise views on any issue remain clouded in vague allusions. At best, these ministers achieved the same level of formal education as their Baptist counterparts. Migrating west from a somewhat broader territory than their brother clergy (several came from New England, for example), they nevertheless displayed little direct familiarity with the details of the Enlightenment. William McKendree, eventually the bishop most interested in the Southwest, was born in King William County, Virginia, received a rudimentary education in country schools, fought in the Revolution, and soon thereafter began preacing on the Cumberland circuit.[18] His friend James O'Kelly was imbued with Commonwealth ideas of republicanism and led a revolt against the Methodist episcopacy. McKendree certainly gained from his friend's familiarity with republican notions, and in the 1790s O'Kelly told him that the Methodists could create "a republican, no slavery, glorious Church."[19] But McKendree turned his back on the O'Kelly rebellion and instead became one of the closest advisers to Bishop Asbury; in 1800 McKendree went west as presiding elder. The influence of the O'Kelly movement on his thought should not be overstated. McKendree had imbibed some vague Commonwealth ideas of republicanism, to be sure; but the concepts of the Enlightenment were much more subtle and complex than he seems to have understood. Arguments from John Locke, Charles Montesquieu, and Thomas Gordon held little place in even the best-informed mind among pioneer Methodist preachers. Again, as with Baptist ministers, these were not igno-

17. Elmer T. Clark, ed., *The Journal and Letters of Francis Asbury*, 3 vols. (Nashville, 1958), 1:712, 2:151; see also Donald Mathews, *Slavery and Methodism* (Princeton, 1965), pp. 17-18.

18. Robert Paine, *Life and Times of William McKendree, Bishop of the Methodist Episcopal Church*, 2 vols. (Nashville, 1869-70).

19. Ibid., p. 139; see also Ancel Bassett, *A Concise History of the Methodist Protestant Church* (Pittsburgh, 1877), p. 323.

rant men; rather, they restricted their interests to their religion and concentrated their intellects upon the immediate needs of the laity.

Out of this group of Methodist ministers, the one who left the clearest record of his antislavery views was John Ray. Little given to sophisticated "modern" thinking, Ray adopted an aggressive style and maintained his coarse ways. When, for example, he was asked by a group of doctors and lawyers why he rode a fine horse instead of an ass, such as was used by Jesus, he replied, "For the simple reason . . . that there are no asses to be obtained—they turn them all into lawyers and doctors."[20] During his rounds of the circuit, he seldom stayed with slaveholders, and when a preacher was proposed at conference for licensing, Ray always opposed any candidate who owned slaves.[21] Once when a slaveholder began to cough violently during one of Ray's sermons, Ray interrupted the talk to shout, "Cough it up, Brother, cough it up. Get all the wool out of your throat and you can serve God a great deal better."[22] Ray provided no clear and coherent theological or theoretical argument against slavery. Indeed, he provided his congregations with little theory on any subject. He took the method of Methodism very seriously and demanded proper behavior as service to God, continually reminding Methodists of the route to salvation. But subtle, fine points or clever arguments held no interest for him. Even more than their Baptist colleagues, such Methodists as Ray had remarkable confidence in their insights, confidence necessary for survival in the West, but they had little time or patience to justify the sureness of their vision.

Pioneer Presbyterians and Slavery

Presbyterians had the smallest following of the three denominations in the eighteenth-century Southwest. Their first Kentucky

20. A. H. Redford, *The History of Methodism in Kentucky*, 3 vols. (Nashville, 1868-70), 1:131.

21. Arnold, *History of Methodism in Kentucky*, pp. 99-100.

22. John Ray, "Memoirs" (typed copy), p. 4, Methodist Historical Society, Lake Janaluska, N.C.

congregation met at McAfee's Station in 1779, but six years later the territory could claim only twelve Presbyterian congregations, with fewer still in Tennessee.[23] Among the Scotch-Irish migrants, who had moved from Pennsylvania to western North Carolina and then to Kentucky and Tennessee, Presbyterians were well respected, and they often became community leaders.[24] When in 1789 a group of Scotch-Irish followed the lead of Presbyterian laymen west from Campbell County, Virginia, to southeastern Kentucky, one of their first acts was to construct a Presbyterian church. Yet such communities were rare in the hinterlands; outside of such towns as Lexington and Nashville, Presbyterian influence was slight. The Transylvania Presbytery, for example, complained that its members could not work together, scattered as they were "up and down in small settlements."[25]

In viewing such social issues as slavery, Presbyterian ministers could at least draw upon their education, which was considerably more advanced as a rule than that of most other western clergymen and, indeed, than just about anyone else in the West. Clerics educated at Princeton or Hampden-Sidney would snort disapproval at their more popular but semiliterate Baptist or Methodist competitors. Probably fewer than twenty preachers of the denomination toured the two states of the West before 1800; of these, four had attended Hampden-Sydney College, four Liberty Hall, and two—James Crawford and Samuel Doak—had graduated from Princeton (then the College of New Jersey). Doak was the first Presbyterian minister in Tennessee (in 1778); as a typical Presbyterian clergyman, he immediately began plans for a literary institution.[26] Born in 1749 of Scotch-Irish parents in Augusta County, Virginia,

23. Walter B. Posey, *The Presbyterian Church in the Old Southwest, 1778-1838* (Richmond, Va., 1952), p. 20; see also Robert Davidson, *History of the Presbyterian Church in the State of Kentucky* (New York, 1847), p. 60.

24. Will A. McTeer, *History of the New Providence Presbyterian Church, Maryville, Tennessee, 1786-1921* (Maryville, 1921), p. 14; see also W. T. Knott, *History of the Presbyterian Church in What Is Now Marion County and the City of Lebanon, Kentucky* (N.p., n.d.), pp. 7-21; Robert L. Kincaid, *The Wilderness Road* (New York, 1947), pp. 167-168; William E. Railey, *History of Woodford County, Kentucky* (Baltimore, 1838), pp. 289-290.

25. Minutes, Transylvania Presbytery (typed copy), p. 4, HFPC.

26. Posey, *Presbyterian Church*, p. 19.

he worked on his father's farm until he was sixteen. After he joined the church he attended grammar school near his home, and in 1773 he entered the College of New Jersey, graduating two years later. He worked as a tutor at Hampden-Sidney for a few years, but soon decided his calling was as a missionary to the West. He helped write the constitution for the abortive state of Franklin in 1784, and he is traditionally given credit for the provision calling for a state university.[27]

It is little wonder that these sophisticated preachers, so different in many ways from the Baptists and Methodists, showed much greater familiarity with the writings of the Enlightenment. David Rice, the spiritual leader of western Presbyterians, proved in his various writings that he was well acquainted with modern notions of liberty and equality. Moreover, his opposition to deism as a mutation of Enlightenment ideas remained absolute; he warned the faithful to "stop your ears against profanity and infidelity, whether they come from the poor or rich, the vulgar or polite, the little or the great ment of the world."[28] Even these ministers, however, spent little time expressly analyzing modern writings. Instead, their consciousness of the Enlightenment remained passive and many of the Presbyterian writings tended to be derivative, familiar echoes of eastern thought. Sources of their thought can easily be traced but originality is less in evidence.

It is, of course, little wonder that the best-developed, most completely argued attack upon slavery by a southwestern minister was by a Presbyterian. David Rice was the preeminent Presbyterian leader of the antislavery forces and one of a very few leaders in Kentucky who called for a practical solution to what they insisted would be the new state's most glaring flaw. Even Bishop Asbury wrote Rice to praise his views on the "natural rights of Mankind." Born in the tidewater county of Hanover, Virginia in 1733, Rice learned opposition to slavery from his parents. He attended the College of New Jersey, receiving the finest education available to Presbyterians in the colonies, and although he did not graduate,

27. William B. Sprague, *Annals of the American Pulpit*, 9 vols. (New York, 1857-69), 3:392-397.
28. David Rice, *An Essay on Baptism* (Baltimore, 1789), p. 74.

he received his license to preach in 1763. He then traveled through Virginia, often preaching to congregations of blacks. Although he contemplated a move west into Kentucky immediately after the Revolution, attracted by the cheap land, he felt that "the spirit of speculation was flowing in such a torrent that it would bear down every weak object that stood in its way." He overcame his scruples in 1783 and made the long trek over the mountains, soon to become the unofficial leader of western Presbyterians. A seemingly tireless man, he wrote circular letters, led services for numerous congregations, and supported the beginnings of the Kentucky Academy.[29]

Rice, a student of Samuel Davies, stood theologically in the Edwardsian tradition.[30] But when Edwardsians in New England began to create a New Divinity, with its careful logic and lack of interest in evangelical preaching, such neo-Edwardsians as Rice tended to follow the path set out for them by John Witherspoon: religion must teach morality, and a Scottish common-sense morality at that. Confronted by the abundant immorality of the West, Rice realized that moral reform activities were necessary preconditions to the more complex indoctrination of his many flocks. He promoted education, opposed capital punishment, argued against dueling, and supported temperance. When he found time, Rice tried to teach about the contents of Scripture, but concern with the moral decay of the southwest demanded most of his time. His primary goal was to an end to slaveholding.

Rice threw his considerable energies into his crusade against slavery in Kentucky, expending his greatest effort at the Kentucky Constitutional Convention of 1792, at which he represented Mercer County. As one of seventeen antislavery men at the convention, Rice was one of only five opponents of slaveholding who owned no slaves. Six other ministers and five active Presbyterian or Baptist laymen came to the convention to oppose slavery and Rice

29. On Rice, see Robert Bishop, *An Outline of the History of the Church in the State of Kentucky during a Period of Forty Years; Containing the Memoirs of Rev. David Rice* (Lexington, 1824), pp. 223-287; Vernon Martin, "Father Rice, the Preacher Who Followed the Frontier," *Filson Club Quarterly* 29 (1955): 324-330; Sprague, *Annals of the American Pulpit*, 3:140-145.

30. See Sprague, *Annals of the American Pulpit*, 3:140-145.

served as spokesman for this group.[31] It was an extremely difficult task. The antislavery faction was divided upon the specific mode of emancipation which should be added to the constitution. Rice argued for universal but gradual emancipation and apparently represented a middle position among antislavery men. He presented his beliefs in an impassioned speech, which might serve as an archetypical example of how a minister can fail to understand the difference between a sermon and a political address. As a work of political rhetoric, his comments were doubtless a failure; the address brooked no compromise, it assaulted the sensibilities of his audience by condemning the lustful nature of the slaveholder, and it focused upon broad theoretical and moral issues, dismissing practical concerns as insignificant. The influential, well-educated leader of the plantation faction, George Nicholas, made quick work of Rice's plea. By focusing exclusively upon the property right, Nicholas galvanized a majority of the delegates, and when Rice's proposal lost in a preliminary vote, the minister resigned. Although he may have hoped to receive a mandate from his constituency, he was replaced by an antislavery judge, who finished out Rice's term at the convention without making much effort to fight against the peculiar institution.

In spite of its political shortcomings, Rice's address, which was in effect a revision of an earlier pamphlet he had published, deserves careful attention, not only because of Rice's standing among the religious leaders of the eighteenth-century West but also because it represents the first step in the development of a coherent religious understanding of the nature of the most glaring moral problem in the region. Indeed, Rice began his analysis with a tight personal focus. Echoes of the Scots ring throughout the first sections; he asserts this his "happiness has been greatly diminished" by thinking about the plight of his fellowmen. He worries about the "load of misery that lies on [slaves], and the load of guilt on us for imposing it on them."[32] The guilt, according to Rice, would be contagious: "I view their distresses, I read the

31. Joan W. Coward, *Kentucky in the New Republic: The Process of Constitution Making* (Lexington, 1979), pp. 36-47.

32. David Rice, *Slavery Inconsistent with Justice and Good Policy* (Philadelphia, 1792), p. 3.

anger of Heaven, I believe that if I should not exert myself, when, and as far, as in my power, in order to relieve them, I should be partaker of the guilt." As Garry Wills has so brilliantly shown in his analysis of the Declaration of Independence, happiness for Thomas Jefferson implied the Scottish notion of a moral sense, and that most assuredly would have been the case with Rice, a man clearly in the Witherspoon tradition.[33] Moreover, happiness required disinterested benevolence, and hence its denial led to guilt. Here Rice might have quoted Francis Hutcheson: "Negligence, which made on incapable of doing justice, argues a prior culpable defect of good dispositions. And 'tis here that the guilt properly lies."[34] In this sense, inaction can be as evil as action.

A slave, Rice continued, is "a human creature made by the law the property of another man creature and reduced by mere power to an absolute, unconditional subjection to his will." In Rice's eyes, this law was just only in the instance of vicious conduct. "In no other case, if my conceptions are just, can it be vindicated on principles of justice or humanity." Here, again, Rice relied upon his training in the Scots. Although Jefferson's reliance upon the same roots had produced simpler prose, Rice reaches the same conclusion: "As creatures of God we are, with respect to liberty, all equal." If that liberty is infringed upon, taken by force, such an action must be considered robbery.[35]

The white man's insistence upon slavery had, in Rice's analysis, no basis in law. More, it was an absurd claim in moral terms. "Did it come from heaven, from earth, or from Hell? Has the great King of heaven, the absolute sovereign, disposer of all men, given this extraordinary right to white men over black men?" Such a claim degrades the white men: in insisting upon it, "we plead for the disgrace and ruin of our own nature." Rice stressed the fundamental immorality of slavery as a violation of God's work. Broaching a subject that would continually recur in southwestern clerical discussion of the institution, Rice attacked the destructive

---

33. Garry Wills, *Inventing America* (New York, 1978).

34. Francis Hutcheson, *A System of Moral Philosophy*, 2 vols. (1755; reprint, New York, 1968), 1:230.

35. Rice, *Slavery Inconsistent*, p. 3.

force of slavery upon the black family. "The relation of husband and wife, of parent and child are founded on the laws of nature." In violating those laws, the master denies God's will. Moreover, some masters opposed religious training. Thus the law "supports in a land of religious liberty, the severest of restrictions." To a meeting dominated by Jeffersonians, this was a particularly harsh accusation.[36]

With much less passion and conviction, Rice continued his analysis by focusing upon the putative subject of his address, the fact that slavery was based upon bad policy. A slave was expected to obey the laws of a government that failed to protect his rights, allowed him no property, and in fact provided him with nothing but punishment. A slave was therefore "in a state of war with his master, his civil rulers and every free member of society." What possible good was a policy, he asked, that created a group of people in whose best interest it was "to subvert the government and throw all into confusion," with results that could all too clearly be seen in the recent events in the West Indies.[37]

Moreover, Rice argued, slavery ruined the lives of whites. It bred idleness, and a lack of industry would surely breed vice. The youth of Kentucky were drawing to "gaming, theft, robbery or forgery." Slavery also made whites prideful; they gained the habit of scorning their fellowmen who had to toil in the fields. Rice concluded that the only solution to these problems was emancipation. He realized that this would come as an economic hardship to some, but he nevertheless argued that the masters had to absorb their losses, for it made little sense to compensate someone for the loss of that which he had stolen: the freedom of blacks. Emancipation would, he admitted, result in the intermarriage of the races, and he acknowledged that this issue troubled him. But he saw his reaction as a simple matter of pride and an evil only in its approach; once intermarriage began, it would seem natural. He followed this remarkably naive comment with the suggestion that intermarriage was at least better than the covert sexual alliances of master and slave, which was "absolutely dishonest, perfectly

36. Ibid., p. 4.
37. Ibid., pp. 12, 13.

sinful and extremely criminal."[38] If his audience had been attentive thus far, here they surely began to rebel.

One great problem worried Rice: the Bible, some had argued, supports slavery. Rice responded that a careful reading of the Old Testament should reveal that slavery was always limited to the life of the slave and that slaves forfeited their freedom not because of the color of their skins but because of crimes or folly. In the New Testament, Paul seemed to support slavery, but Rice viewed this as contrary to the "righteous and benevolent doctrines, and duties taught in the new Testament." Rice argued that Paul avoided proclaiming his antislavery views out of fear of Roman reprisals.[39]

The abolition of slavery could not be avoided, Rice believed, but it must not be immediate, for "we have rendered [slaves] incapable of enjoying and properly using this their birthright." First, there should be a legislative ban on the importation of slaves into Kentucky. Second, any child born after a certain date would be free and must be educated by the master of his parents.[40] In a letter to a fellow preacher, Rice suggested that he would have been pleased if abolition began under religious rather than legal auspices, "because then it would appear to be the general effect of the power of truth and of the justice and benignity of the religion of Jesus."[41]

In concluding his remarks, Rice focused upon the central moral issue of slavery: its sinfulness. Here once again he followed Hutcheson's language. Rice distinguished between a natural evil, which he defined as a practical one, and a moral evil, which he defined as a sin. Many of the consequences of slavery may have been natural evils, but "enslaving our fellow creatures is a moral evil." To be sure, emancipation might produce certain natural evils. It would be inconvenient, and it would create discord. But, he asked, "shall we persist in corrupting and ruining" human nature "in order to avoid the natural evils we have already produced?" Here Rice stands apart from many of the southeastern

38. Ibid., pp. 17, 19-21, 27.
39. Ibid., p. 31.
40. Ibid., p. 34.
41. David Rice to James Blythe, December 11, 1799, Shane Collection, Presbyterian Historical Society, Philadelphia.

evangelicals examined by Donald Mathews, who found themselves compelled to avoid the determination that slavery was a sin.[42]

A combination of Rice's background in the Scots and his strong personality may explain why he took a stand avoided by many other clergymen. But another clue to his reasoning lies in his last comment of the speech. He argued that, in creating a separate state from Virginia, Kentuckians had a singular opportunity: "It depends upon our free choice, whether we shall be born in this sin, or innocent of it."[43] The phrasing, of course, plays a bit with Edwardsian rhetoric, and it therefore foreshadows the less deterministic language of the soon-to-blossom Great Revival. But it also emphasizes one initial interpretation of the possibilities of the new culture of the Southwest. Echoing many other frontiersmen in American history, Rice suggests that the Southwest, a new region, could make a fresh start by freeing itself from the bonds of slavery. Here is the image of the New Jerusalem.

Limits on Frontier Antislavery Thought

Rice, Barrow, and Ray represented the articulate antislavery faction within southwestern churches, a faction that had limited success. Methodists, with their more rigid structure, attempted to settle the issue at the general conference level; although the rules changed in their severity, Methodists' basic condemnation of slavery remained in force throughout the eighteenth century. The Christmas Conference of 1784 ruled that slavery was "contrary to law of God and an abomination."[44] No southwestern Methodist minister in the eighteenth century gave any indication of disagreeing with that statement. In the other two evangelical denominations, antislavery statements regularly emerged from clerical meetings. The Transylvania Presbytery, when considering the question, "Is

42. Rice, *Slavery Inconsistent*, p. 12. See Mathews, *Religion in the Old South*, p. 74.
43. Rice, *Slavery Inconsistent*, p. 13.
44. David R. McAnnally, *Statement of Facts in Regard to the Official Acts of the Methodist Episcopal Church, on the Subject of Slavery* (St. Louis, 1856), pp. 10-11.

slavery a moral evil?" answered in the affirmative.[45] The 1791 meeting of the Elkhorn Baptist Association drew up a memorial to the state constitutional convention advocating abolition.[46]

Yet if the most outspoken and best-known preachers advocated some form of abolition, why did most churches remain silent? Where did the opposite reside? As would be true during the Great Revival, the opposition did not stand up and clearly identify itself; no eighteenth-century minister in the Southwest explicitly defended slavery. Instead, some ministers tried to muffle or silence antislavery pronouncements. The Baptist Salem Association was asked in 1789, "Is it lawful for a member of Christ's church to keep his fellow creature in perpetual slavery?" The question could not be put any more concisely, but rather than answer, the association decided it was "improper to enter into so important and critical a matter at present.[47] No meeting of Methodists in the eighteenth-century Southwest left an explicit condemnation of slavery in its records, a remarkable circumspection shared by the Presbyterians. When the Transylvania Presbyterians condemned slavery, they almost immediately hedged on the issue. They argued that "all persons who hold slaves" were not to be considered caught in a web of sin. Yet they declined to say who was caught in that web if not slaveholders. Such artful dodging had long been practiced in the Southeast. Eighteenth-century evangelical churches, fighting against the authority of established Anglicanism, could seldom afford the luxury of wholehearted expressions of antislavery. Indeed, such evasion on potentially divisive issues has characterized other churches in other regions in eras of great stress, as witness the promulgation of the halfway covenant in New England, at least in part the product of an attempt to avoid the decline in conversions.[48] The failure of attempts by antislavery clergymen to end the

---

45. Minutes, Transylvania Presbytery, p. 178, HFPC.

46. J. H. Spencer, *A History of Kentucky Baptists*, 2 vols. (Cincinnati, 1885), 1:184; Minutes, Elkhorn Baptist Association, Tennessee (1791), BHS; Frank Masters, *A History of Baptists in Kentucky* (Louisville, 1953), pp. 80-81.

47. Spencer, *History of Kentucky Baptists*, 2:47.

48. Minutes, Transylvania Presbytery, p. 178, HFPC. On the halfway covenant and declension, see the cautions in Robert Pope, *The Half-Way Covenant* (New Haven, 1969).

peculiar institution cannot be explained completely by referring to the careful work of a secret opposition. Instead, a variety of factors joined with such opposition to doom the abolitionist cause and indeed threatened the general enterprise of promoting religion in the transappalachian South.

The frontier itself presented the first and most obvious obstacle to concerted antislavery activity. The Southwest was separated by a great mountain range from areas these ministers considered civilized. Until the end of the Revolution, Indians frequently attacked white settlements. Immigrants often failed to understand the problems they would face, for example, many early settlers in the damp area at the falls of the Ohio (later Louisville) contracted rheumatism because they wore moccasons instead of more substantial footwear.[49] Improvisation was often necessary; rather than wasting his energy building a cabin, so the tradition goes, the first settler in the Louisville area lived in a hollow sycamore tree.[50] Many ministers complained about the weather, for often their clothing and housing were inadequate. Moreover, the clergy felt compelled to travel frequently from settlement to settlement, which required hearty constitutions. This mode of life demanded endurance from young ministers, and for the elderly or infirm it was torture.[51] Francis Asbury was only forty-five years old when he first ventured into Tennessee in 1790, but he recorded that "the unsettled state of my stomach and bowels make labour and life a burden."[52]

The general clerical complaint about poor pay served as the focus for such practical concerns. Rare was the situation of John Gano, who was invited west and supported by wealthy patrons.[53]

49. Ben Casseday, *The History of Louisville from Its Earliest Settlements till the Year 1852* (Louisville, 1852), pp. 34-35.

50. J. Stoddard Johnston, ed., *Memorial History of Louisville from Its Settlement to the year 1896*, 2 vols. (Chicago, 1896), 1:38; see also Casseday, *History of Louisville*, pp. 48-49; Moore, *Frontier Mind*, pp. 13-20; James Hall, *Sketches of the History, Life and Manners in the West* (Philadelphia, 1835), p. 240.

51. Garrett, *Recollections of the West*, pp. 15-16; see also James Smith, "Tours into Kentucky and the Northwest Territory," *Ohio Archeological and Historical Publications* 16 (1907); 357.

52. Clark, ed., *Journal and Letters of Francis Asbury*, 1:632.

53. John Gano, *Biographical Memoirs* (New York, 1806), pp. 119-121.

More often the clergy struggled along as part-time farmers, craftsmen, or teachers. One minister made his living as a tinkerer.[54] The more devoted the minister, of course, the more likely he would be to go hungry. William Burke, a Methodist preacher, recalled his travel on the Salt River circuit in Tennessee: "I was reduced to the last pinch. My clothes were nearly all gone. I had patch on patch and patch by patch, and I received only money sufficient to buy a waistcoat; and not enough to pay for the making, during the two quarters I remained on the circuit.[55] David Rice tired of waiting for payment for his preaching and refused to hold services in Danville. Rather than producing money, this action provoked Tom Johnson, "the drunken poet of Danville," to write a satirical poem directed against Rice:

> Ye fools, I told you once or twice,
> You'd hear no more from chanting R——e;
> He cannot settle his affairs
> Nor pay attention unto prayers;
> Unless you pay up your arrears.
> O how he could in pulpit storm,
> And fill all hell with dire alarm!
> Vengeance pronounce against each vice,
> And more than all cursed avarice,
> Preach'd money was the root of ill,
> Consigned each rich man unto hell;
> But since he finds you will not pay,
> Both rich and poor may go that way . . .[56]

Certainly not all frontiersmen showed so little sympathy for the poverty of these ministers. One reason for the limited support received by the clergy was that, in this period, in many churches, religion was primarily the business of women.[57] It was a poor area

54. Drake, *Pioneer Life*, pp. 224-225.

55. James B. Finley, *Sketches of Western Methodism: Biographical Historical and Miscellaneous; Illustrative of Pioneer Life*, ed. W. P. Strictland (Cincinnati, 1854), p. 41.

56. John W. Townsend, ed., *O Rare Tom Johnson, Kentucky's First Poet* (Lexington, 1949), p. 20.

57. Mann Butler, *A History of the Commonwealth of Kentucky* (Cincinnati, 1836),

to begin with, and men often refused to part with what little money they had to support a cause that held little interest for them.

In the midst of practical troubles, it is little wonder that these pioneers had so little energy or time to fight against slavery, if indeed they wanted to. It would have taken almost all of their time to keep house and home together, grow the crops, and preach to those who would listen.

Second to the problem of the frontier, these evangelical clergy shared a complicated relationship with their congregations. Orthodoxy could be sacrificed in this backward area for the purpose of serving the needs of the flock. Many churches desperately sought clerical leadership. On alternating Sundays a Baptist minister would typically serve two or three churches. The Presbyterians of Little Mountain and Springfield congregations in Kentucky, "being destitute of the Regular and State Means of Grace" and sensing themselves "Reduced to a Dilemma Under the Prospect of Raising our families in Such a situation," pleaded for the services of either one of two ministers.[58] Preachers also, of course, created a need for themselves, especially the heroic Methodist circuit riders, who slept on the ground and in hovels and then awoke to bring their message to any and all southwesterners who would listen. No less heroic were their followers, who would walk miles through the forest to hear the gospel preached by the rider, who might not return for several months.

Although most members of the congregations probably came with the best of intentions, ministers found an occasionally hostile response to their sermons; some frontiersmen came only to heckle or quarrel with the "holy man." Many of these preachers had faced opposition to their work in the East. One Baptist minister in Virginia was attacked by two young men who began dunking him in a pond and asking if he believed. On the threat of a third

---

p. 20; see also Cartwright, *Autobiography*, pp. 23-24, contrasting the views of his mother and father on religion.

58. Little Mountain and Springfield churches to Howe, October 4, 1794, in Joseph Howe Papers, Shane Collection, Presbyterian Historical Society, Philadelphia.

dunking he answered, "I believe . . . you intend to drown me."[59] In North Carolina, James McGready, a Presbyterian, had been attacked by "wild Sinners" who formed a mob and burned his pulpit.[60] In the Southwest, attacks on clergymen were seldom so violent. Hecklers usually contented themselves with issuing disparaging comments about the preacher's ideas, clothes, morality, and general existence from a seat in the back of the meeting hall. Some ministers, such as John Ray, developed retorts that would be the envy of a twentieth-century stand-up comic.

In the face of such difficulties with their congregations, the orthodox clergy attempted to stabilize the southwestern churches. Respectable numbers of the faithful were necessary if meetings were to succeed, and each denomination worried about gaining and keeping members. Therefore, the clergy emphasized in their sermons the central importance of regular attendance. They also promoted the erection of church buildings, realizing these would provide significant symbols of order and and respectability. In addition, the churches began to concern themselves with various forms of social control. Virtually every southwestern church in the eighteenth century engaged in long, complicated processes of church discipline.[61] It would overstate their power, of course, to claim that these churches successfully controlled the behavior of all members of southwestern society, for most of it remained well outside their grasp, and churchmen continually complained about the spread of disbelief. Instead, the strict moral standards served as an emblem, a badge of membership. Methodists, for example, could take pride in their reputation as the "families in the neighborhood . . . who did not keep or drink whiskey."[62] To be sure, church regulation of members' lives could lead to unpleasant incidents when popular members strayed from the moral norm.

59. Spencer, *History of Kentucky Baptists*, 1:248-249.
60. Finley, *History of Russellville and Logan County, Kentucky*, pp. 9-11.
61. Minutes, Transylvania Presbytery (1789-1795), HFPC.
62. Leland Meyer, "The Great Crossings Church Records, 1795-1801," *Register of the Kentucky State Historical Society* 34 (1936):5, 12, 13; see also Zachariah F. Smith, *The History of Kentucky from Its Earliest Discovery and Settlement to the Present Date* (Louisville, 1895), p. 367.

Membership, in fact, liberated members from the anonymous, lonely existence of the frontier yet at the same time churches tended to isolate their members.[63] Few ministers in the eighteenth century considered undertaking revivals; spreading the moral strictures of their church to the heathen white remained of little concern to most of the clergy, and it was backsliders, not scoffers, who posed the real threat to the future of these churches, since only a limited number of southwesterners paid close attention to clerical pronouncements. Barely a quarter of eighteenth-century southwesterners belonged to any church, and a smaller percentage could have been considered active in their religious community. A vast majority of men who had settled the region had little use for the concepts of morality and justice preached from the pulpits every Sabbath. Perhaps aware of their lack of influence, only a very few ministers, such as David Rice, attempted to engage in the political process at any level. Perhaps most important, many antislavery ministers felt obliged to couch their pronouncements in conciliatory words for fear of alienating prospective members. To be sure, the watch-care of the Saturday meetings could examine the hearts and actions of present members with rigorous standards; but the more public exercises on Sunday, and especially the sermon, had to be somewhat muted. Southwestern conditions did not permit the luxury of complex obstacles to membership. Although ministers had neither the time nor the energy to proselytize on a full-time basis, they could not disregard the opportunity of catching a few new converts in their nets. Each the watch-care aspects of congregational activity could go only so far; if, under the clergyman's leadership, the church demanded a form of behavior not agreeable to most members, a crisis might develop. Fear both of scaring off prospective volunteer members and of causing a split within the congregation forced ministers to mute their antislavery arguments. Each church might condemn the idea of slavery as an abstraction, but even David Rice opposed the notion of making antislavery a "term of communion." The fear of the consequences of too ardent antislavery activity was made all

63. Drake, *Pioneer Life*, p. 206.

too clear in several Baptist churches which split into unreconcilable factions in the 1790s over slavery.[64] Especially in the last decade of the century, with losses of members continuing each year, the fear of driving indigent masters from the churches, never to be replaced, cooled the ardor of all but the most enthusiastic of antislavery ministers. Indeed, by the mid-1790s, virtually all comment on the problem of slavery disappeared from southwestern church records, not to be revived until the floodtide of the Great Revival.

This fear of division over specific issues was not merely based upon paranoic fantasy. Internal dissent profoundly threatened the continued growth of southwestern religion. Baptists came west in Regular and Separate factions, the latter rejecting such organizing principles as constitutions, the Philadelphia Confession of Faith, or even rules of decorum.[65] Throughout the remainder of the century, several attempts to effect a union failed.[66] The Methodists suffered a schism when James O'Kelly called for the reduction of the power of bishops. At the 1792 General Conference in Baltimore, he proposed that the conference undertake systematic review of all bishops' appointments, especially concentrating on circuit riders. When the conference defeated his proposal, O'Kelly organized the Republican Methodist church.[67] James Haw, a particularly energetic preacher, joined the schism and helped to popularize the cause in the West.[68] Adam Rankin, a Presbyterian born in western Pennsylvania, arrived in Kentucky in 1784.[69] His presence as one of the first Presbyterians in the area led to the first general meeting in Kentucky, in Cane Ridge in 1785, and he settled in Lexington, the intellectual center of the West.[70] By 1792, however,

---

64. Rice to Blythe, December 11, 1799, Shane Collection, Presbyterian Historical Society, Philadelphia; see also Redford, *History of Methodism in Kentucky*, 2:250-255, on the effect of antislavery on church membership.

65. Spencer, *History of Kentucky Baptists* 1:148.

66. Ibid., 1:482-483.

67. For the basics of the O'Kelly schism, see Bassett, *Concise History of the Methodist Protestant Church*, pp. 13-74.

68. Arnold, *History of Methodism in Kentucky*, pp. 37-39, 42; Redford, *History of Methodism in Kentucky* 1:47-48.

69. Davidson, *History of the Presbyterian Church*, pp. 94-97.

70. Bishop. *Outline of the Church in Kentucky*, p. 140.

his support for a radically literal version of Psalms (and his violent opposition to the use of the Watts adaptation) led to a trial before a committee of the Kentucky Presbytery, at which he was convicted of schism. He then took his supporters out of the Presbyterian church and established his own denomination, the Associate Reform church.[71]

The forces at work in these various divisions were remarkably similar. In none of the dissident movements did the leadership originate in the West; each new offshoot of evangelism adapted an idea initially popularized by easterners. Moreover, each movement centered around a charismatic leader: Rankin, Haw, and William Bledsoe. The last, the leader of the Separate Baptists, had claimed that he had found two hen's eggs on which were written "the day of God's judgment is near." With the eggs as evidence of God's will he staged a great revival in his church, one of a very few in the eighteenth-century Southwest. The discovery also helped him solidify his position as the leader of the Separates.[72] Finally, in each movement innovation opposed established ideas in the denominations, as traditional notions of church organization and government fought new ones. When in 1795 William Burke debated Haw over the question of the episcopacy, Burke's supporters cried, "give us the old way."[73]

Such potential destruction of the evangelical enterprise, weakening an already fragile set of churches through factionalism, clearly worried many ministers. By the 1790s, then, the three evangelical denominations appear to have reached a spirit of compromise, fearful of too much controversy, avoiding such vexed questions as slavery if at all possible. A substantial change in the prestige and power of the churches was required to move them from this uneasy stasis. When that change came, however, it was more an earthquake, a revolution. Led by a new generation of clergymen, the Great Revival would cause a complicated and painful reassessment of all matters, and among these the slavery issue held a prominent position.

71. Davidson, *History of the Presbyterian Church*, pp. 88–94.

72. Spencer, *History of Kentucky Baptists* 1:175; see also Forrest Calico, *History of Garrard County, Kentucky* (New York, 1947), p. 10.

73. Finley, *Sketches of Western Methodism*, p. 48.

PART TWO

THE REVIVAL
GENERATION

Clergymen of the eighteenth-century Southwest were united by several shared experiences. All had migrated from the East, mostly from Virginia and North Carolina. All had suffered the inconveniences of the frontier life; poor food and shelter, difficult travel. All had to cope with a populace that often ignored them and frequently opposed their efforts. Whatever their differences in theology and personality, the pioneers were a generation, a cohort, as is shown in their similarities. Few had the interest, training, or temperament needed for detailed doctrinal preaching; rather, most pursued practical topics in their sermons. They worried about their well-being, for that was often threatened. They complained about the sad state of religion in the West, and they could take no solace in the size of their congregations.

Around the turn of the century, a new group of ministers, many of whom had recently come west, begun to take over the religious affairs of the Southwest. This second generation did not so much supplant the pioneers, many of whom remained in place after the turn of the century, as its members overwhelmed the first generation with the Great Revival, which they ushered into the region. Indeed, the revival created this second cohort of southwestern ministers as much as the ministers created the revival. The success of the awakening reflected upon a few clergymen in Kentucky, Tennessee, and small areas in the territories to the south. Such men as the McGee brothers of North Carolina and Barton Stone from Virginia made their fame in the West and remained in the region to nourish the work.[1] Such outside agitators inspired an enthusiasm beyond the imagination of the pioneer clergymen. The easterners had brought with them an extraordinary tool, an exceptionally powerful weapon against disbelief: the camp meeting. The origin of the device is obscure, although Barton Stone remembered something similar from his college days in North Carolina.[2] Whatever their origins, the camp meetings became the dominant technique of revivalism in the first decade of the century, with week-long gatherings of men and women, who traveled great distances to the almost fairlike experience of the power of the Holy Spirit. The meeting, together with the enthusiastic preaching and simple, easily communicated doctrine, served as the hallmark of the Great Revival in the Southwest.[3] Completing the new generation were ministers converted in the revival, men such as Peter Cartwright, the most fascinating and amusing of southwestern ministers. Little interested in the brave struggles of the pioneer generation, Cartwright and his fellow preachers saw the churches through young and often uncompromising eyes. As far as most members of this generation were concerned, the churches belonged to them, and what had transpired in the past was little more than prologue.

Eastern migrants found western churches different in several respects from those at home. The real threat to western religion was never deism or liberalism. Far from being a hotbed of modern views, most of the Southwest suffered a lack of any religious sentiments, save the scoffing taunts of disbelief. To be sure, Lexington inhabitants read Paine and other deists with enthusiasm,

1. On these figures, see Catherine Cleveland, *The Great Revival in the West* (Chicago, 1916); John Boles, *The Great Revival in the South* (Lexington, 1972). On another major figure in the revival, see John Opie, "James McGready: Theologian of Frontier Revivalism," *Church History* 34 (1965): 445-456. Also of interest is Ralph Morrow, "The Great Revival, the West, and the Crisis of the Church," in John McDermot, ed., *The Frontier Reexamined* (Chicago, 1967), pp. 65-78.

2. John Rogers, ed., *The Biography of Barton W. Stone* (Cincinnati, 1847), pp. 7-8.

3. McFerrin, *Methodism in Tennessee*, 1:338; Davidson, *History of the Presbyterian Church in Kentucky*, pp. 141-169; Spencer, *History of Kentucky Baptists*, 1:514-521.

but the vast majority of westerners lived far from the reaches of civilization, and clergy, as we have seen, were more likely to worry over the general disbelief of the masses than over the intellectual threat posed by the elite.

The theology of the pioneer generation had created anything but a coherent system. Most of the Baptists and Presbyterians held certain orthodox assumptions; they subscribed to limited atonement, election, and justification of the saints, all expressed in stiff, formal, and undeveloped sermons, if the extant examples are representative. Such ministers had instead stressed practice, and in this sense they had much in common with Methodists. In this environment, the revivalists did not have to fight very hard against entrenched, orthodox preaching.

Most members of the revival generation in the Southwest had no memory of revivals. By the turn of the century, a high proportion of the inhabitants had either been born or raised in the region. The frontier experience was all they knew, and the heritage of the Great Awakening would have, at most, been limited to stories told by elderly relatives. More often than not raised in disbelief, and seldom troubled by the pioneer preachers who were trying to hold together and small flocks as best they could, the children of the West were fallow ground for ministers of an evangelical and revivalistic bent.

For all of these reasons, the Southwest was ripe for revival. The challenge of disbelief was more easily approached than that of belief in enlightened religion; the lack of theological sophistication allowed the simple message of the revival to penetrate; no memory of the Great Awakening meant no fear of it. Ministers also found that the development of the region in other ways opened up opportunities for revival. Much of the land in Kentucky and Tennessee was now settled; many of the greatest horrors of the frontier, including the fighting between whites and Indians which had made this the "dark and bloody ground," had subsided. A period of boom had come to the Southwest, and the inhabitants had begun to want some community of their own akin to eastern culture.

In exploiting the opportunities the Southwest offered them, the revival ministers did not see themselves as a generation, although their demographic characteristics clearly show their similarities. Most of this second generation migrated from the East (88.4 percent), although for the first time a noticeable group of western ministers had been born and raised in the region (11.6 percent). Among the migrants, 49.7 percent came from Virginia, 33.3 percent from other parts of the South, and 17 percent from the North or abroad. Of the Virginia migrants to Kentucky, about whom the most information can be generated, more members of the second generation than of the first were from upland sections of the state. Only 10.2 percent came from coastal or tidewater counties (as opposed to 25 percent in the first cohort), 30.7 percent came from piedmont counties, and 42.9 percent grew up in the Shanandoah Valley or the Blue Ridge Mountains, an area of little slaveholding, slight influence of Anglicanism, small farms, and some antipathy for eastern ways. The remaining ministers came from the Appalachians or from the counties bordering on North Carolina.

Once in the West, this revival generation was the most peripatetic of any cohort of western ministers. Forty-one percent stayed in the state to which they migrated, as opposed to 58.7 percent of all western ministers. Fully 41 percent (as opposed to 29 percent of all ministers) preached in one other western state during their careers. Twelve percent preached in two other states, and 6 percent traveled to three other southwestern states during their ministries. Of the second-generation ministers who migrated to Kentucky, 25.3 percent also moved to Tennessee, 17 percent also preached in Mississippi, 28.6 percent spent some of their time in Ohio, 5.5 percent eventually moved to Missouri, and 2.7 percent found their way to Alabama. Of those who moved first to Tennessee, 44.9 percent also preached in Kentucky. In short, the second generation created a true regional network of ministers, a leadership class that could control the revival through the migration of clergy.

Although not as long-lived as members of the first cohort, ministers in the second generation very seldom died at a young age. Eighty-two percent lived over the age of fifty, and 49 percent died after the age of seventy. The age at which members of the revival cohort joined the western clergy (either by migration or ordination) reveals a remarkable bifurcation. Among them 41.8 percent were very young (under the age of twenty-five), and 37.8 percent were mature (over the age of thirty). Indeed, 12.4 percent of the members of the second cohort were older than forty when they began their western ministry, almost all of these eastern migrants bringing the gospel to the frontier; 18.4 percent were twenty or younger. This alliance of discontented but mature eastern-trained ministers and very young western preachers may help explain some of the vitality of the revival. Eastern-trained ministers, of course, held most positions of authority: 90 percent of the educators, 85.7 percent of the Methodist presiding elders, and 77.8 percent of Baptist Association moderators came from the East during the years of the revival. In all, 87 percent of the positions of authority in western churches (educators, presiding elders, leading revivalists, association moderators, editors, urban preachers, Methodist bishops, authors, and missionaries) were filled by eastern migrants.

Although many of the most interesting personal characteristics cannot be quantified for this cohort, available sources do suggest that the ministers of the revival were the most poorly educated of any of the generations of western clergymen. Only 4.6 percent had received college educations, as opposed to 15.9 percent of all southwestern ministers before 1860. This is not to say that members of the cohort disapproved of education: their support more than doubled that of the previous cohort (7.2 percent as opposed to 3.4 percent). But their relative lack of education may provide a partial explanation for their eagerness to experiment with new techniques, which they could then teach to future preachers.

As a group, these ministers began to consider the social implications of their revival. They did not remain unified, however, but fell into three camps in line with their attitudes on the revival. To make sense of their views on slavery, therefore, I feel obliged to devote one full chapter to an analysis of the ideological factions that developed during the fifteen years of revivalism. Once such divisions are fully understood, the nature of the factions dividing over the problem of slavery will become clear. Approximately the same people who opposed the revival tended to oppose abolition;

those who radically favored the revival radically supported abolition; those who took a moderate position on one issue, by far the majority, chose a moderate viewpoint on the other. I will further argue that revival ideology and views on slavery did not exist in a simple causal relation, but rather that each shaped and influenced the other.

CHAPTER 2

Clerical Factions in
the Great Revival

Although the dramatic events of the Great Revival in the Old Southwest have been analyzed with great success by several writers, no careful analysis of the ideology of the factions the revival created among southwestern clergymen has yet been written to compare with such events as the Unitarian controversy in Boston.[1] Yet to understand the attitude toward slavery taken by members of the clerical generation of the Great Revival, it is critical to understand the tensions generated by their experiences in the period of religious awakening. A paradox of many revivals is that, although the motive is always evangelical and typically catholic, the end result is frequently the unleashing of sectarianism. The intention is to unify Christians, whether as a prelude to the millennium or as a check against disbelief, to form a society of the faithful in a new territory, or to revivify piety in an old one. The product, ironically, is division, whether over the revival itself, the merits of a leading preacher or doctrine, the relative importance of emotion and intellect, or the centrality of works as opposed to grace. The divisions are both internal and external; not only are opponents of the revival lined up against proponents, but special interests within the ranks of revivalists fight among themselves. Of course, to some extent such battles depend upon the nature of

1. On the Great Revival, see Boles, *Great Revival in the South*, and Cleveland, *Great Revival in the West;* on the Unitarians, see Howe, *Unitarian Conscience.*

65

the regional culture in which the revival takes place. Less rigid and highly structured regions such as the Old Southwest or the burned-over district of the early 1830s became virtually boiling stews of sectarianism. More stable and orderly regions, such as the Southeast in the early nineteenth century, faced little sectarian strife during the course of the revival. The pattern of revivalism in western New England is an example. During the final decade of the eighteenth century a spirit of awakening began to grow in the Connecticut River valley, in part the product of a reaction against what some clergymen considered the deistic excesses of the revolutionary phase of the Enlightenment in America. Further, a new interpretation of Calvinist doctrine, the "new theology" of Samuel Hopkins, encouraged a quickening of religious feeling. The new awakening was also influenced by the old spirit, which had never fully disappeared. The leaders of the revival placed limits on enthusiastic excesses, and a rapprochement took place between the survivors and the heirs of the parties of the Great Awakening. Thus the revival in the Connecticut River valley was as much a continuation of the past as a beacon for the future.[2] In the Southwest, the situation was radically different, and the factionalism of the revival in Kentucky, Tennessee, and the northern sections of the new territories to the south was a product of the Old Southwest's fresh experience.

The first camp meeting, which could be said to have begun the Great Revival, was held at the Red River meeting house in Kentucky in June 1800. By midsummer reports that souls were being saved poured out of the region, and on August 8, 1801, the meeting at Cane Ridge, which one participant likened to a gathering of "Gideon's army," shook the nation.[3] Some ministers were

2. On the Second Great Awakening in New England, see Charles R. Keller, *The Great Awakening in Connecticut* (New Haven, 1943); Henry F. May, *The Enlightenment in America* (New York, 1976), pp. 318-320; Perry Miller, *The Life of the Mind in America* (New York, 1965), pp. 3-36; Donald Mathews, "The Second Great Awakening as an Organizing Process," *American Quarterly* 22 (1969): 23-43; Joseph W. Phillips, *Jedidiah Morse and New England Congregationalism* (New Brunswick, 1983).

3. Boles, *Great Revival in the South*, pp. 52-55; Theophilus Armenius, "Account of the Rise and Progress of the Work of God," *Methodist Magazine* 2 (1819: 223.

shocked by the seeming disorder of the camp meeting. One reported: "At first appearance, these meetings exhibited nothing to the spectator, but a scene of confusion. They were generally opened with a sermon; near the close of which, there would be an unusual outcry; some bursting forth into loud ejaculations of prayer of thanksgiving for the truth."[4] Soon, writhing converts filled the meeting, some falling to the ground, some dancing, some howling, some crying. More and more people would join in these exercises over the course of a week-long meeting, until few remained who had failed to feel manifestations of the Holy Spirit. Some pioneer ministers saw these events as a great work of God; many others seem to have been frightened or appalled.

Older ministers stressed the shocking interdenominationalism of the revival, a nonsectarian quality that tended to blur distinctions that suddenly became very important to these pioneers. Baptists tended to be less active in the camp meetings, but Presbyterians and Methodists frequently led joint services. One observer recalled: "It was then difficult to discriminate between a Presbyterian and a Methodist preacher, or member; they preached together, and shouted together—for stiff, sullen, dry formality was then not much in vogue."[5] The two ministers often credited with setting off the Great Revival, the McGee brothers, symbolize this cross-denominational unity. John preached as a Methodist minister; William was at least putatively a Presbyterian. According to John McGee, "the difference of doctrines was not sufficient to dissolve those ties of love and affection which we both felt."[6] Baptist ministers had less interest in camp meetings because they already reached a wide audience and did not need the publicity the

---

The impossibility of counting the number of converts is particularly clear in the Old Southwest of this period; reports on the meeting at Cane Ridge varied in the count by a factor of ten.

4. Richard McNemar, *The Kentucky Revival* (Cincinnati, 1807), p. 23; Spencer, *History of Kentucky Baptists*, 1:515.

5. Garrett, *Recollections of the West*, p. 42; see also Paine, *William McKendree*, pp. 334-346. When James Haw left the Methodists to join the Presbyterians, his new denomination required him to apologize for making unkind remarks about Bishop Asbury. See Redford, *History of Methodism in Kentucky*, 1:60-61.

6. Davidson, *History of the Presbyterian Church in Kentucky*, p. 263.

meetings provided, but the Presbyterians and Methodists needed to take extraordinary measures to bring their message to the people. They therefore forgot their disagreements for a time and united their efforts.

If the denominations had united merely for organizational purposes, many ministers would have disapproved but few would have rebelled. Doctrine was affected, however, and a crisis resulted. The disorder of interdenominational meetings could not help but affect what would be preached, for if one tree stump served as the platform for an old-style Calvinist and the next a vigorous Arminian, confusion would replace conviction. Further, the revival generation ministers soon realized the importance of quantity in conversions. All of the accounts of Cane Ridge and similar meetings stress the size of the crowd, and the total conversion of a community began to take on great importance. The tactical reason was obvious: if 80 percent of a community was saved, the evil effects of skepticism and scoffing could be avoided. Further, the spirit might then spread, "running like fire,"[7] from one settlement to the next. With these considerations, preachers tended to avoid theological tenets that might disrupt the progress of the revival. Of the two competing doctrines, the Arminianism of the Methodists was soon generally stressed, and orthodox Presbyterian thought as outlined in the Westminster Confession was all but ignored. Some Presbyterian evangelicals later argued that they had always been troubled by elements of the orthodox faith, especially the notion of a restricted atonement. More to the point, however, the free grace of the Methodists was simpler to accept than was the seeming restrictiveness and elitism of orthodox determinism, and the teachings of orthodox Presbyterianism were too complicated and hard to explain. A dry discourse on election, reprobation, justification, and sanctification had no place in the swirling life of the camp meeting. Preachers who tried to present such materials soon found that they were talking to themselves. Although the clergy seldom mentioned personalities, much of the rancor that arose derived from bruised or inflated egos for the marketplace of ideas in the camp meetings made the clergy themselves an issue. Several

7. Clark, ed., *Journal and Letters of Francis Asbury*, 2:226.

preachers became major celebrities in their areas; readily recognized, they developed personal followings. Famed for their gifts, they would frequently travel beyond their localities to spread the revival. Several joined together into a preaching clique, which soon took on party characteristics; ministers who disagreed with the clique were condemned, and a party platform developed. Jealousy and accusations of pride came from those less admired by the crowd.

These issues became the fundamental causes of a major split within the ranks of the clergy, as the ministers divided into three antagonistic groups. The first group, the most enthusiastic preachers, became increasingly radical. Most of these men were Presbyterians, as were the most conservative ministers. The radicals preached a simple, catholic religion and expended much of their energy attacking clergy who scrupled over the problems of the revival. A moderate center predominated, members of which saw value in the Great Revival and were convinced, for the most part, that it was the work of God. They nevertheless feared that elements which they termed excessive would destroy true religion, replacing it with godless enthusiasm. Almost all the Methodists belonged in this second group, although they were more tolerant of enthusiasm than were moderates in other denominations. Most Baptist ministers joined this camp as well; their participation in the revival was always the most restrained and cautious of any interdenominational mingling. A few Presbyterians attempted to maintain a moderate posture, but their clergy was the most thoroughly polarized. A third faction opposed the revival. Primarily made up of Calvinist Presbyterians, these clergymen saw the revival as a delusion fostered by Satan. These conservatives were the remnants of the first generation of southwestern ministers, the pioneers.

Radical Revivalism

The acknowledged leader of the radicals was Barton W. Stone, as hard a worker as any preacher in the first years of the revival, both admired and respected by many of his fellow clergy. John Carr, a Methodist preacher in Tennessee, remembered Stone as "a great and good man. He was a man of remarkable humility and modesty. These traits of his character were known wherever he was known."[8] John P. Campbell, a quintessential conservative, describes a different man, one with a passion for virulent personal attacks. Campbell also accused Stone of heresy: "It is of little consequence what name is chosen for his designation, whether it be Sabelliam, Socinian, Deist or Infidel."[9] The man who inspired these conflicting opinions was born in Maryland in 1772. His father died when Stone was an infant, and the family moved to Pittsylvania County, Virginia. Well educated in the local schools, he spent much of his time reading the Bible; he took delight in books on all subjects, especially such popular novels as *Peregrine Pickle* and *Tom Jones*.[10] Having decided early in his life to become a barrister, he entered Guilford Academy in North Carolina. A great revival was then taking place at the school, led by James McGready, but Stone associated with the scoffers. A friend persuaded him to listen to McGready preach, and Stone was soon converted.

Rapid shifts in mood characterized Stone throughout his life. After his conversion, he struggled with Calvinist theology, alternately despairing and rejoicing over the state of his soul. A great deal of hesitation preceded his decision to join the ministry, soon after he began to preach, and he temporarily gave up his calling to teach school at a Methodist academy in Georgia. He attended the annual Methodist conference in Charleston, and there is some indication that he considered joining the Methodist ministry. While in Georgia, he met some French refugees from the Reign of Terror, from whom he surely learned of modern writers. The history of his youth indicates great confusion over his identity, his beliefs, and his ambitions. He was an energetic young man, fascinated by new ideas.

Following another bout of soul-searching, Stone received his license from the Orange Presbytery in North Carolina. He soon headed west, answering a call from the Cane Ridge and Concord

8. John Carr, *Early Times in Middle Tennessee* (Nashville, 1857), p. 89.

9. John P. Campbell, *Vindex, or the Doctrines of the Scriptures Vindicatedd, against the Reply of Mr. Stone* (Lexington, 1806), p. 5.

10. Rogers, ed., *Biography of Barton Stone*, p. 4.

churches in Kentucky. To become minister to the two churches, however, he was required to receive ordination, and he unfortunately disagreed with the Westminster Confession of Faith on the Trinity, election, reprobation, and predestination. Because these tenets consistuted the core of the Presbyterian creed, Stone naturally expected the church to reject his application. It is some indication of the great need for clergy among Presbyterians, however, that he was allowed to accept the Confession "as far as I see it consistent with the word of God." He soon demonstrated that he did not see much he liked. He rejected Calvinism as "among the heaviest clogs on Christianity in the world. It is a dark mountain between heaven and earth, and is amongst the most discouraging hindrances to sinners from seeking the kingdom of God."[11] In early 1801 he attended a camp meeting led by James McGready and was so impressed by this method that he led protracted meetings in both of his churches. In August 1801 he invited many of the neighboring evangelical preachers to a camp meeting in a field near his Cane Ridge church, certainly the most famous meeting of the Great Revival.

Four other Presbyterians shared Stone's enthusiasm for the revival. Along with Richard McNemar, John Thompson, John Dunlavy, and Robert Marshall, Stone began to use the name "New Light" to characterize the prorevival forces of his denomination. He summarized their doctrine in his autobiography: "God loves the world—the whole world, and sent his Son to save them, on condition that they believed in him—that the gospel was the means of salvation—but that this means would never be effectual to this end, until believed and obeyed by us—that sinners were capable of understanding and believing this testimony, and of acting upon it by coming to the Saviour and obeying him, by obtaining salvation and the holy spirit." This statement contained as thorough a rejection of Calvinism, or at least of Calvinism as he understood it, as Stone could manage in a limited space. McNemar termed the Calvinist system "the old bed of sand" upon which the structure of religion was unsafe, and each agreed that the future of religion depended upon the repudiation of that system.[12]

11. Ibid., pp. 30, 34.
12. Ibid., p. 45; see also McNemar, *Kentucky Revival*, pp. iv, 27.

Their first point of dispute was over the nature of God. Some argued that Calvin's belief in a wrathful, vengeful God contradicted the gospel, which describes Him as a God of infinite love. The wrath seen by Calvin, in fact, was "nothing else but his holy nature standing in opposition to sin."[13] This fact, Stone explained, is also apparent in the conversion experiences of all Christians. When they are renewed in His image, they feel love and love alone; if God were wrathful, a true convert would experience that wrath as well. The radical theories, then, attempted to raise the question of the proper stress Christians must give to the various elements of God's makeup. Although they certainly did not wish to minimize divine hatred of sin, they wished to return emphasis to His love, arguing that orthodox Presbyterians had created a caricature of God as cruel, ill-tempered, and hardly attractive to potential believers. From a very different perspective, some Connecticut divines had at the same time begun to sense this aspect of Presbyterianism as well.

Much more controversial was the second element of the radical attack, which centered on the question of Christ's atonement. Marshall and Thompson renounced their New Light beliefs in 1811, at least in part because they felt Stone's explanation of the atonement placed the faction on the outer fringes of Christianity.[14] The atonement of Christ is the theological issue of the purpose and function of the death of Jesus. Stone argued that the Westminster Confession of Faith, the central document of Presbyterian orthodoxy, takes a legalistic view of the crucifixion, in which Christ is seen to assume the debt of man to God, making himself liable for the penalty, death. Stone condemned this notion as unscriptural, arguing that orthodox ministers had invented it to bolster belief in election and justification. Moreover, if Christ paid for man's obligation to obey the law, then He in effect accepted sin and sinning, which Stone found unacceptable. The Westminster view, according to Stone, had transformed the holy concept of atonement into little more than a business transaction, and Christ

13. Barton W. Stone, *Atonement* (Lexington, 1805), p. 6.
14. Robert Marshall and John Thompson, *A Brief Historical Account of Sundry Things in the Doctrines and State of . . . the Newlight Church* (Cincinnati, 1811), p. 7.

became not the Savior but a pawnbroker. After a series of other objections, Stone finally suggested that the Westminster view was profoundly heretical because it suggested the existence of two Gods, one purchasing forgiveness from the other.[15]

Stone's proposed new interpretation of the atonement rested on his notion that atonement means "at one." Therefore, the crucifixion was intended to unite man and God. Christ did not die to appease God (for then He would be appeasing Himself), but rather to give Christians faith, not only in Christ's blood but in what it stood for, the love, grace, and mercy of God.[16] The importance of this interpretation of the atonement is not in its originality; Stone's thought contained bits from numerous theologians. Rather, it suggests that on the most central element of Christian thought orthodoxy had obscured the true elements of faith. Richard McNemar used the harshest language he could muster when he proclaimed that "the foundation of a lasting union could not be laid until the rubbish was cleared out of the way."[17] In place of the complex and outmoded doctrines of orthodoxy the New Lights "held forth the promise of the Gospel in their purity and simplicity, without the contradictory explanation and double meaning, which scholastic divines have put upon them to make them agree with the doctrines of the confession."[18] As a third element of their thought, then, New Lights believed that converts could and would fully understand the fundamentally simple teachings contained in Scripture.

The fourth fundamental doctrine was the Arminian notion that grace is available to all who desire salvation. Stone faulted Calvinism for obscuring the simple purity of the gospel, which he believed must touch the hearts of all who hear it. Instead, he argued, the Calvinists took the perverse stance that only those who were already saved deserve to hear the gospel preached. Moreover, Stone contended that "Calvinism spawns a slothful attitude among Christians, for there would be no room for inde-

15. Stone, *Atonement*, pp. 3-4, 7, 10-12, 15-16.
16. Ibid., pp. 20-27.
17. McNemar, *Kentucky Revival*, p. 36.
18. Presbytery of Springfield, *An Apology for Renouncing the Jurisdiction of the Synod of Kentucky* (Lexington, 1804), p. 4.

pendent action in a strictly predestined world."[19] His certainty
that election was false doctrine, he recalled, came from his experiences in camp meetings. He had always felt confused as to the
purpose of election. "In this state of perplexity I remained till I
want to see the work of God in the lower parts of this state. There
my mind was filled with admiration at the work...I saw that
faith was the sovereign gift of God to all sinners, not the act of
faith, but the object or foundation of faith, which is the testimony
of Jesus, of the Gospel; that sinners had power to believe this
Gospel, and then come to God and obtain grace and salvation."[20]

Preaching these four basic tenets, the New Lights created a
significant following. In style they were aggressive, occasionally
belligerent, and usually self-righteous. In a sense, however, their
posture was defensive. Perhaps more than their opponents among
the Presbyterians, the New Lights were conscious of the threat
posed by deists and atheists. McNemar described prerevival Kentucky as suffering from widespread deism.[21] Although his observation was probably exaggerated, McNemar's certainty of the immi-
nent danger was all-abiding. The solution to this desperate situation,
according to the New Lights, was a lively and simple religion.
They saw orthodox Presbyterians as troublesome less because of
their attacks upon New Light theology than because they were
easy targets for the barbs of disbelievers. In short, the second
generation saw the remnants of the first as hopelessly dull, tiresome,
and out of step. Therefore, at least in part, Stone and his faction
moved beyond passionless theological discussion into the world of
rough-and-tumble debate as a rear-guard action against deism while
at the same time hoping to destroy orthodoxy in the Southwest.

This important point should not be understated. For all of their
theological trappings, these radicals realized that they had to gain
the attention of the southwestern laity if they were to accomplish

19. Stone, *Atonement*, pp. 14, 17.

20. Barton W. Stone, *A Reply to John P. Campbell's Strictures on Atonement*
(Lexington, 1805), p. 6.

21. McNemar, *Kentucky Revival*, p. 10; see also John P. Campbell, *Strictures
on Two Letters* (Lexington, 1805), p. 24; David Rice, *An Epistle to the Citizens of
Kentucky, Professing Christianity* (Lexington, 1805), p. 7.

their great goal, the transformation of western religion, followed by the transformation of the world. As the most vigorous spokesmen of the revival generation, these ministers understood well the nature of southwestern society; it was lively, disorderly, exciting, and dangerous. Whereas the pioneer ministers had attempted to create small, devout, protective communities of Christians, through solid if uninspired practical sermons and careful organizations, the second generation, in its most radical form, stressed dramatic meetings and controversies. The pioneers established a base from which the radicals could launch their revival, a fact seldom acknowledge by the Stoneites. Yet to expand from that base, the radicals felt, required the expenditure of a great deal of evangelical effort. Their goal was not simply to make converts; rather, they intended to take over the regional culture, to remake it to their own specifications. As I will argue in Chapter 3, this goal refects a powerful millennarian element in the New Light thought, never completely articulated yet always to some degree present.

The New Lights presage much of the spirit of revivalism in the burned-over district of western New York, where outbursts of millennial thought occurred at regular intervals. There, too, the most radical aspect of the revival was the work of new ministers, a second generation of western New York clergymen. The revivals in the early nineteenth-century Connecticut River valley, by contrast, remained relatively free of radical revisions of orthodox doctrine. The social conditions of Connecticut's culture, old, stable, and relatively secure, allowed careful planning of the revival impossible in western New York or the Old Southwest.

Conservative Opponents of the Great Revival

No single leader emerged to oppose the work of the radicals, for the opposition consisted of several groups with markedly different objections. Some Baptists found the revival excessive and even frivolous. Elijah Craig, in an essay primarily concerned with the greed of some ministers, considered it unnatural that "boys of ten years old, are used as instruments to carry on the great work of

God, while learned and able ministers stand and look on."[22] Baptist disapproval generally came from successful pioneer ministers, who saw little to be gained and much to be lost from the activities of the revival. They generally expressed their disapproval by refusing to participate in the joint camp meetings.

The developing intellectual elite in Lexington gave even less attention to the revival. Certainly, deists felt little inclination to attend camp meetings, except perhaps to scoff. An occasional convert came from their ranks, but what little notice they gave was scornful. The redoubtable Tom Johnson wrote a poem about a woman named Celia, who passed wind at a revival service.[23] More often, the work of the evangelicals was ignored. There was no mention of the Great Revival in any of the four Kentucky newspapers, for example. The huge camp meetings would hardly have passed unnoticed by the editors, so their lack of interest is particularly striking. John Breckinridge, Jeffersonian senator and a leading social figure in Kentucky, ignored the religious agitation; his admirer, Robert McAfee, who was studying law at the time, wrote that "it was firmly impressed on my mind that a man could not be religious and a lawyer at the same time."[24]

The clearest, most direct, most complex opposition to the work of the radicals came from a handful of Presbyterian preachers who felt that Calvinism, discipline, and learning had to be protected from revivalistic excesses. These clergymen seemed out of place in the Southwest. All had moved west as members of the pioneer generation, and as Presbyterians in the Southwest of the eighteenth century they had refused to countenance the regional culture of

22. Elijah Craig, *A Few Remarks on the Errors That Are Maintained in the Christian Churches of the Present Day* (Lexington, 1801), p. 36.

23. Townsend, ed., *O Rare Tom Johnson*, pp. 17-18.

24. Posey, *Presbyterian Church*, p. 25; Niels Sonne, *Liberal Kentucky* (New York, 1939), p. 22; Lowell Harrison, *John Breckinridge, Jeffersonian Republican* (Louisville, 1969), p. 155; Robert McAfee, "Life and Times of Robert McAfee," *Register of the Kentucky State Historical Society* 25 (1944): 222. On disinterest in religion, see John W. Townsend, *Kentucky in American Letters* (Cedar Rapids, 1913), pp. 23-24; Thomas D. Clark, *The Rampaging Frontier* (1939; reprint, Bloomington, 1964), p. 30. Antireligious southerners recited a popular story about a Methodist minister who traded his horse for a rich man's wife; see *History of the Ohio Falls Cities and Their Counties*, 2 vols. (Cleveland, 1882), 1:213-214.

the frontier and instead tried to behave as though they were still in the East. In many ways they resembled the New England clergy of the same period, who had to cope with the horror of party politics and, although rejecting that specter, were drawn into its clutches as they became loyal Federalists.[25] In the same sense, the antirevival Presbyterians tried to protect their constrained but secure role in the turn-of-century Southwest, and in attacking the controversies caused by the revival, they became controversialists. John Poage Campbell, Robert Bishop, and Adam Rankin led the attack. There were several connections among them: Campbell had been a student of Rankin's, and both had been students of Archibald Scott, a mild-mannered Virginia preacher who felt that the central concern of a minister should be catechizing the young. Bishop was a follower of Rankin, to whom he dedicated one of his essays.[26]

The radicals had expended little energy defending the divine influence that created the revival; they were satisfied that the spirit manifested itself in the meetings and exercises. Their opponents, therefore, suggested that demonic influence had produced the revival. Rankin in particular, made it his cause to prove that the revival was largely the work of the Devil. He began his argument by defining delusion as the conviction that that which is false is true, based upon the Hebrew for "cunning fable" and the Greek for "efficacy of error."[27] (Such scholarly posing permeated his work.) God uses delusions, Rankin believed, for two purposes. First, they can be corrective: by their foolishness they point out the truth more clearly by means of contrast. Second, they can be judicial, forcing some to suffer delusion as punishment for their sins.[28]

25. See Donald M. Scott, *From Office of Profession: The New England Ministry, 1750-1850* (Philadelphia, 1978).

26. Sprague, *Annals of the American Pulpit*, 3:388; see also Edward Humphrey, *Memoirs of the Rev. Thomas Cleland, D.D., Competed from His Private Papers* (Cincinnati, 1859); Robert Bishop, *A Legacy to Vacant Congregations* (Lexington, 1804).

27. Adam Rankin, *Review of the Noted Revival in Kentucky* (N.p., 1803), pp. 11-12; see also John P. Campbell, *The Doctrine of Justification by Imputed Righteousness Considered, in Letters to a Friend* (Danville, 1805), p. 4.

28. Rankin, *Review of the Noted Revival*, pp. 35-48.

Rankin believed that several tests could be used to recognize delusion. First, one must look for "pride of heart, or high-mindedness." That is, one must be suspicious of all who proclaim themselves or their work to be important. Second, one must be watchful of those who seem easily to attract a large following, for "deluded guides have the power to lead us." Third, one must be wary of any "corruption of the means of grace," for those who are deluded will try to lead us away from a proper faith in Christ. Fourth, any form of fanaticism should be studiously avoided because deluded leaders frequently "follow one commanded duty to the neglect of all others." Fifth, it is dangerous "when a people build all their hope upon their practices without any respect to their principles." In other words, because principle is the cause and practice the effect, a concentration on practice tends to make the motive unclear and, therefore, in error. Sixth, it is usually a sign of delusion "when church officers dispense with ecclesiastical government." Seventh, one should distrust those who place their "faith in new revelations and visions of God, as man." (This criticism seems to have been directed particularly at the Shakers.) An eighth danger sign is "a greater confidence in our own experiences and feelings, than in divine revelation." Ninth, and especially dangerous, is "extravagant affection, such as falling into dead fits, strong convulsions," and all the many exercises that were manifested at the camp meetings.[29]

Rankin found all these characteristics of delusion present in the Great Revival. Further, its leaders used many of these manifestations to justify the notion that the revival was a portent of the "beginning of the millennium."[30] Rankin agreed that something out of the ordinary was happening, but not that it was a miracle. It did seem that the revival failed to respect character, that all converts were convinced of their sinfulness, and that they spoke only of Christ and God during the exercises. But Satan had been known to perform similar acts in the past. The ordinary functions of the Holy Spirit, Rankin claimed, bore no resemblance to the

29. Ibid., pp. 66-70.
30. Ibid., p. 26; see also John P. Campbell, *The Passenger; or a Religious Ramble through Kentucky and Ohio* (Lexington, 1804), p. 9.

activities of the revival. Further, the special influence of God was reserved for those who, like Paul, had shown a powerful enmity toward religion in its true form. Only Satan had the power to work such wonders as were present in the revival.[31] It is some measure of how far Rankin was from the man-centered world of the Enlightenment that he never considered that the revival might simply be the work of man. Yet one of the authors he brought forth to support his argument was David Hume; Rankin showed no awareness that Hume might not share his understanding of the truth and efficacy of Calvinist teaching.

Addressing the true believers, Rankin presented his list of enemies. He included atheists, Unitarians (who reject the Trinity), infidels (who reject revelation), usurpers (who reject the government of God), Christian deists (who meddle with God's laws), legalists (who hold that Christ paid for the sins of all men), apostates (who view all religion as hypocrisy), and blasphemers (who appeal not to God but to the Devil). All of these enemies, he felt, thrived in the revival. He admonished proper Christians to maintain a pure Christian behavior, perfect unity, and proper distance from their enemies. They should be explicit in their views on Scripture, never waver from the worship of God "according to your profession," and never let practice "give your profession the lie."[32]

Rankin shared many characteristics with the fanatics he condemned. His battle with the Presbyterian establishment over the use of the Watts translation of Psalms had already given some a taste of his occasionally hysterical personality. John Campbell presented a much less strident refutation of the radical position, grounding his comments in a defense of Calvinist doctrine. After an exchange of pamphlets with Stone, however, Campbell lost some of his scholarly detachment. "There is a dwarfish, sickly, ill-favored thing, pretty generally baptized charity, which has done infinite mischief in our country. She has an angel's name, but is a brat of darkness" because she allows debauchery and error to run rampant. The charity of the Bible is clear-sighted, but this

31. Rankin, *Review of the Noted Revival*, pp. 35-48.
32. Ibid., pp. 66-70.

evil form is accompanied by "a yielding, careless pliancy of heart, a fondness for novelty and change, and a restless, ungovernable impatience of restraint."[33]

Whereas Rankin had concentrated his efforts upon the errors within the practice of the revival, Campbell concentrated on the mistakes of radical theology. His first point of substantive disagreement was on the nature of God. He deplored the rejection of the old style of preaching in which "the wrath of God, and the terrors of his law, pierces the conscience."[34] In its place he found "Deism in a Christian garb," in which "God is love, and love only." In reducing God to love without wrath, Stone had created "a feeble, inefficient God."[35] Lacking wrath against sinners, God would fail to punish them, content instead to love them for their sins. This, he felt, tainted God with sin, and he found it an absurd proposition.

The second element of the radical program, the issue of atonement, drew much of Campbell's attention. After a tiresome and complicated analysis, Campbell rejected Stone's notion that Christ was merely a witness to a bond between God and man. Instead, Campbell stressed Christ's role as mediator between the two parties. In this role, Christ undertook "to endure the penalty of death" for man. Christ humbled Himself to restore man, "restoring the honors of a law which he had not violated, suffering for guilt which he had not personally incurred, and making reparation for wrongs he had never done."[36]

Robert Bishop, provided the most direct answer to the third point of the New Light doctrine, that Calvinist doctrine is obscure and unnecessary. All sects, he pointed out, have their creeds and confessions. Those who reject creeds embrace at least the tenet that creeds must be rejected. Until Christians no longer disagree, "every sect will find it necessary to have some sort of a creed or confession," and those who write tracts to do away with creeds are like the monk who published a book condemning publishing.[37]

---

33. Campbell, *Vindex*, pp. 7-9; see also Campbell *Strictures*, pp. iii-iv.
34. Campbell, *Vindex*, p. 151.
35. Campbell, *Strictures*, p. 14.
36. Campbell, *Doctrine of Justification*, pp. 22–23.
37. Robert Bishop, *An Apology for Calvinism* (Lexington, 1804), pp. 35-37.

Bishop was particularly appalled that untrained clergy increasingly dominated over the course of the revival. Piety, he argued, is never enough in religious leaders, for there then remains no check upon ignorance and stupidity: "Babes, and sucklings, idiots, and the deaf and the dumb, may, by the power of grace, be conformed to God's image; but no man in his senses will say, that any of these are qualified for being Gospel ministers."[38] The function of a minister is to guard against error, and to do so he needs sufficient knowledge.

The fourth element of the radical program, the concept of free grace, excited and angered all the opponents of the revival. Many of the conversions, Campbell felt, were "a mere self-wrought, mechanical thing; the child of fancy and delusion."[39] The key to Stone's delusion, Campbell concluded, was that his system of free grace depended upon selfishness. Because Stone believed that justification "is produced by faith, an act of my own, which no divine power is requisite to enable me to exercise, I then more than ever must think his views chargeable with selfishness." That is, Stone argued, each individual has the power to accept God's grace; Campbell responded that this idea smacks of pride because the all-important act in the course of salvation depends not upon God but upon man. "From such a system," Campbell proclaimed, "every honest heart should recoil in horror . . . to embrace it,—to act upon it,—to meet eternity upon it,—is to be UNDONE!"[40] Bishop echoed these sentiments and stressed the orthodox notion that human will is free, but only free to sin: "In refusing the offers of salvation, men must act according to their own wicked inclination."[41]

These clerics tended toward hysterical extremes when faced with the extremism of their opponents, yet they also tended to trot out all the old explanations of their faith when attacked. This

38. Bishop, *Legacy*, p. 13.
39. Campbell, *Vindex*, p. 52.
40. Campbell, *Doctrine of Justification*, pp. 8, 11.
41. Bishop, *Apology for Calvinism*, p. 11; see also John Lyle, "Diary and Journal of a Missionary Tour within the Bounds of the Cumberland Presbytery Performed in the Year 1805" (typed copy, p. 10, HFPC).

reaction made for a curious mixture of styles; within a few pages, a violent diatribe would be followed by an unimaginative and dull summary of some element of orthodox thought. This tension reflected a general uncertainty and confusion in the minds of these men. Content to preach old and safe doctrine to small but stable congregations, they faced a seemingly uncontrolled and uncontrollable force in the revival. Preachers new to the West disrupted presbytery and session meetings with new and often obnoxious ideas. Little wonder their opponents' prose suffered the schizophrenia of mild-mannered theology coupled with bitter invective. They knew, or sensed, that preachers of their style and concerns would never dominate in the West. This new, vital, vibrant, simplistic, and terribly threatening religion was the wave of the future, and theirs was a remnant of the past. As representatives of the pioneer generation, they felt their control disintegrating, and they decided to fight.

Moderate Clergy and the Great Revival

Most of the western clergy considered themselves neither radicals nor conservatives on the issue of the revival. Instead, they adopted a detached and moderate stance. The form of moderation differed from denomination to denomination. Presbyterians had to show the most care in expressing their opinions because their church was the most wracked with dissension. The typical Presbyterian moderate, therefore, tried to express as few opinions as possible. Methodists had united in defense of the revival, and they recognized the benefits it brought them. They therefore seldom commented on it, except to express a general sense of pleasure at the state of affairs. Baptists retained their limited list of simplified orthodox beliefs, which amounted to infrequent affirmations of basic doctrines such as antipedobaptism and original sin. They directed their attention, for the most part, to more practical concerns. The Arminianism of the radicals offended them, but none expressed particular outrage over it. More important, they received a great increase in membership from the revival. So, although they recognized a possible threat to orthodox thought implicit within the revival, they nevertheless cautiously supported the awakening because it was producing impressive number of converts.

Many moderates had recently joined the clergy, and some, such as Peter Cartwright, were themselves converts in the revival. They were, then, cohorts of the radicals, shaped by experiences that were shared by the leaders of the revival. Such ministers felt their natural connections were with the radicals, although they could not bring themselves to follow the extreme views of Stone and his friends. Many other moderates were older and had been pioneers themselves but had also regularly objected to various aspects of pioneer thought. David Rice, for one, saw the revival as a wonderful fulfillment of many of his deepest wishes, although, as we will see, he could not tolerate many of its wilder aspects. Both groups were active in the revival, hostile to the conservatives, yet remained unconvinced that New Light thought should be embraced wholeheartedly.

Although a complex group, moderates all shared several concerns over the course the revival had taken. They recognized the possibility and threat of excess, of mindless, uncontrolled religious "error." One Presbyterian worried that such error might result because the western controversialists were, in his eyes, a bit dim-witted; "Oh for some enlightened Missionaries or Ministers from New England to go as laborers among them with that blessing which has so often followed some of them."[42] It is particularly ironic that this minister appealed to other migrants to save the West from its latest troubles. In a letter to William McKendree, Asbury worried that the revival might backfire on the Methodists, as it had on the Presbyterians: "The spirit of error, superstition and schism is rising and spreading in the west, when it is dying in the east."[43] In his first, subdued comment on the revival, David Rice worried that "an ardent zeal, too often united with a certain spiritual pride, and strong self-love, is apt to inspire some persons, of an enthusiastic temperament, with vehe-

42. Charles Coffin, "Tennessee Journal" 1800–22, Presbyterian Historical Society, Philadelphia.
43. Clark, ed., *Journal and Letters of Francis Asbury*, 3:412.

ment impulses, to preach the gospel."[44] Two years later, in 1805, his mood had turned grim. The many attacks by Stone and his colleagues on Calvinism had led Rice to think that the revival was nearing the end of its usefulness. As a period of prosperity is followed by afflictions, so, he believed, "a time of revival in religion is frequently followed by great error and delusion." Revivals, he explained, generally begin with great outpourings of piety: "The spirit of the Lord is poured out upon ministers, they are anointed to preach the gospel, and stirred up to labor with more than usual diligence and faithfulness." Formalists become more lively, backsliders return to the church, the Bible gains respect, the Sabbath is honored, and, in general, "gross immoralities are carefully and conscientiously avoided." Unfortunately, Rice warned, the revival is followed by a "time of declension, backsliding and desertion." Such declension has several causes: spiritual pride, enthusiam, formalism, the personal fame of some preachers, emphasis of one doctrine over all others, improper discipline, and general contentiousness. He felt the Great Revival was the genuine work of God, but he also saw signs of error. Too little doctrine was being explained, especially that of the final preseverance of the saints, which all too often was replaced by Arminianism. Although this doctrine gave "great comfort and consolation...to believers on condition of their faithfulness," it failed to inform "them in what that faithfulness consists, of what degree it is requisite, of suggesting one reason for them to hope they will continue faithful."[45]

Rice and Asbury were disturbed almost as much at the disorder of the revival as at its tendency to produce error. Discipline, Rice argued, was essential. He thought the revival churches had used the wrong method for adding communicants: "Too disproportionate a regard is paid to experiences; too little to knowledge and sound profession." Significantly, this thought led Rice to the conclusion that all evangelical denominations should thank Presbyterians for maintaining knowledge, in much the same way Presbyteri-

44. Synod of Kentucky, *A Serious Address to the Churches under Their Care* (Lexington, 1804), p. 18.
45. Rice, *Epistle to the Citizens of Kentucky*, pp. 4–22, 32.

ans should thank the bishops of the Church of England, who had stood as a bulwark for Christianity "against the many formidable and violent attacks of its foes."[46] Asbury generally expressed confidence that order might be maintained even in the face of the revival: "We shall prevail, we do prevail, God is with us, better and better, order everywhere." Occasionally, however, he worried about the fate of Christianity in the West. Although Methodists had maintained their harmony, he feared the "heretical and schismatical jaws" into which the other denominations had fallen.[47]

In spite of reservations that members of the moderate clergy occasionally expressed, in general they were pleased with the achievements they saw. Rice thanked God, for "he has made the wilderness a fruitful field."[48] An observer writing from Lexington in 1801 commented enthusiastically that the revival "appears like a fire that had been long confined."[49] The notion of a holy fire that would burn down all disbelief appeared time and again in the moderate writings. The most comprehensive moderate defense of the revival came from David Thomas, a Baptist preacher in Kentucky. He objected to Rankin's attack in particular because he not only wanted to correct errors but desired "to explode the whole work, as a sanguinary machination, calculated by the infernal spirit, to inveigle and betray the souls of men." Thomas considered this notion nonsense, for the many positive elements of the revival, that it had "made better husbands and wives, parents and children, masters and servants, and every domestic relation,"[50] proved that it was divine work. To be sure, there were shortcomings;

46. Ibid., pp. 34–35.

47. Clark, ed., *Journal and Letters of Francis Asbury*, 3:400, 332.

48. David Rice, *A Sermon on the Present Revival of Religion, etc., in the Country* (Lexington, 1803), p. 3; see also Synod of Kentucky, *Serious Address*, p. 3.

49. *Gospel News, or a Brief Account of the Revival of Religion in Kentucky, and Several Other Parts of the United States* (Baltimore, 1801), p. 3.

50. David Thomas, *Review of the Revival* (Lexington, 1803), pp. iii, 12. See also Minutes, Long Run Baptist Association, Kentucky (1805), BHS; "Article of Agreement for School," Robert Marshall Papers, Presbyterian Historical Society, Philadelphia; *Minutes of the "Original" Cumberland Presbytery, 1803–06* (Louisville, 1906), p. 12; Minutes, Transylvania Presbytery, p. 413, HFPC. These ministers also encouraged patriotism; see James McChord, *National Safety* (Lexington, 1815), p. 29.

some meetings, for example, were the scene for "lewd" activity. Nevertheless, the revival amounted to "pure sterling gold" although " some dross has, no doubt, been mixed in." Rankin was a fool to expect perfection, Thomas believed, "until the final restitution of a degenerate and fallen world."[51]

Certain important benefits had resulted from the revival, and these helped support the case the moderates wished to make. By 1803 the Baptists in Kentucky had 15,695 communicants and 219 churches. Eleven years before there had been 4,373 members and 84 churches.[52] Each of the denominations experienced similar growth. Baptists benefited additionally from the temporary union of the Regular and Separate factions, which was negotiated by ten clergymen, five from each side, in 1801. They agreed to several terms, including faith in the scriptures, original sin, perseverance of the stains, baptism of the converted, and mutual aid among the churches. Two elements were to be tolerated: those who preached that "Christ tasted death for every man" and those who wished to "keep up their associational and church government as to them may seem best."[53] A minor split on personal rather than religious grounds occurred two years later, but the basic union lasted into the middle of the next decade, when the subject of missions divided loyalties once again.

Methodists benefited the most from the revival. With the radical Presbyterians fighting Calvinists, Methodists could easily capture members, and indeed they were accused of shrewdly seizing control of the West through the use of camp meetings, which were usually run by Methodist clergy. Asbury was conscious of the great advances of his church when he wrote, "Kentucky, which was a few years ago a dangerous frontier, is the centre of the western front of our empire where we behold a second part of the new world."[54] Never the dominant power in the

51. Thomas, *Review of the Revival*, p. 22.
52. *American Baptist Register*, p. 24.
53. Spencer, *History of Kentucky Baptists*, 1:546.
54. Clark, ed., *Journal and Letters of Francis Asbury*, 3:299.

West, a position held by the Baptists, Methodists nevertheless had gained great respectability and prestige.

The moderates concerned themselves with aspects of church activities which were generally ignored by the other parties. They showed great interest in the religious needs of settlers who began to move into the new territories to the south. This frontier was just as forbidding as Kentucky and Tennessee had been thirty years before. Early immigrants faced Indian attacks, scarce food, and a rough, uncharted land.[55] In 1807 McKendree and Asbury assigned Jacob Young to the Natchez region, but they had to argue him into agreeing to go.[56] The settlers were often less than pleased to see a preacher come to save them. In St. Stephens, in the Mississippi territory, "a local tradition represents a Baptist preacher visiting the thrifty town and expressing a desire to preach the gospel. He was summarily seized, placed in a canoe, rowed to the opposite side of the river, and warned that if he again set foot within the limits of the town, he would be promptly tarred and feathered."[57] Nevertheless, the moderate clergy took missionary tours south, went east to raise money for more missions, and tried to extend their empire into these new lands.

A good deal of interdenominational rivalry continued throughout the period of the revival. One pamphlet debate pitted John Cleland, a Presbyterian, against Jacob Heard, a Methodist. Cleland attacked the Methodists as opportunists, prostitutes of the gospel, and generally sinister creatures. Heard was particularly incensed at the attack because Cleland had participated in the camp meetings,

55. Z. T. Leavell and T. J. Bailey, *A Complete History of Mississippi Baptists from the Earliest Times*, 2 vols. (Jackson, 1904), pp. 18-24; B. F. Riley, *History of the Baptists of Alabama* (Birmingham, 1895), p. 12. For a more general picture, see Margaret Des Champs Moore, "Protestantism in the Mississippi Territory," *Journal of Mississippi History* 29 (1967): 358–370.

56. Gene R. Miller, *A History of North Mississippi Methodism, 1820-1900* (Nashville, 1966), p. 13; see also John Jones, *A Complete History of Methodism as Connected with the Mississippi Conference of the Methodist Episcopal Church, South* (Nashville, 1908), p. 15; Marion E. Lazenby, *History of Methodism in Alabama and West Florida* (N.p., 1960), p. 31.

57. Riley, *History of the Baptists in Alabama*, p. 14.

at which time "he made high professions of a catholic spirit, and seemed very desirous of having union and fellowship with the Methodists."[58] On the other side, Peter Cartwright was known to have invaded at least one solidly Presbyterian neighborhood, where he converted much of the population to Methodism.[59]

Most of the interest in regular church business came from the moderates. They kept busy ordaining church officers, trying to collect money for various causes, building churches, holding association meetings, and, in general, keeping the institution together. Moderates also were obliged to act as the judges and juries over members who offended the public decency, such as the minister who was stripped of his clerical authority after he had been found drunk several times.[60] In addition, moderates informally tried to maintain a sense of dignity and respectability among the ministers. One mature preacher was known for his caustic criticisms of the talents of his fellow clergy. He once stunned a new itinerant in the middle of the young man's sermon when he looked up to the pulpit and yelled, "Quit that smacking of your lips."[61] When Peter Cartwright was elected deacon, it was with the proviso that "the president give him a caution to be more serious."[62]

Each of the factions had a unique view of the direction the church should take. Moderates were receptive to new ideas but relatively cautious and slow in their implementation. Opponents of the revival believed that new ideas threatened the essence of Christianity, and they threw all their efforts into reestablishing the old order. The radicals wished to destroy the tired beliefs and structures they saw everywhere around them. The first group saw

58. Jesse Head, *A Reply to the Arguments Advanced by the Rev. Thomas Cleland* (Lexington, 1805), p. iii.

59. Walter B. Posey, *Religious Strife on the Southern Frontier* (Baton Rouge, 1965), p. 223.

60. Minutes, Transylvania Presbytery, p. 262, HFPC; Minutes, Bethlehem Baptist Church, Kentucky, Historical Commission of the Southern Baptist Church, Nashville (hereafter cited as HCSBC); Minutes, South District Baptist Association, Kentucky (1814), BHS.

61. H. C. Northcott, *Biograpy of Rev. Benjamin Northcott* (Cincinnati, 1875), pp. 77-78.

62. William W. Sweet, *Methodism in American History* (New York, 1933), p. 111.

the revival as nothing more than a quickening of the religious spirit, and they rejected the notion that the millennium was at hand. The second group felt certain that, if anything, the revival was the forerunner of an age of darkness. The third, however, expressed great hope that the "reign of grace" was at hand. One predicted that the millennium might come as early as 1823.[63]

The three groups based their formulations upon distinct world views. The orthodox opinion of those opposed to the revival showed residues of the doctrines of the established churches of the past century. The conservatives thought religion was a social verity, about which little fuss should be made. Catechizing the young, ordaining only those who met the highest standards, providing preaching to the already converted, they viewed their occupation, and the world, as ordered, secure, and proper.

The radicals believed that religion and life were elements in a process of experiment. They viewed the orthodoxy of their opponents as rigid, stodgy, lifeless, dry, and mechanical. In place of such a creed, they saw an open, exciting set of possibilities. Uncertain of what the future promised, they nevertheless felt a need to rush toward it. Theirs was both an acceptance of and insistence on the variety and mystery of divine experience and human life.

In the intentions of the central group lay the future of religion in the West. Their caution was telling, for they were willing to reap the benefits of the revival, but not at the expense of an excess of wild enthusiasm. Unwilling to speed headlong into the future, they insisted upon consultation and compromise. As long as the more extreme factions remained active, however, this essentially cautious stance was constantly threatened, buffeted in the winds of controversy. Above all, such ministers understood the special importance of the revival, and although filled with anxiety, they found their allies more often among the radicals who loved the revival than among the conservatives who remained firmly linked to the past security of small, pioneer congregations.

63. Rice, *Epistle to the Citizens of Kentucky*, p. 14; James McChord, *The Morning Star, or Precurser of the Millennium* ... (Lexington, 1813).

CHAPTER 3

Southwestern Antislavery
during the Great Revival

Slavery proved to be one great test of the distinction between the revival and pioneer generations of clergy, with the moderate component of the revival group taking the more complex and, in preactice, the more controversial position. Such moderates expressed powerful antislavery views although the issue upset and confused them. Radical revivalists adamantly refused to join any antislavery society, adopting an anarchistic attitude toward secular organizations, yet they agreed in principle that slavery was a great and manifest evil in southwestern society. Religious conservatives, continuing the pioneer tradition, generally opposed abolition. Conservatives, as I will argue in Chapter 4, did not provide ringing defenses of slavery. Such defenses were rare in the region for several decades. Rather, conservatives tended to feel that antislavery was but one more perversion of orthodox thought by modern innovation, particularly troubling because of its social ramifications.

The revival, then, made the clergy examine carefully their relation to society. Radical and moderate revivalists looked forward to the remaking of man and thereby the establishment of a virtuous world. They varied, however, in the degree of commitment they were willing to give to the notion that the millennium was at hand. Not even Barton Stone showed complete confidence in the imminence of the rule of Christ. Almost all the religious moderates and radicals were confident that their great awareness of God's purposes would enable them to guide less fully aware

Christians down the path of righteousness. They were optimistic about the chances of man if he followed their lead, but they recognized that their lead did not go unquestioned. Dissension and confusion within the ranks of the clergy seemed endemic to the revival; no one voice rose above the others to lead the way. The rise in piety was welcome, but how much it would translate into concrete action was never clear.

An equally troubling obstacle to the renaissance of society was that slavery was rapidly becoming a central element in the economic structure of the Southwest. By 1810, 17 percent of the population in Tennessee consisted of slaves.[1] In a few counties half of the population was black.[2] Slaves had rapidly been moved into the new territories to the south. Revivalists increasingly began to recognize the power of the institution to disrupt their hoped-for new world.

Radical Revivalists and Slavery

The vigor of the attack on slavery depended, in large measure, upon each minister's confidence in the imminence of the millennium. Radical revivalists, who based their beliefs most completely on progress, if not toward the millennium at least toward an earthly, Christian utopia, had the least interest in engaging in direct and detailed attacks on the institution. They seldom mentioned slavery. Believing that society would be totally transformed through the agency of the Holy Spirit, the radical revivalists provided little detailed analysis of problems in the modern world. They were usually content to contemplate the future, free of the work of Satan, when "the all-conquering Jesus will ride on the chariot of his gospel, gaining victory after victory, until his empire shall spread from pole to pole."[3] It was missing the point to look at specific sins for the truly saved were released from sin, could follow the inner light, and would therefore have exemplary behavior.

1. Charles Hedrick, *Social and Economic Aspects of Slavery in the Transmontane prior to 1850* (Nashville, 1927), p. 23; see also Caleb Patterson, *The Negro in Tennessee* (Austin, 1922), p. 212.

2. Railey, *History of Woodford County, Kentucky*, p. 7.

3. James McGready, *Posthumous Works* (Nashville, 1837), p. 26.

Embedded in the radical beliefs was an anarchistic strain. Radical revivalists rejected worldly law, culture, and tradition, as demonstrated most clearly in their repudiation of creeds and confessions and especially in their attacks on John Calvin. In place of such systematic beliefs, each Christian was a worship God according to his feelings. The government and laws of man would crumble, replaced by those of God. Although premillennialists, these radicals saw the future as promising peace and order rather than simply judgment and destruction. The revival, they felt, was not controlled by the normal forces of man-made law; its participants came from all elements of society and behaved unconventionally. As Barton Stone mused, "How persons, so different in their education, manners and natural dispositions; without any visible commander, could enter upon such a scene, and continue in it for days and nights, in perfect harmony, has been one of the greatest wonders that ever the world beheld."[4] Human tradition had to be rooted out, and a higher law would replace it.

Fundamental to the radicals' anarchism was a distrust of church government. Soon after the Kentucky Synod tried McNemar for heretical beliefs, the radicals gave up their official relation with the Presbyterian church and formed an independent presbytery of Springfield. Only a year later, they gave up even this limited connection with tradition and wrote the "Last Will and Testament of the Springfield Presbytery." Stone quite his congregations, fearing the constraints of the traditional minister-church relation.[5] He also objected to error institutionalized within the conventional and traditional churches: "Witness the parties, the bitterness, the envy, the cold formality, and deadness, which exist to the disgrace of the Christian religion. Truth, and truth only, will make us free."[6]

Such anarchism made questions of social reform seem trivial; instead, a revolution was called for. To be sure, Stone freed his slaves, but not as an example to the rest of society. Rather, his act of emancipation seems to have been passive, as though the slaves

4. McNemar, *Kentucky Revival*, pp. 36, 31.
5. Rogers, ed., *Biography of Barton Stone*, pp. 50-55.
6. Stone, *Atonement*, p. 36.

ceased to be his property, not because he became convinced of the evil of slavery but because they became superfluous. He simply disemburdened himself, inspired by "a sense of right, choosing poverty with a good conscience, in preference to all the treasures of the world. This revival cut the bonds of many poor slaves; and this argument speaks volumes in favor of the work.[7] In short, antislavery was never, for the radicals, an end in itself, any more than were temperance or opposition to gambling. Rather, these views reflected true conversion.

Several of the radicals joined the Shakers, an act which took them out of society altogether. Stone was shocked by this turn of events,[8] but some saw it as a logical move because the followers of Ann Lee believed that the millennium was at hand and that they were to be the judges of humanity. They joined together in communities of the saved and rejected all worldly activities, including slavery. The opponents of the Shakers, however, characterized the sect as a form of slavery, in which the community leader served as master.[9] This view underlines all the more clearly that the anarchism of the radicals did not provide the primary motive for opposing slavery; rather, slavery, especially American Negro slavery, must be abandoned because it was an element of the sinful government of man. Under the rule of God, however, some other form of slavery might be appropriate and just. In this sense, the radicalism was all-encompassing, and slavery was less important than ideology.

Moderate Revivalists and Slavery

Moderate revivalists shared the theological notion of the government of God with their brothers in the radical camp but were

7. Rogers, *Biography of Barton Stone*, p. 44.

8. Stone, *Reply to John P. Campbell's Strictures*, pp. 66-67.

9. James Smith, *Shakerism Detected* . . . (Paris, Ky., 1810); James Smith, *Remarkable Occurrences, Lately Discovered among the People Called Shakers; of a Treasonous and Barbarous Nature, or Shakerism Developed* (Paris, Ky., 1810). On Shakers in general, see Edward D. Andrews, *The People Called Shakers: A Search for the Perfect Society* (New York, 1953); C. Allyn Russell, "The Rise and Decline of the Shakers," *New York History* 49 (1968):29–55.

much less confident that the prophecy of Revelation was unfolding in the early nineteenth-century Southwest. As we have seen, their view of the revival tended to be complex and somewhat ambivalent. Uneasy with the confusion and occasional chaos the revival brought with it, moderates nevertheless understood its practical value: warm bodies now occupied once empty pews. Such success could excuse a great deal of chaos. Their practical bent, however, suggests the route moderates would take on social issues. The miraculous transformation of southwestern society seemed no more likely than was the miraculous transformation of southwestern souls. The anarchism of the New Lights held no appeal for moderate revivalists. Indeed, much as was the case with revivalists in the Connecticut River valley, southwestern moderates saw the revival as a chance to reform, not to overthrow, their regional culture. Order, restraint, and care were their watchwords during the revival, and these concepts shaped their reform ideas well. As a consequence of the moderate goal of leading southwestern society forward, such clergymen tended to assume a divine sanction for the basic laws, creeds, rules, and confessions of Kentucky and Tennessee, the emblems of civilized Christian society which prevented Indians and heathen whites from taking over the region. These clergy hoped to promote the reform of society in such a way as to conform earthly government to Christian ideals.

Among necessary reforms, the abolition of slavery was the most troublesome. Prohibition of the use of alcohol required personal sacrifice and government intervention. Other reforms, such as sanctions on gambling and dancing, would place constraints on culture. Sabbatarianism necessitated the restriction of normal functions of business. Each of these reforms, therefore, required distinct tactics. Merchants had to be made to understand the merits of a day of rest. Politicians had to be taught the evils of drink. The moderate revivalists felt, naively of course, that such sins would give way to the wishes of the righteous.

But direct action would be insufficient to abolish the ever more important institution of slavery in the Southwest. Simply lobbying one element of society would have had little effect on so complicated an evil. The clergy had to face the challenge of removing one of the cornerstones of southwestern society. Slavery was a vital economic institution, as much a part of southwestern agriculture as the seasons. It was also an important element of the social structure, which some preachers had begun to liken to a family relationship.[10] Government sanctioned the institution and provided numerous laws to secure its regular and smooth operation. And because the clergy regularly stressed the sinful nature of man, they could hardly have ignored the psychological pleasures masters received from owning slaves. They certainly recognized the physical pleasures as well, for the ministers often acknowledged that miscegenation was a fact of life in slaveholding societies. Church records regularly cited "yellow" members of their congregations. The matrix of slavery and society, then, made the business of abolition much more than simple reforming activity; because it was so dominant in southwestern society, slavery became, for many ministers, too great a challenge to overcome. Some, as we shall see, fled the region because of it, and some others held their tongues and remained in place.[11]

Another obstacle to antislavery was its potential conflict with an important tenet of the revival: the necessity of universal conversion. Some Baptists and Presbyterians still believed in the doctrine of election, but free grace had gained great popularity among the clergy. If churches excluded slaveholders, however, a sizable group of influential citizens would be lost to the revival. Drunkards were seldom the leading members of society, so sermons on temperance hardly blemished and often enhanced the success of the evangelical mission. Slaveholders posed a much greater threat. With their substantial prestige and economic power, they could have opposed the clergy's attempt to save the West from infidelity. Moreover, slaveholders provided much of the funding for financially hard-pressed churches. Ministers who remembered the hard times at the end of the eighteenth century might well be loath to alienate the only truly wealthy members of southwestern society.

A final obstacle to abolition, an intriguing counterpart to the fear of jeopardizing the source of church income was that as the

10. Minutes, South District Baptist Association, Kentucky (1812), pp. 3-4, BHS.

11. See Jordan, *White over Black.*

revival continued, clergy began to achieve noticeable status in society. Even the conventionally humble Methodists had, on occasion, begun to dress in fashionable style and adopt current mannerisms. Members of Nashville society looked to Henry Bascom, a young, brash Methodist minister, to find out the latest fashions from the East.[12] As ministers achieved this respectability, they felt less certain that an upheaval of society through the abolition of slavery was needed. Few ministers, of course, acquired great wealth and power, but once even a few gained increased prestige, their inclination toward sacrifice weakened. Such status considerations might easily be overstated, however, as they surely have on countless other issues in American history. Status concerns certainly typified the more established, conservative clergy in the cities and larger towns of the region, as I will argue in Chapter 4, but were seldom expressed by most revival ministers. The most serious result of a change in status for southwestern clergy was that many more ministers had slaves of their own. Statistics do not exist enumerating slaveholders among the clergy, but more and more frequently church governments cited ministers for their participation in the peculiar institution. Preachers expressed fewer condemnations of slavery when they saw other ministers ignoring church sanctions as brazenly as the richest plantation owners in the West.[13]

These interrelated problems should have severely restricted the enthusiasm for antislavery by the moderate southwestern ministers had it not been for several powerful influences in the opposite direction. The evangelical churches had a strong antislavery tradition with a long history of decisions against chattel slavery in each denomination. The central governments of both the Presbyterian and Methodist denominations had long opposed slavery. Wesley was often quoted in debates over slavery for having called it the "execrable sum of all vilanies [sic]," and he encouraged antislavery activities in all Methodist societies. To be sure, some retreat on the issue could be detected in the eighteenth century, but in the main both denominations continued their opposition to the peculiar

12. Moses Henkle, *The Life of Henry Bidleman Bascom* (Nashville, 1894), p. 63.
13. William W. Sweet, *The Rise of Methodism* (New York, 1920), p. 203.

institution. Enthusiasm was less apparent in the Baptist church, which lacked effective national organization. Nevertheless, many influential and important Baptist preachers had participated in the fight against slavery.[14]

Antislavery activities were also supported by the argument that slavery was an unchristian institution. Ministers frequently noted that most slaveholders failed to bring their servants to church. Masters often abused and mistreated slaves, and they failed to educate them, so it was difficult for the slaves to follow Christian teachings. Moreover, as many ministers pointed out, the New Testament seemed to provide much ammunition against slavery. Although biblical arguments could and would be trotted out on either side of the issue, the Gospels and the word of Christ in the beatitudes suggest that Christ's sympathies lay with the oppressed and not the oppressors.

Such arguments missed the point, according to some antislavery clergymen. Slavery was primarily a practical rather than a doctrinal problem, and moderates had always been at their best when dealing with practical issues. For the most part they promoted a working faith, free of the debates and attendant confusions over God's will which came from radical revivalists and their opponents. Therefore, a practical problem such as slavery had great appeal, in large measure simply because it was not necessarily theologically troublesome. No disputes that went to the heart of Christianity would erupt from a debate over slavery; no divisions of a theological nature would result. Within this context, moreover, a curious paradox resulted. A radical stance on slavery, a demand for immediate, total abolition, might well issue from a moderate position on the fundamental issues of the revival. On this practical rather than theoretical issue, revivalists could hope to attract converts who would have little to say about the course of the revival but who would approve of its antislavery aspect.

One final factor favoring antislavery views was the proximity of western states and territories that were free of slavery. Ohio in

14. See Jeffrey B. Allen, "Were Southern White Critics of Slavery Racists? Kentucky and the Upper South, 1791–1824," *Journal of Southern History* 44 (1978): 169-190, is an enthusiastic account of the virtues of antislavery activists.

particular, served as a repository for antislavery thought and a conscience for the slaveholding West. Clergy in Tennessee and Kentucky had constant interaction with ministers in Ohio through letters, official meetings, and personal visits,[15] so the expressions of antislavery sentiment which frequently emerged in the churches of the Old Northwest were communicated south, encouraging antislavery thinking. Here interregionalism mattered because the inner workings of the regional culture could not provide enough stimulation for southwestern ministers who were concerned about slavery.

Moderate clergy in each denomination responded in complex ways to the various forces at work on their consciences and intellects, trying to force them this way or that on the issue of slavery. The internal logic of each denomination in large measure fixed the limits of antislavery activity for individual southwestern clergymen. Obviously, this is not to say that the position ministers took on any social issue, particularly slavery, was a simple product of internal denominational pressure. All of the issues I have just discussed, be they intellectual, social, ethical, political, or practical, played into their decisions. But these clergymen had to see all of the divisive issues of the revival and all of the complexities of southwestern culture within the context of denominational thought. As was true of the eastern New England Unitarians and the western New England evangelicals, the specific nature of denominational development was the central concern for these ministers of the Old Southwest. It was to church government that each minister was ultimately responsible, and therefore close examination of antislavery notions within individual denominations is necessary. In short, no simple causal model will be useful. To say that the moderates were simply a product of southwestern society ignores their frequent attachment to theological and sectarian movements. Yet to see them merely as products of the professionalization of the clergy, as representatives of theological or institutional trends within the denominations, minimizes their participation within the regional culture. The best model is that denominational

15. William W. Sweet, *Religion on the American Frontier,* 4 vols. (Chicago, 1931-46), 4:152-155.

factors provided the context for their thought, the limits beyond which they were loath to tread, but society and individual belief explain movement within the denominationally set parameters.

Baptists divided most severely over the issue of slavery. Their major problem stemmed, ironically, from their greatest strength: Baptists were the most powerful and well-established ministers in the region. As we have seen, the pioneer generation of Baptist ministers had to gauge their comments to the audience with whom they conducted secular affairs during the week. Revivalists continued to find that success in the localities of the Old Southwest brought with it some degree of, or at least concern about, worldliness. In short, Baptists were the most likely among the region's clergymen to have status concerns. The most successful Baptists, secure in their possessions and eager to maintain the staus quo, saw abolition as a threat to their way of life. This group included mostly former Separate Baptists, who had always been the most conservative members of the denomination. Separates distrusted all authority, and they saw their religion as fundamentally individualistic. Any rules against slavery necessitated meddling in the affairs of true Christians, which the Separates opposed as much for moral as for personal reasons. Naturally, then, the first break in the union of Regulars and Separates resulted from a dispute over the ownership of a slave.[16]

As a consequence of the anxiety among the Separate Baptists over slavery, the various Baptist associations in the West evaded the problem each time it was raised. In 1805 the Elkhorn (Kentucky) Association decided that it was "improper for ministers, churches or associations to meddle with emancipation from slavery or any other political subject."[17] Ten years later, the Cumberland River (Tennessee) Association followed Elkhorn's lead. It felt that churches should stay out of the debate over the future of slaves: "We think it would be best to wait for the dispensations of Providence, and pray to God for the happy year of their deliverance to commence."[18]

16. Spencer, *History of Kentucky Baptists*, 1:553.

17. Minutes, Elkhorn Baptist Association, Tennessee (1805), p. 2, BHS.

18. Minutes, Cumberland River Baptist Association, Kentucky (1815), p. 2, BHS.

Occasional comments which members raised about the proper treatment of slaves caused Baptist associations no little anxiety. In a circular letter on duties of Christians, including slaves, members of the South District (Kentucky) Association disclaimed any interest in "discussing the question of slavery." They consequently avoided listing the duties of masters to slaves.[19] In 1808 the Mississippi Association received a letter from a member church inquiring about what actions to take toward a member who mistreated his slaves. The reply was a recommendation "to the several churches belonging to our connection to take notice of any improper treatment of their members toward their slaves, and deal with them in brotherly love, according to the rules of the gospel."[20] Such mild and ambiguous directions typified Baptist comments on the subject.

During the first years of the nineteenth century, several preachers promoted antislavery and founded emancipation societies. David Barrow continued as the leading Baptist spokesman for abolition, now joined by Carter Tarrant, an early settler of Kentucky, who led numerous meetings in opposition to slavery. By 1805 the emancipationists had stirred up enough controversy that the North District (Kentucky) Association expelled Barrow, claiming that he propagated "doctrines that are unsound or pernicious to peace and good order."[21] Several abolitionist preachers soon left their associations, and in 1807 they joined together as the Licking-Locust Association, with 190 members; Carter Tarrant was elected moderator.[22] Other Baptist associations shunned this upstart group, declaring that it would be "imprudent (under the present state of things) to intermeddle therewith."[23] Nevertheless, the association took advantage of the democratic structure of the denomination to form a dissenting group. Only among Baptists, indeed, could an

19. Minutes, South District Baptist Association, Kentucky (1815), pp. 3-4, BHS.

20. *A Republication of the Minutes of the Mississippi Baptist Association* (New Orleans, 1849), p. 13.

21. Spencer, *History of Kentucky Baptists*, 1:189, 2:120.

22. Minutes, Licking-Locust Baptist Association, Kentucky (1807), p. 1, BHS.

23. Minutes, Long Run Baptist Association, Kentucky (1811), p. 2, BHS; see also George W. Ranck, *History of Lexington, Kentucky* (Cincinnati, 1972), p. 119.

association be formed that might take a hard and fast position on slavery, although the most adamant antislavery baptists isolated themselves by forming the association. Little wonder that the Licking-Locust Association remained small, eventually leaving for the more supportive environment of Illinois.[24]

It is also not surprising that Presbyterian moderates gave scant attention to slavery because they were occupied with other controversies. The records of meetings over the first decade and a half of the nineteenth century consequently mention slavery infrequently. In the 1809 meeting of the Kentucky Synod, the assembled members ordered their presbyteries to take steps that "may seem prudent to secure the religious instruction of the slaves." Soon afterward, however, the synod lifted the suspension of a member of the Concord Church in Kentucky who had been convicted of selling a slave at auction.[25] The Presbyterian government in the Southwest was therefore no less equivocal than the Baptists on the issue of slavery.

Several individual Presbyterians vigorously favored abolition in spite of the denominational government's disinterest. James Barnes and Hugh Bass enthusiastically fought for the cause, following the dictates of their consciences on the issue.[26] Robert Marshall, a teacher and Presbyterian minister, sent a child of a local slave to a subscription school. When the school refused her admittance, Marshall wrote the schoolmaster, expressing his sorrow "that difficulty should occur respecting one child merely because her skin is not of the same colour with others."[27] Two of the most important preachers of the revival among the moderates also promoted antislavery. Isaac Anderson founded a manumission society in Knoxville, and David Rice continued his fight against slavery until his death in 1816.[28] These were mostly individual

24. Sweet, *Religion on the American Frontier,* 1:564-607.

25. Minutes, Kentucky Synod (1809), Presbyterian Theological Seminary, Louisville; ibid. (1810).

26. Posey, *Presbyterian Church,* p. 79.

27. Marshall to William West, Robert Marshall Papers, Shane Collection, Presbyterian Historical Society, Philadelphia.

28. Will A. McTeer, *History of New Providence Presbyterian Church, Maryville, Tennessee, 1786-1921* (Maryville, 1921), pp. 40-44.

activities, however. Presbyterians never organized a body of anti-slavery supporters in the period to match the Baptist Licking-Locust Association.

For a number of reasons, Methodists in the Southwest came most easily into the antislavery camp. The denomination had experienced no major division over the revival, and so antislavery was not lost in the wash of other troubles. Moreover, the Methodist church had the most hierarchical organization of the three evangelical denominations, and its leader, Bishop Francis Asbury, continued to oppose slavery vigorously for most of the period of the revival. The advantages of Methodists over the other two denominations are obvious. Presbyterians had no clear-cut leadership and broke into a variety of factions, as we shall see, over the issues of the revival. Baptists could evade the issue by learning the decision on the efficacy of slavery to local organizations. Methodists, out of respect for their leaders and a sense of the antislavery tradition flowing from Wesley, could not easily ignore the need for abolition (although Asbury's views would later change, as will be apparent in Chapter 4). Beyond their need to respect the beliefs of the leadership, Methodist ministers also found that they had the least to lose in advocating so fundamental and crucial a reform. Almost no Methodist minister, as far as the records show, owned a slave in the early years of the revival; most, indeed, were itinerants with few worldly possessions. Theologically, their thoroughgoing commitment to free grace, with its emphasis on works, tended to encourage an active reforming spirit, as would become apparent later in the burned-over district, where Methodists and doctrinally loose Presbyterians created a vast wave of reform. In the Old Southwest of this period, most Baptists and Presbyterians, who still tended to advocate deterministic elements of American orthodoxy, felt somewhat less certain about the need for moral reform.

During the period of revival, members of the Western Methodist Conference passed several strongly worded resolutions against slavery and began to implement these decrees. In 1806, for example, they admitted Benjamin Wofford on trial, but only after he provided "for the emancipation of his two slaves, now in South Carolina." Soon, however, such vigorous antislavery activities began to disappear. In 1808 the ministers ordered the expulsion of any member who sold slaves out of "speculative motives."[29] By Asbury's interpretation, a slaveholder had to emancipate his slaves only if he behaved "unjustly, inhumanely or covetously."[30] The conference consequently became a tribunal, judging the slaveholders' motives. Because the clergy could spare little time to evaluate each case, conferences tended to allow a grace period before requiring divestiture. For example, Samuel Sellars was allowed to keep his fourteen-year-old slave "until he is 22 years of Age."[31] The Tennessee Conference, founded by antislavery ministers, had little interest in compromise, however, and forced Asbury to sign a directive expelling any Methodist who owned a slave.[32]

Peter Cartwright and Benjamin Northcott typified the antislavery Methodists in the Southwest. Both took resolute and uncompromising stances on the issue of slavery, and they regularly preached their views.[33] Much more vehement in his antislavery views, however, was James Axley. An imposing individual, Axley was "very broad and compactly built, formed for strength; his step was firm, his face was square, complexion dark, eyebrows heavey [sic]; dressed in the costume of our fathers, with Straight-breasted coat, and broad-brimmed hat projecting over a sedate countenance."[34] He was hardly an intellectual; when he was admitted on trial, the conference termed him "a man of undoubted piety, but small gifts."[35] He used his talents to reform society, leaving the fine points of theological debate to others. When a slaveholder came to join his congregation, Axley told him he could hold no church office; his sole activities, so long as he owned slaves, would be "to pay and obey."[36] Axley believed that the

29. Sweet, *Rise of Methodism*, pp. 114, 148.

30. Clark, ed., *Journal and Letters of Francis Asbury*, 2:480.

31. Sweet, *Rise of Methodism*, p. 181.

32. Mathews, *Slavery and Methodism*, p. 181.

33. Northcott, *Biography of Rev. Benjamin Northcott*, p. 88; Cartwright, *Autobiography*, pp. 188-189.

34. Finley, *Sketches of Western Methodism*, p. 232; Cartwright, *Autobiography*, p. 93.

35. Sweet, *Rise of Methodism*, p. 94.

36. Redford, *History of Methodism in Kentucky*, 1:424.

direct, even insulting approach was the only proper address to such monstrous sinners as slaveholders.

Although the Methodists took the most vigorous antislavery stance during the revival, their enthusiasm fell off as the revival waned. McKendree suggested that the Tennessee Annual Conference should use caution if it had to deal with the subject of slavery.[37] The number of clergy who owned slaves increased. In 1812 the Tennessee Conference altered its prohibition on ownership if the master were motivated by "justice and mercy."[38] Many clergy saw these as ominous indications of a future trend, and some moved out of the slaveholding territory. As I will argue later, this declining enthusiasm for antislavery had complex roots in the development of southwestern religion.

The Antislavery Thought of Moderate Revivalists

As a group, the antislavery ministers created a series of arguments on moral and practical grounds with which to attack slavery. To be sure, because of the denominational differences among these moderate revivalists some issues were stressed over others; nevertheless, a complex set of beliefs emerged to unite them into a moderate revivalist antislavery "mind." Hardly primitives, these ministers often expressed their abolitionist ideas in as persuasive and sophisticated a manner as arguments proposed by antislavery ministers in the East.[39] But they produced no single, systematic attack on slavery; their views much be pieced together from often fugitive sources.

Following their commitment to moral issues over all others, moderate revivalists worked their way through a set of broad ethical and moral objections to the peculiar institution. Although, unlike ministers of the pioneer generation, moderate revivalists usually stopped short of declaring slaveholding a sin, the Ken-

37. Paine, *William McKendree*, p. 216.
38. Redford, *History of Methodism in Kentucky*, 1:261, 282-284.
39. See Alice Adams, *The Neglected Period in American Antislavery* (1908; reprint, Gloucester, Mass., 1964).

tucky Synod echoed David Rice's notion of a "moral evil." This ambiguous characterization depends upon a distinction between thought and action in which a moral evil is a sin and a practical evil is merely the unpleasant consequence of an action. The Presbyterians spent little energy on such moral considerations, however. Instead, moderates tended to stress the inappropriate moral and ethical consequences of slavery, avoiding the issue of the moral basis of the institution. A moderate poem argued that God must be distressed when "He sees immortal creatures / Converted into herds; / Abused by proud oppressors, / Who fancy they are Lords."[40] / Moderate revivalists tended to contrast the master's abuses of slaves' humanity with the attitude of Christ, who treated all men, from thieves to wise men, as equals. There is at least some echo here of moderate Enlightenment views, but what is most significant about this category of moderate objections is the infrequency of its appearance.

Much more significant as a moral objection was the moderate revivalist assertion that slavery was contrary to the word of God as contained in the Bible. In organizing an antislavery church, a group of Baptists wrote that they differed from other Baptists only in that they believed "perpetual, hereditary, involuntary and unmerited slavery, is contrary to the Gospel of God." Here and elsewhere, the moderates tended not to follow a literalist interpretation of the Bible, in contrast to both of the other camps in the clergy. Instead of following close arguments throughout Scripture, moderates were willing to accept a broader, looser construction when they felt it was appropriate. Carter Tarrant concentrated upon text in his use of Scripture for antislavery purposes, but he always blurred the apparent and obvious sense of the verses he quoted. For example, he argued that Genesis 9:25 has nothing to say about perpetual slavery; the verse reads, "And he said cursed by Canaan; a servant of servants shall he be unto his brethren." Tarrant argued that this passage is not what it appears to be, Noah's prophecy; Noah had no power to curse anyone. Instead, he was simply stating a fact, that Canaan was a slave. Tarrant

40. Levi Purviance, *The Biography of Elder David Purviance* (Dayton, 1848), p. 49.

examined other passages in a similar manner, with equally great capability to ignore the obvious. In trying to explain Christ's failure to condemn slavery, Tarrant used a similar exegetical technique. Instead of purposefully ignoring the obvious meaning of Christ's words, Tarrant was forced to put words into Christ's mouth. Christ, Tarrant argued, condemned slavery by implication. Jesus could hardly have condemned all the evils in the world. The true Christian is expected to understand that there are many evils of which Christ was not aware or which He assumed His followers should avoid.[41] Moderates were willing to argue that Scripture in general implied a condemnation of slavery and that read with a proper understanding of its meaning, the Bible is abolitionist. In this way these early nineteenth-century moderate revivalists presaged the thought of the abolitionists emerging out of the burned-over district.

The simplest moral objection to slavery issued by these moderate revivalists was an extension of their condemnation of the low state of morality in the Southwest, one of the issues that had propelled the revival to its considerable success. If Christians failed to eliminate slavery, Tarrant argued, "it is not unlike reproving a gambler, and then sitting down and keeping game for him."[42] Axley had achieved fame throughout the West for his "Sermon on the Abominations": "Freemasonry, whiskey, smoking, fashion and slavery." Aid to the poor, temperance, and similar reforms were frequently advocated by the same reformers.[43] Everywhere around them they felt that decay was growing, and the revival was the only hope for society. They were not particularly talented organizers; they did not lead a full-fledged reform movement. But their linking of slavery to other issues again previews the developments of reform in decades to come.

41. Carter Tarrant, *The Substance of a Discourse Delivered in the Town of Versailles, Woodford County, State of Kentucky, April 20, 1806* (Lexington, 1806), pp. 27, 11-12, 16.

42. Ibid., pp. 27-28.

43. Redford, *History of Methodism in Kentucky*, 1:418-423; Labon Jones, *A Brief Memoir of the Rev. Samuel Ayres Noel...* (Louisville, 1846), p. 83; Walter B. Posey, "The Development of Methodism in the Old Southwest, 1783-1824" (PhD. dissertation, Vanderbilt University, 1933), pp. 104-5; John Ewell, *Life of Rev. William Keel* (Noah, Tenn., 1884), p. 93.

Detailed, practical problems of the institution of slavery received greater emphasis in the writing of antislavery moderates than did the moral shortcomings of the peculiar institution. In these writings the fundamentally pragmatic nature of moderate revivalism showed through. Especially in central Kentucky and Tennessee, where more slaves lived than in the rest of the Southwest, clergy had numerous firsthand experiences of the system. They particularly objected to the separation of families, a problem for which they seldom had a satisfactory solution save the total abolition of slavery. One Baptist association was asked, "What shall be done with a black member having his wife taken from him and removed to a different part, he marry another?" It could only suggest that churches "act prudently and tenderly toward that afflicted people."[44] The Glen Creek Baptist Church "reproached its members who separated by sale a Negro woman and her child."[45]

A second practical problem moderate ministers stressed was the failure of masters to provide slaves with a proper education. Much of the agitation on this point came, not surprisingly, from Presbyterians, who saw education as a necessity. The Kentucky Synod stressed the careful "religious instruction of Slaves held by members of our connections,"[46] and the Transylvania Presbytery argued that this was as important as the education of white youth. The failure of masters to provide their slaves with proper religious training was not lost on the Baptists either. It showed, Carter Tarrant argued, the fallacy of the notion that slavery was a Christianizing force. Slave traders had not gone to Africa to covert the natives; if that had been their intention, "they might have carried books and gone to have preached to them in their own country."[47] Under slavery, these ministers argued, slaves usually remained in darkness, seldom allowed to receive the word of God.

A third element that the antislavery ministers condemned was

44. Minutes, Long Run Baptist Association, Kentucky (1812), p. 2, BHS.

45. Walter Posey, "Baptist Watch-Care in Early Kentucky," *Register of the Kentucky State Historical Society* 34 (1936): 314-315.

46. Minutes, Kentucky Synod (1809), Presbyterian Theological Seminary, Louisville.

47. Tarrant, *Substance of a Discourse*, p. 18.

the cruelty of slavery. Especially repulsive were the hypocritical actions of Christian masters who were meek and gentle with their white brethren but demanding and violent with their slaves. Axley preached that the women in his church would sit in their pews "as sweet and smiling as if you were angels." Yet if he visited them at home, he could hear "the sound of slaps, and the poor slave girl screaming, and the sister whaling and trouncing Sally in the kitchen as hard as she can."[48]

Cruelty was related to a fourth problem, the low morality of both slaves and masters, which, the clergy argued, was a direct product of slavery. White youth became insensitive to the sufferings of their fellowman; instead, they assumed a false pride, became lazy, and were cursed with avarice.[49] Slaves, on the other hand, "were convicted of lying, stealing, conjuring, drinking and adultery."[50] These slaves, remarkably, were members of a Baptist church; others had, if it were possible, lower morals.

A fifth problem intrinsic to slavery was less frequently cited, but those who mentioned it spoke in extraordinarily dramatic terms. Miscegenation was both a racial and a moral problem. Peter Cartwright stressed the latter element in his autobiography. He noted that "young masters are often tempted and seduced from the paths of virtue," which was both a sin in itself and a source of "domestic disquietude." That is, white wives and mothers suffered from "heart-embittering feeling" when they saw the "thousands of mixed blood around them."[51] It is revealing that Cartwright stressed the effects on whites of miscegenation; that slaves "tempted and seduced" their masters implied, of course, the subtle racist point that black women were the aggressors, the beneficiaries rather than the victims of adultery. It is tempting, however, to overstate the degree of racism present in these ministers and to condemn them too stridently with modern concepts of social equality. As members of a regional culture fully and

48. William Milburn, *The Pioneers, Preachers and People of the Mississippi Valley* (New York, 1860), p. 372.

49. Tarrant, *Substance of a Discourse*, pp. 9-10; see also Charles Osborne, *Journal of the Faithful Servant of Christ* (Cincinnati, 1854), p. 98.

50. Posey, "Watch-Care," p. 314.

51. Cartwright, *Autobiography*, pp. 128-129.

determinedly committed to the notion of black inferiority, the moderate, antislavery ministers were unusually conscious of the capabilities of blacks; for example, they frequently encouraged slave aspirations toward the ministry. To be sure, they showed no understanding of the intricacies of slave culture, but it was, after all, their business to show no interest in any society but the one they felt was ordained by God. Even these reformers shared in some of the sexual mythology Winthrop Jordan has painstakingly described, but their calling meant that such concepts were part of a complex belief structure that included countervailing notions of the humanity of blacks.[52]

Because their antislavery beliefs reflected the moderate concentration on practice rather than theology, one would expect such ministers to generate an array of specific ideas on how to end slavery. Such was not the case. Doubtless their failure to unite their churches behind an antislavery crusade explains to a great extent their failure to develop a full-fledged antislavery program. In general, the churches had concluded that they could not risk the revival for the sake of slaves. Individual preachers did not remain inactive, preaching the evils of slavery but doing nothing about it. To do so would have violated the revivalist desire to create awakening, through whatever technique might be available. Specific moderates freed their own slaves, proselytized, and organized. Robert Donnell, for example, actively moved from town to town in Tennessee organizing manumission and antislavery societies.[53] Others chose nonparticipation: Benjamin Northcott used slaves for laborers but only if he could treat them as if they were free and give them wages they could keep.[54]

The revival, for the moderates, had not been in any sense a political event. It might usher in a change for society but not through the conversion of the leaders of society. That revivalist technique would await Charles Grandison Finney, who used it with uncommon skill. The moderates, indeed, tended to distrust

52. Coffin, "Tennessee Journal," November 5, 1806; Jordan, *White over Black*.
53. David Lowry, *Life and Labors of the Late Rev. Robert of Alabama, Minister of the Gospel in the Cumberland Presbyterian Church Connell* (Alton, Ill., 1867), pp. vvi-xi.
54. Northcott, *Biography of Rev. Benjamin Northcott*, p. 88.

those members of society whom they felt might try to capitalize upon the awakening; they looked askance, for example, at the charlatans who tried to profit financially from the camp meetings. Unlike the radicals, who saw a truly political message of transformation in the Great Revival, moderates remained separate from that sphere. Organized, secular campaigns remained beyond the moderate imagination, and disruption of social standards barely occurred to them. Moderate advocates of antislavery worried that they would be suspected of fomenting slave unrest. Carter Tarrant explained that he "never told an African that he or they ought to be liberated, but have uniformly urged the necessity of their obedience, honesty and industry."[55] Moderates believed that the proper function of a religious abolitionist was the conversion of other Christians to antislavery. Some taught their students the fundamentals of antislavery;[56] others campaigned within the church governments to pass rules against slavery. A few tried to go beyond such circumscribed activity and unite with secular leaders to promote legislative abolition, but in general the moderate revivalists undertook diffuse and formless actions in dealing with the peculiar institution.

This circumscribed form of action on slavery is perhaps best exemplified by the moderates' actions toward slaveholding members. Axley felt that "no slaveholder could be saved in heaven, or was a proper person to be admitted into the church."[57] The Kentucky Synod, in its *Memorial on Slavery*, argued that no southwestern Presbyterian church should allow union with slaveholders. The members who wrote the manifesto saw "slavery as a moral evil, very heinous, and consequently sufficient to exclude such as will continue in the practice of it from the privileges of the church."[58] On a few, admittedly rare, occasions, an abolitionist found the idea of communion with slaveholders so repugnant that he seceded from his church. William Hickman "came forward and informed the church that he was distressed on

55. Tarrant, *Substance of a Discourse*, p. 8.
56. McTeer, *History of New Providence Presbyterian Church*, p. 43.
57. Redford, *History of Methodism in Kentucky*, 1:418-422.
58. Minutes, West Lexington Presbytery, Kentucky, 1:23-24, HFPC.

account of the practice of slavery as being tolerated by the members of the Baptist Society, therefore he declared himself no more in union with us, of the Elkhorn Association."[59]

Hickman had found himself facing the unwillingness of moderates to act upon their beliefs in any coherent or systematic way. Indeed, after a brief separation from his church, he returned to the fold. Much more to the liking of the moderate revivalists, whatever their beliefs about the sinfulness of slaveholding, was to preach to the masters, hoping to bring about a change of heart. David Purviance, an unflinching enemy of slavery, persuaded his father, father-in-law, and most of the members of his church to free their slaves.[60] The failure to develop a full-fledged antislavery program, a product of the various reasons for avoiding antislavery discussed above, meant that these ministers failed to act at precisely the point at which their power was at a peak and that antislavery in the region was probably doomed.

59. Ermina J. Darnell, *Forks of Elkhorn Church* (Louisville, 1946), p. 29; see also Minutes, West Lexington Presbytery, Kentucky, 1:23-24, HFPC.
60. Purviance, *Biography of Elder David Purviance*, p. 49.

CHAPTER 4

Opposition to Antislavery in the Period of the Revival

The revival produced debate on myriad issues, from sanctification and justification to temperance and missions. Yet the central fact that distinguished southwestern society from the rest of the West, slavery, never received intense scrutiny. Antislavery ministers vigorously promoted their views in meetings, pamphlets, sermons, and lectures. Their opponents, however, remained silent, at least in public. The churches failed to take any coherent position on slavery; abolitionist preachers complained of harassment and more and more ministers owned slaves. Nevertheless, despite this implicit support of the peculiar institution, no minister came forward with a direct proslavery statement.

The silence of the proslavery forces is perhaps the great puzzle in the history of slavery and southwestern religion. How, then, did this opposition so effectively thwart the goals of a highly organized antislavery movement, and how did it avoid taking a public stand in favor of the peculiar institution? The answer suggested in the following pages to both questions can go only far as the sources allow, using clerical debate to suggest a complex set of explanations. The silence of close to two centuries will, of course, never be completely broken. Nevertheless, in this period, antiabolition sentiment was expressed in myriad actions and opinions by those who quietly promoted the continuation of slavery, either because of apathy or fear of disruption, as well those who articulately defended the peculiar institution.

Opposition to Antislavery

Sentiments in favor of slavery abounded among the southwestern laity. Newspapers constantly advertised for runaways, such as Anthony, who was "artful in telling stories." Transactions among slaveholders also frequently appeared; one Kentucky master, for example, offered to sell two slaves or trade them for whiskey. Similar expressions of the assumed validity of slavery made their way into laws of the states. The Kentucky legislature, for instance, included, in a law on fee collection, strict regulation of the relations between collectors and slaves. Travelers to the Southwest often commented on the importance of slavery to the residents they met. The peculiar institution had become a central feature of southwestern life and thought.[1]

Slavery and Church Governments

Although low-keyed and subtle in their actions, the antiabolition clergy accomplished their major objective, preventing the churches from taking an uncompromised position in opposition to slavery. The Baptist church, with a loose state and national structure, never took a clear stance. In 1807 the Salt River Church asked the Long Run Association whether it would be "consistent with good order for the Baptist churches of our union to invite those preachers to preach among us, that hath withdrew from among us, on account of slavery." In its answer, the association stressed its interest in avoiding the subject even at the cost of losing the services of good preachers: "it is considered imprudent (under the present state of things) to intermeddle therewith." Only a few Baptist churches ever raised issues related to slavery, and fewer answered the questions they raised. On June 11, 1808, the West Fork Meeting House discussed the question, "Does this church hold with perpetual slavery or not?" The question was laid over until the next meeting on July 9, at which the members present decided it "inexpedient to enter into a discussion [of slavery] at

---

1. *Clarion* (Nashville), August 31, 1803; *Reporter* (Lexington), April 23, 1808; *Argus of Western America* (Lexington), February 7, 1817.

present."[2] In short, the Baptists either failed to address the question of slavery or discussed the issue and immediately abdicated all responsibility.

Presbyterians, surprisingly, paid scant attention to the matter. During this period the denomination was undergoing great turmoil in the West, and no one wanted another divisive issue. Yet the silence should be partly attributed to the vague recommendations of the General Assembly. In 1812 the members of the assembly opposed slavery, but they attached the qualification that regard should be taken for the "safety and happiness of the master and slave."[3] This phrase provided the necessary loophole for slaveholding Presbyterians: ministers cited examples of freed slaves who had undergone severe moral deterioration after emancipation, and tales of the good and kind master were told frequently. Rather than promote abolition, some churches in the West began to encourage education for the slaves or, at the very least, "the Catechetical instruction of youths and slaves."[4] Presbyteries passed resolutions condemning slavery, yet the Kentucky Synod reinstated the one member suspended by the Concord Church for selling a slave. Many Presbyterians opposed slavery in a general way, but they failed to construct and implement a workable and consistent program of abolition.

Of the three evangelical denominations, the Methodist church undertook the most vigorous attack against slavery. Nevertheless, even the Methodists finally arrived at a qualified, crippled set of regulations regarding the holding of slaves. By 1808 the General Conference had bowed out of the issue, leaving it to the annual conferences.[5] The Western Conference that year adopted a rule

2. Minutes, Long Run Baptist Association, Kentucky (1802), p. 2, BHS; Minutes, West Fork Baptist Meeting House, Nashville, June-July 1808, HCSBC; Spencer, *History of Kentucky Baptists*, 1:185.

3. Posey, *Presbyterian Church*, pp. 75-76.

4. Minutes, Kentucky Presbytery, 1812, Presbyterian Theological Seminary, Louisville for a different view, see J. E. Alexander, *A Brief History of the Synod of Tennessee, from 1817–1850* (Philadelphia, 1890), p. 52.

5. Lucius Matlack, *The History of American Slavery and Methodism, from 1780 to 1849; and History of the Wesleyan Methodist Connection of America* (New York, 1849), p. 31; Mathews, *Slavery and Methodism*, p. 26.

prohibiting the purchase or sale of slaves "from speculative motives." The same rule, however, permitted traffic in the internal slave trade if the dealer were acting in the cause of "mercy or humanity."[6] The conference provided a complicated system for evaluating these motives. The 1812 Kentucky Conference made the rule even less clear, eliminating the question of speculative motive. Instead, any transaction now had to be judged strictly as to its "justice and mercy." In 1817 the conference declared that each action against a slaveholder would be reconsidered if "the laws of the State continue rigidly to oppose the emancipation of slaves." The same conference elected a slaveholder to the position of elder, despite the requirement of the previous conference that he emancipate his slaves. Not only did he keep the slaves he already owned; he had recently purchased "a negro boy." Nevertheless, it was "the opinion of the chair . . . that it was not a violation of the rule."[7] The Tennessee Conference remained the single repository of uncompromised antislavery views, and in 1819 a major debate erupted, producing the strongest antislavery rule in the West. The conference decided "not to receive any one into its membership, or ordain any local preacher who was a slave holder."[8] This decision was an anachronism, however; no effective rule could last much longer among the southwestern Methodists.

The sincerity of antislavery preachers during the period of the revival is unquestionable. Many worked hard; Carter Tarrant, David Rice, and many others had organized large groups of clergymen in the cause. Nevertheless, more and more antislavery ministers, seeing a bleak future for the area, began to move north to the frontier settlements in Illinois and further west. Hugh Bass, a Presbyterian abolitionist, left for Illinois,[9] as did the Licking-Locust Association of antislavery Baptists. Many others relocated in Ohio, maintaining their contacts with southern clergy but freeing themselves of the burden of slavery. James Booty moved from Kentucky to Mt. Pleasant, Ohio, in 1816, and he immediate-

6. Sweet, *Rise of Methodism*, p. 148.
7. McFerrin, *History of Methodism in Tennessee*, 2:282-284, 463-467.
8. Arnold, *History of Methodism in Kentucky*, p. 48; Redford, *History of Methodism in Kentucky*, 2:500-504.
9. Posey, *Presbyterian Church*, p. 79.

ly founded The *Philanthropist*, an antislavery newspaper.[10] The son-in-law of Benjamin Northcott, a leading Methodist minister, also fled the growing proslavery atmosphere in the Southwest. One writer suggested that Harriet Beecher Stowe might have used him as the model for John Vantramp in *Uncle Tom's Cabin*.[11] All of these ministers said that they fled the Southwest as the result of a mixture of frustration and moral outrage; they saw no point in remaining where their sermons against slavery received scant attention from either fellow clergy or their congregations.

Slaveholding and Revival-Period Churches

In spite of the regulations and restrictions and some impressive moral arguments, the habit of owning slaves increased among the remaining clergy. There is no good way of measuring the scope of this phenomenon, but it is suggestive that two early and vigorous opponents of slavery, James Blythe and William Hickman, both had bought slaves by 1810.[12] Disputes over the ownership of slaves began to interrupt the business of church meetings. These arguments arose not over the morality of slavery but over business considerations. The Elkhorn Association of Baptists in Kentucky divided in 1805 over the dispute between Jacob Creath and a fellow parishioner involving their financial arrangements surrounding the purchase of a slave girl.[13] The Red River Baptist Church in Tennessee entertained a complicated dispute over the slave of a slave.[14] These church records do not indicate any moral outrage over the subject; rather, the clergy seem to have accepted the normality of slaveholding.

The increase in the numbers of slaveholders in the church was accompanied by a corresponding increase in churchgoing slaves. Methodists kept the most complete account of this phenomenon, and a study of individual church records indicates that they had

10. Osborne, *Journal of the Faithful Servant of Christ*, p. xii.
11. Northcott, *Biography of Rev. Benjamin Northcott*, pp. 60-61.
12. Darnell, *Forks of Elkhorn Church*, p. 30; Posey, *Presbyterian Church*, p. 85.
13. Spencer, *History of Kentucky Baptists*, 1:311.
14. Minutes, Red River Baptist Church, July 19, 1816, HCSBC.

more slave parishioners than did the Presbyterians and somewhat fewer than the Baptists. Table 3 shows the relative size of the black and white membership of the Methodist church for the thirty-year period surrounding the revival.

Table 3. Black and white membership in the Methodist church, 1790–1819

Year	Area	White	Percent	Black	Percent
1790	Western Conference	1,104	98	19	2
1791	Western Conference	1,205	96	49	4
1792	Western Conference	2,221	93	158	7
1793	Western Conference	3,007	94	182	6
1794	Western Conference	3,208	96	135	4
1795	Western Conference	2,999	98	155	2
1796	Tennessee	503	92	43	8
	Kentucky	1,666	95	84	5
1797	Tennessee	534	93	42	7
	Kentucky	1,740	97	57	3
1798	Tennessee	528	92	49	8
	Kentucky	1,550	97	51	3
1799	Tennessee	580	93	49	8
	Kentucky	1,672	96	65	4
1800	Tennessee	681	92	62	8
	Kentucky	1,626	93	115	7
	Natchez	60	100	0	0
1801	Tennessee	681	92	62	8
	Kentucky	1,626	93	115	7
	Natchez	60	100	0	0
1802	Tennessee	2,436	93	183	7
	Kentucky	1,377	94	82	6
	Natchez	100	100	0	0
1803	Tennessee	3,668	93	276	7
	Kentucky	3,985	96	186	4
	Natchez	85	98	2	2
1804	Tennessee	4,476	93	322	7
	Kentucky	3,311	95	174	5
	Natchez	100	98	2	2
1805	Tennessee	5,578	93	416	7
	Kentucky	3,718	94	243	6
	Natchez	74	54	62	46
1806	Tennessee	5,619	94	354	6
	Kentucky	3,955	96	180	4
	Mississippi	132	65	72	35

Table 3. (Continued)

Year	Area	White	Percent	Black	Percent
1807	Tennessee	5,968	94	412	6
	Kentucky	4,276	96	192	4
	Mississippi	283	75	92	25
1808	Tennessee	6,599	94	454	6
	Kentucky	4,095	93	324	7
	Mississippi	335	81	80	19
1809	Tennessee	5,563	93	404	7
	Kentucky	4,342	92	385	8
	Mississippi	279	73	101	27
1810	Tennessee	7,265	92	591	8
	Kentucky	5,513	93	404	7
	Mississippi	263	73	97	27
1811	Tennessee	8,365	92	716	8
	Kentucky	6,965	93	518	7
	Mississippi	390	77	119	23
1812	Tennessee	10,101	92	853	8
	Kentucky	7,410	93	562	7
	Mississippi	639	81	150	19
1813	Tennessee	15,290	91	1,469	9
	Kentucky	7,799	93	660	7
	Mississippi	1,067	82	240	18
1814	Tennessee	14,902	92	1,354	8
	Kentucky	6,712	93	474	7
	Mississippi	1,067	82	240	18
1815	Tennessee	16,304	91	1,515	9
	Kentucky	6,969	93	509	7
	Mississippi	1,691	81	404	19
1816	Tennessee	15,248	91	1,443	9
	Kentucky	6,647	92	579	8
	Mississippi	1,576	77	478	23
1817	Tennessee	15,507	93	1,136	7
	Kentucky	5,669	90	637	10
	Mississippi	1,531	79	410	21
1818	Tennessee	15,316	91	1,564	9
	Kentucky	6,647	91	662	9
	Mississippi	1,623	79	430	21
1819	Tennessee	16,116	92	1,395	8
	Kentucky	7,290	89	875	11
	Mississippi	1,846	83	389	17

Source: Minutes of the Annual Conferences of the Methodist Episcopal Church (New York, 1840)

The table reveals several facts about the nature of slave member-ship in the Methodist church. First, although blacks never reached the proportions in the churches that they held in the population as a whole, and in Kentucky and Tennessee never exceeded 11 percent of church membership, they made up a clearly present minority. Almost every church in the Southwest had some black members. Second, the figures tend to obscure the rise in slave population. The great increase in church membership between 1802 and 1807 caused the proportion of blacks in the church to stabilize, but a steady rise in the proportion began in 1808. This rise was especially pronounced in Kentucky, where black membership rose from 4 percent in 1803 to 11 percent in 1819. In Mississippi and in such highly concentrated areas as the Nashville District, greater numbers of blacks attended churches. In Nashville, for example, slaves constituted 12 percent of the Methodist membership in 1810.[15] In the smaller Watauga circuit, during the same year, black membership exceeded 15 percent of the church population. The church in Tennessee as a whole showed a less dramatic increase, and the proportion of slaves remained around 8 percent through-out the period. In part, this stability was owing to the rapid development of the Tennessee church in the late eighteenth century, which meant that evangelizing slaves occurred earlier than in other parts of the Southwest. Moreover, the late eighteenth-century figures are so small that the 8 percent black membership is hardly revealing. More significant is the rise between 1806 and 1815. A third conclusion that one may draw from these figures is that Methodists had an ever-increasing interest in providing religion to blacks during the revival. On occasion, as in the sudden burst of slave membership in Natchez between 1804 and 1805, these efforts produced dramatic results.

The presence of blacks in the churches regularly brought to the fore the question of the moral recitude of slavery. Churches often were forced to deal with critical issues of the institution: the proper relation of master to slave, the moral problems inherent in the traffic in human flesh, and the importance of the slave family. Such issues frequently impinged upon the lives of white parishio-

---

15. *Minutes of the Annual Conferences of the Methodist Episcopal Church* (New York, 1840), p. 182.

ners who sat next to slaves. Certainly ministers, trained to observe the actions of their flocks and encourage improvement, found themselves contemplating these issues and painfully taking sides in the debate over them.

It is nevertheless true that a significant number of religious westerners, although mentioning the peculiar institution, seldom wanted to discuss its implications. Slaveholders and slaves came to church, antislavery men protested the existence of slaveholding, yet each attempt to force abolition on the churches failed, and antislavery clergy fled the region in dismay. No one issued a proslavery appeal, but slavery's elusive defenders somehow had enormous success.

Opposition to Antislavery Activity

Among the Presbyterian clergy, the few active opponents of antislavery tended to come from the more conservative wing of the church, the Calvinist opponents of revival excess. Typical of these clergymen was William Montgomery, a scholar and a sincere Calvinist, who moved from South Carolina to Mississippi in 1811 to become president of Jefferson College. Like many southwestern proslavery clergymen, Montgomery was also a slaveholder.[16] The great conservative champion John Poage Campbell, in his newspaper the *Evangelical Record and Western Review*, supported mission societies, Sabbath schools, Bible societies, church repairs, and numerous other benevolent activities; abolition, however, did not appear on his list.[17] In his newspaper and in other works, Campbell commented on almost every conceivable aspect of the religious life of the West. His failure to include antislavery indicates, at best, benign neglect, although it fits with much of the rest of conservative opinion. The conservatives opposed the revival because it disrupted the status quo. Campbell argued for the preservation of a "real, practical Christianity,"[18] by which he meant one that bothered no one and maintained a high level of respectability and

16. George Howe, *History of the Presbyterian Church in South Carolina* (Columbia, 1883), 2:180-181.
17. *Evangelical Record and Western Review* 1 (1812):6; 2 (1813):170.
18. Campbell, *Vindex*, p. 5.

dignity. Just as radical reforms within the church could only damage it as a social edifice, so any attack on society, such as antislavery, would impinge upon the mild and inoffensive work which Campbell and his peers promoted. It was better for ministers to point out the ominous features of the great earthquake of 1812, Campbell apparently felt, than to cause parishioners to question basic social assumptions. One ally, James McCalla, confidently attacked "gay dress, gay furniture, and gay equipage."[19] yet he avoided the deeper problems of his society, the inequities of income, the fighting and drunkenness, and the question of Negro slavery. Such conservative Presbyterians revealed no impulse to defend slavery. Ignoring the problem, however, served as a type of defense. Of course, without diaries and personal letters from these conservatives, it can never be known whether their failure to discuss slavery was intentional. It is perhaps conceivable that such well-informed conservatives could have missed the many continuing debates on the efficacy and morality of the peculiar institution. As was the case with the nonbarking dog in the Sherlock Holmes story, the inferences we can draw from an absence of information depend upon the context in which that absence appears. In this instance, the context in which these clerics worked was full of the discussion of slavery. Their failure to address the issue is therefore all the more significant.

Methodists faced much the same problem as Presbyterians. They wished to appeal to as many westerners as possible, and the issue of slavery could only be divisive. More and more, talented clergy purchased or inherited slaves, so that the bishops had to decide between the morality of slavery and the effectiveness of their mission to the West. In 1810, while visiting Tennessee, Asbury sadly commented that, for fear of alienating his host, "I dare not complain when I see the wretched fate of the poor Africans in slavery."[20] In 1812 Asbury announced to the Ohio Conference that Methodist clerics should avoid the issue of slavery.[21]

19. *Case of Maccalla against Blythe, Tried before the Synod of Kentucky in September, 1814* (Chillicothe, Ohio, 1814), pp. 21, 6, 18; see also Carr, *Early Times in Middle Tennessee*, p. 46.

20. Clark, ed., *Journal and Letters of Francis Asbury*, 2:653.

21. Henkle, *Life of Henry Bascom*, p. 384.

Eight years earlier he had begun to retreat from an unqualified antislavery position, refusing to support an effort to strengthen the antislavery position of his church.[22] Bishop McKendree seems to have moved in the same direction, fearing that the slavery issue would cause an irreparable rift in the church.[23] Neither man supported slavery; on the contrary, each had often expressed strong antipathy toward it. Both nevertheless decided that the promotion of abolition was tactically unwise.

Methodists who owned slaves or promoted the weakening of denominational antislavery regulations had also begun to achieve social status. Henry Bascom was well known in the Southwest as a dandy who dressed as well as if not better than any member of the laity. Learner Blackman gained great esteem by completing the first wholly successful missionary tour of Mississippi, and he then took charge of the Methodist church in Nashville.[24] Thomas Douglas also worked in Nashville, and he virtually ran the missionary society of the Tennessee Conference.[25] Gilbert Taylor, a graduate of a Philadelphia medical school, had been a doctor on General Jackson's staff. Except for Blackman, each of these preachers opposed abolition in the 1819 dispute over the slave rule in the Tennessee Conference.[26] Not every Methodist preacher who had achieved some degree of prestige and respectability also opposed abolition; nevertheless, in general, the clergy who opposed abolition also saw status as important, whereas those such as Cartwright and Axley, who opposed slavery, had little interest in social prestige. Moreover, the antislavery Methodists tended to use revival techniques whereas the proslavery preachers, such as Blackman, stressed the value of missions. The difference was in emphasis; no Methodist actively opposed either approach. The better-educated clergy found missions more intellectually appealing than the often inexplicable workings of the spirit in revival.

22. Mathews, *Slavery and Methodism*, p. 26.
23. Henry B. Bascom, *Methodism and Slavery* (Frankfort, 1845), p. 8.
24. Arnold, *History of Methodism in Kentucky*, pp. 399-40.
25. Sprague, *Annals of the American Pulpit*, 7:352-354.
26. McFerrin, *History of Methodism in Tennessee*, 3:163-166, 160-162; Lazenby, *History of Methodism in Alabama and West Florida*, p. 93; Gene R. Miller, *A History of North Mississippi Methodism, 1820-1900* (Nashville, 1966), p. 61.

Clergymen who felt that Methodists should take their proper role in respectable society also tended to consider missions more dignified. When the 1819 Tennessee Conference rejected the applications of two slaveholders to the ministry, many of these clergy signed a letter of protest, stressing the violation of the "order and discipline of our Church,"[27] Order, dignity, and respectability meant, to these men, established churches, large congregations, and, when necessary, heroic missions. Moreover, opponents of abolition saw nothing necessarily wrong with wealth, and southwestern society measured wealth by the number of slaves one owned. The most bothersome possible reform, in light of these aspirations, was the abolition of slavery. Abolition would disrupt the church, alienate the wealthier and more respectable laity, and require some personal sacrifice. The time for suffering, for uncertainty, and for inflexible morality, many Methodists felt, had long since passed.

Whereas such conservative Presbyterians and Methodists felt uneasy about revivals and the disorder they aroused, conservative Baptists scrupled instead over missions. Baptists never joined to any great degree in the interdenominational meetings of the revival, preferring smaller meetings of their own.[28] Even those preachers who enjoyed interdenominational activity rejected the Stonite radicalism. Yet such ministers as John Taylor had led revivals before the turn of the century, and they continued to do so in the period of the Great Revival. The real threat, many of these preachers felt, was the encroachment of centralized authority, especially in the form of societies and associations on a state or national level. In particular, they disliked the new movement for missions to the unchurched. Part of the stimulation for domestic missions came from the success of the Baptists' most important competitors, the Methodists. Through the use of circuit riders, Methodists had converted large areas of the West, especially in Tennessee.[29] In addition, the benevolent empire, the organized

27. McFerrin, *History of Methodism in Tennessee*, 3:160–162. Although several revival period ministers took part in this dispute, it is more appropriate to discuss the debate in Chapter 5.

28. O. W. Taylor, *Early Tennessee Baptist, 1769-1832* (Nashville, 1957), p. 155.

29. Riley, *History of Baptists in Alabama*, p. 47.

moral reform movement of early nineteenth-century New England, had started to address the problem of irreligion in the world with the founding of the American Board of Commissioners for Foreign Missions. The notion of both foreign and domestic missions at first received some support in the West among Baptists. Stark Dupuy founded the *Kentucky Missionary and Theological Magazine* in 1812,[30] and several Baptist associations voiced their approval of foreign missions.[31] In 1814, the Baptist General Conference (for foreign missions) held its first meeting in Philadelphia and appointed Luther Rice to promote the work among the many Baptist associations.[32]

When Rice arrived at the Concord Association in Tennessee, most members gave him a warm reception, but one minister expressed misgivings. Some of his brother clergy asked Daniel Parker if he wanted to contribute anything to the mission association. "His reply was—No; he had no counterfeit half dollars; if he had he would have thrown in, but as he had none, he would not throw away good money for such an object."[33] Parker was born in Culpeper County, Virginia, and raised in extreme poverty. Converted in Georgia, he arrived in Tennessee in 1803 as a Baptist preacher.[34] He was known as a hard worker and a good preacher, and he was a particularly devout Calvinist. Gradually he became one of the most important and influential figures in the church in Tennessee. When Baptists began to organize missionary societies in Tennessee, Parker at first took a neutral stance. As his popularity increased, however, he reexamined the issue and informed the Concord Association that if it did not drop the missions from consideration, he would "burst the Association."[35] Parker had by

30. Spencer, *History of Kentucky Baptists*, 1:569, 347.

31. Minutes, Russell Creek Baptist Association, Kentucky (1813); Minutes, Long Run Baptist Association, Kentucky (1815); Minutes, Elkhorn Baptist Association, Kentucky (1819); Minutes, Salem Baptist Association, Tennessee (1815); all in BHS; Kendall, *History of the Tennessee Baptist Convention*, p. 37.

32. Spencer, *History of Kentucky Baptists*, 1:569.

33. Kendall, *History of the Tennessee Baptist Convention*, p. 38; John Bond, *History of the Baptist Concord Association of Middle Tennessee and North Alabama* (Nashville, 1860), p. 27.

34. Kendall, *History of the Tennessee Baptist Convention*, p. 37.

35. Bond, *History of the Baptist Concord Association*, pp. 28, 26.

this time devised a hyper-Calvinist "Two-seed Theory," in which he argued for particular atonement and election and against missions, education, Sunday schools, and instrumental music. God never created a human being who would eternally suffer, Parker believed; instead, He had planted a good seed in Eden in the form of Adam's soul in union with Christ. Eve and Satan had, in some mysterious way, created a bad seed that dominates the soul of most humans so they cannot be saved. Each man has either the good or the bad seed planted in his body at birth, and no amount of religion can change his destiny.[36] Some opponents of Parker recognized this view as antinomianism, proclaiming his followers "a privileged class, who dwell in a region of unshaken security and lawless liberty, while the rest of the Christian world are, in their opinion, the vassells [sic] of legal bondage, toiling in darkness and chains."[37] The opponents of missions often took the extreme predestinarian stance that there is no need to bring the gospel to those who are already elect.[38]

Not all of those who adopted antimission sentiments stressed the Calvinist argument, however. Instead of using an abstract argument, John Taylor fought missions for practical reasons. First, he objected to the notion that highly educated easterners, through their societies, should dictate the nature of western Baptism. It smelled of the "New England Rat."[39] Moreover, he worried that these new organizations would destroy the integrity of the churches, turning them into clearinghouses for the national organizations.[40] Others feared that these organizations would impinge on personal piety: Theodorick Boulware, a leader of the fight against the missions in Kentucky, stressed "regular industry and prudent economy" in his personal life. The burgeoning eastern movement

36. Jesse Boyd, *A Popular History of the Baptists in Mississippi* (Jackson, 1930), p. 54; J. N. Grime, *History of Middle Tennessee Baptists* (Nashville, 1902), pp. 400-403.

37. James Fishback, *A Defence of the Elkhorn Association and the Terms of General Union Among the Baptists* (Lexington, 1822), p. 13.

38. Spencer, *History of Kentucky Baptists*, 1:572.

39. Bertram Wyatt-Brown, "The Antimission Movement in the Jacksonian South," *Journal of Southern History* 36 (1970): 510; Robert Baker, ed. *A Baptist Source Book* (Nashville, 1966), pp. 79-81.

40. John Taylor, *Thoughts on Missions* (Franklin Co., 1820), p. 6.

for benevolent reform threatened those ministers who expressed such conservative, individualistic piety.[41] Many ministers also found the style of the well-organized, centralized missionary movement repugnant. L. C. Davis, the self-proclaimed "Club Ax" of the church, was a powerful leader in the antimission struggle. Rude and unpolished, "his preaching was a strange conglomeration of ridicule, sarcasm, exhortation, denunciation, pathos, humor and zeal."[42] Such a man would naturally oppose the workings of so calm and cautious a group as a mission society.

What remained of the pioneer generation in the southwestern Baptist church was the antimissionary element. These individualists and chauvinists tried to maintain as much independence from outside interference as possible. Many had been among the first settlers in the West; Warren Cash, Theodorick Boulware, Isaac Steele, Elihu Millikan, and John Taylor all arrived before the turn of the century. Almost all owned their own farms, and most had achieved some prosperity. They had become successful members of their society, and they felt a great need to protect their success. One element of their lives they particularly wanted to protect was the institution of slavery. Taylor was a successful farmer and owned between ten and twenty slaves.[43] Among the societies in the East which he mistrusted he listed "Negro Societies."[44] Perhaps the leading Baptist association opposed to missions, the Licking Association of Particular Baptists, had been formed as the result of a squabble over slavery.[45] What the antimission groups really opposed was a violation of their lifestyles, and antislavery, as much as missions or education societies, stood as a particular threat. In alliance with more moderate opponents of abolition, therefore, the antimission forces successfully prevented any effective movement against slavery in the Baptist church. Carter Tarrant, the leading Baptist abolitionist, felt that he had been

41. Spencer, *History of Kentucky Baptists*, 1:315.
42. Riley, *History of Baptists in Alabama*, p. 27.
43. Taylor, *History of Ten Baptist Churches*, p. 146; Taylor, *Early Tennessee Baptists*, p. 177.
44. Taylor, *Thoughts on Missions*, p. 12.
45. Frank Masters, *A History of Baptists in Kentucky* (Louisville, 1953), pp. 178-179; Spencer, *History of Kentucky Baptists*, 1:606-607.

hunted down and accused of being "an enemy to civil and religious society."[46] The antimission men believed it was their duty to protect that society, and that meant, especially, to protect the peculiar institution.

Elements of Antiabolitionist Thought

Although none of the three groups of antiabolition clergy produced a simple proslavery essay, members of each stressed two elements in their occasional comments on the subject: attacks on abolitionists and catalogs of the duties and rights of masters and slaves. For antimission Baptists, antiabolition diatribes were only part of a larger attack on moral reform that required concerted activity. Even clerics who were disinclined to attack the organizational basis of antislavery argued that the agitation for abolition could only disrupt the proper functioning of religion in the West. Both Asbury and McKendree stressed the importance of maintaining church order at any cost. The North District Association of Baptists expelled David Barrow because he held views "pernicious to peace and good order."[47] When abolitionists tried to exclude slaveholders from the churches, several proslavery clergymen condemned these efforts as sinful attempts to purify the church beyond God's wishes. Thomas Griffin pointed out that not even Abraham would merit membership in the Christian church if the abolitionists had their way. "It appears that some of our Northern brethren [sic] are willing to see us all damned and double-damned, rammed, jammed, and crammed into a forty-six pounder, and touched off into eternity."[48] These clergy warned that many good and important people would be excluded from the practice of Christianity, leaving little more than a small, arrogant elite in place of a thriving, albeit less perfect, church.

---

46. Tarrant, *Substance of a Discourse*, p. 3.

47. Minutes, North District Baptist Association, Kentucky (1805), BHS; see also Ranck, *History of Lexington*, p. 119; Minutes, Russell Creek Baptist Association, Kentucky (1811), BHS.

48. Holland McTyeire, *A History of Methodism* (Nashville, 1884), p. 546.

Clerical opponents of abolition accused the antislavery forces of meddling in politics. Dismissing any moral questions the slavery issue might pose, antiabolition forces argued that it would be "improper for ministers, churches or associations to meddle with emancipation from slavery, or any other political subject, and as such, we advise ministers and churches to have nothing to do therewith, in their religious capacities."[49] Moreover, the antislavery message, these ministers insisted, was potentially dangerous; it called for a form of civil disobedience because several states forbade the emancipation of slaves. Purposeful violation of the law would be disastrous for the churches. In these arguments, propriety lay in fastidious attention to the letter of the law. The anarchistic potential of the revival was repudiated, and the antiabolitionist clergymen instead argued that good citizenship, unquestioning devotion to man-made law, served as the mark of proper Christian behavior. They did not separate church and state, but rather saw the functions of the two estates as complementary and symbiotic.

Together with this attack upon the basis of antislavery action, conservatives began to suggest the beginnings of a proslavery position by outlining the duties inherent in the master-slave relation. The juxtaposition of such an analysis of mutual duties with the attack upon antislavery suggests an incipient proslavery tack; moderate antislavery arguments often included some suggestions concerning the relation of masters and slaves before the gradual elimination of the institution. The outline of social obligations formulated by the ministers, however, did not have behind it the assumption that such obligations would ever end. John Poage Campbell, the archenemy of the revival, insisted in his *Evangelical Record* upon the necessity of fair treatment of slaves by masters. He called upon the master to consider the situation if the roles were reversed.[50] The Transylvania Presbytery encouraged masters to "secure the religious instruction of slaves together with a humane and christian treatment."[51] Conservatives did not intend to encourage overly lenient treatment, however; the Western

49. Spencer, *History of Kentucky Baptists*, 1:185.
50. *Evangelical Record and Western Review* 2 (1813):456–457.
51. Minutes, Transylvania Presbytery, p. 387, HFPC.

Conference put one Methodist minister on trial for "saying masters ought not to correct their slaves"; although he was acquitted for lack of evidence, the conference had made its point—reasonable punishment did not violate Christian morality.[52] Indeed, slaves had a duty to obey their masters as much as masters had a duty not to abuse their slaves. The South Concord Baptist Association of Kentucky spelled out the slave's duties with remarkable care; "Servants then are to be in subjection to their own masters according to the flesh, not only to the good and gentle; but also to the forward—they are not to render eye-service nor answer again (gainsay) nor purloin (pilfer or steal) but to shew all good fidelity."[53] In short, slaves should be passive and submissive even in the face of unchristian treatment.

By stressing the practical aspects of slavery, and by encouraging slaves to submit passively to the institutions, these ministers laid the groundwork for much more complete defense of slavery. I have found no revival-era argument stressing the divine approval of the peculiar institution. This was nevertheless the logical conclusion of their ideas, which became particularly clear when the proslavery ministers attempted to outline the religious duties of slaves. Some clergy argued that such activities should always have the prior approval of masters. The Mississippi Baptist Association cautioned slaves to be "careful to obtain a written permission from their masters or overseers" before assembling for meetings.[54] Black preachers, according to the Providence Baptist Church in Kentucky, must have "the consent of their owner" before the church could sanction their ministries.[55] Slaves usually obtained the required permission, but the fact that the churches felt inclined to bow to the master's wishes on a subject so central to religious concerns is

52. Sweet, *Rise of Methodism*, p. 100.

53. Minutes, South District Baptist Association, Kentucky (1810), BHS.

54. *A Republication of the Minutes of the Mississippi Baptist Association*, 1814; Minutes, Long Run Baptist Association, Kentucky (1810), BHS.

55. S. J. Conkwright, *History of the Churches of Boone's Creek Baptist Association of Kentucky* (Winchester, Ky., 1923), p. 26; Minutes, Bethlehem Baptist Church, Kentucky, p. 24, HCSBC. For an account of the biblical argument in the East, see Loveland, *Southern Evangelicals*, pp. 200-202.

one more indication of the respect they held for the institution of slavery.

This chapter began with a question: why did no direct proslavery statement issue from the southwestern clergy in the period of the Great Revival? The presence and even dominance of proslavery sentiment in the area is unquestionable. Many of the most vocal and enthusiastic controversialists lined up in favor of the peculiar institution, yet no one went to the trouble of putting together a coherent set of arguments in favor of it. One part of the answer to this puzzle is simple—no one wrote such a treatise because it was not needed. The proslavery forces had achieved great success without needing to use a diatribe against their opponents and in favor of their position. The possibility of a backlash was enough of a threat to prevent the writing of such an essay. The proslavery forces seem to have understood that the best way to deal with a reformer is to ignore him. Moreover, the traditions of the churches, and the attitudes of eastern clergy, had a strong antislavery bias. Proslavery proclamations would have caused upheavals within the denominations, which did happen in a few decades. Finally, the lack of comment probably reflected some lack of conviction. Unlike their southeastern counterparts, who had increasingly begun to consider the positive features of slavery, southwestern ministers had not yet reached the point at which they felt comfortable defending the peculiar institution. Why they drew back and remained silent on this point must remain at least partly a mystery.

PART THREE

THE ANXIOUS
GENERATION

Few revivals have continued for more than a generation. Revivals are a time of the quickening of religious sentiment; they stand out in religious history because of the calm periods that frame them, a calm which is the normal state for American churches. The Great Revival began to wane around the time of the War of 1812 for no single, outstanding reason. Part of the explanation may have been the war itself, which distracted in the attention Southwest from matters of the soul. In addition, the leading revivalists were no doubt growing weary; they had been at the business of awakening, with the camp meeting and other devices, for too long to maintain the enthusiasm such work required. I will stress two other, related explanations in the first chapter of this section: changes in the regional culture and in the clerical profession.

However one explains the decline of the revival spirit, by about 1815 ministers were entering the clerical profession who knew only what they had been told about the years of religious upheaval. This group constitutes a cohort, or generation, of southwestern ministers, who had to cope with the conditions of a period of real or perceived decline. The dim and confused religious atmosphere, of course, helped shape their social attitudes, especially on the issue of slavery.

This generation may be compared with other groups of ministers who have had to clean up after upheavals. Donald Scott has shown that evangelicals in the Connecticut River valley reacted to the confusion of the abolitionist upheavals by strengthening their professional standards. At least one interpretation found in E. Brooks Holifield's excellent study of southeastern urban ministers is that they responded to subtle changes in their society by developing complex professional networks. No similar pattern seems to have developed in the burned-over district, where, according to Paul Johnson and Whitney Cross, ministers quickly moved into politics and reform after the first dramatic waves of revivalism; however, the revival did not end in this region after a generation but continued unabated for at least forty years. It is one glaring exception to the generalization that revivals tend to have short lives and therefore an exception to the notion that some ministers will have to cope with the period after the revival's decline.[1]

The postrevival southwestern clergymen share a set of demographic characteristics that make them a cohort. Although still composed primarily of migrants from the East, this cohort was the first to have a substantial native-born population: 31.3 percent of those who began preaching in the Southwest between 1815 and 1829 were born in Kentucky, Tennessee, Mississippi, or Alabama. Of the migrants, 43.6 percent came from Virginia, by far still the single most important source of western preachers. This figure, however had dropped substantially from the 56.9 percent of Virginia-born preachers of the first cohort and the 49.7 percent of the second. Other southern states contributed 41.2 percent, with the remaining 15.2 percent coming from the North or Europe. These figures suggest that the churches in the West were becoming less and less simply branches of Virginia culture, and as they drew their preachers from broader sources, they would be more likely to determine their own course of development. The initial response to this erosion of Virginia influence was the malaise of the 1820s.

The migrants who made up the vast majority of the third

1. See Scott, *From Office to Profession*, pp. 95-111; Paul E. Johnson, *A Shopkeeper's Millennium: Society and Revivals in Rochester, New York, 1818-1837* (New York, 1978), pp. 116-135; E. Brooks Holifield, *The Gentlemen Theologians: American Theology and Southern Culture, 1795-1860* (Durham, 1978), pp. 24-49; Cross, *Burned-Over District*, pp. 211-357.

cohort were considerably less inclined to move around the region that had been members of the revival generation. Whereas only 41 percent of the revival cohort had remained in one western state, 49 percent of the third cohort did. Only 27 percent of the third cohort traveled to one other southwestern state (as opposed to 41 percent of the revivalists), with 14 percent moving to more than one other state (down from 18 percent).

Reflecting the decreasing importance of migrants ministers, positions of status in southwestern churches increasingly went to southwestern-born ministers in the third generation. In this cohort 42.1 percent of the teachers, 37.5 percent of the presiding elders in the Methodist church, and 60 percent of the editors of denominational journals were westerners. Nevertheless, eastern-born clerics still held a majority of all positions of power in the churches (65 percent).

The age characteristics of this cohort showed both continuity and change from those of the revival generation. The age at which ministers entered the western ministry remained remarkably bifurcated. Of the new ministers 43.1 percent were younger than twenty-five, and 33 percent were older than thirty (as compared to 41.8 percent and 37.8 percent in the second cohort). This group was by far the youngest of the four. It was also the least long-lived. Only 34 percent lived past the age of seventy. Although it is impossible to establish precisely why this characteristic would have changed, perhaps the relative youth of the cohort at entry meant that these ministers were not self-selected for heartiness, as the pioneers and the revivalists had to have been to migrate west.

Of the members of the third cohort 10.9 percent had received a college education, more than double the percentage of revivalists (4.6 percent). Yet only 8.5 percent enthusiastically promoted education through teaching or fund-raising. The relative increase in education reflects in part the growth of a few western colleges and the explosion of education opportunities in the East, but the relative lack of enthusiasm for improving education in the West is but one of several important examples of the reticence of this group of ministers to promote change.

The transformation of the southwestern clergy from the revivalists to this new cohort was, of course, neither immediate nor dramatic. Instead, as revivalism slowed down after about 1815, the leaders of the movement lost the predominant role they had held during the awakening. Some revivalists, especially antislavery men, moved north and west; some, most notably David Rice, died; others simply grew old. In the void these events created, third-generation men found pulpits and some prestige. Many entered the ministry after about 1815 to preach in the new settlements south of the Tennessee River. Not men inclined toward activism, their entry into southwestern religious life was characteristically gradual and understated.

In considering the nature of this third cohort of ministers, I shall first describe their attitudes toward slavery and attempt to relate these views to their social position and professional development. It is also crucial to understand the social and theological positions of the one branch of evangelism which emerged and prospered in the region during the fifteen years after the War of 1812, the Disciples of Christ. Finally, I have tried, in this section, to evaluate the thought of these ministers on the issue of slavery by examining the experiences of slaves within southwestern churches. This detour into social history is, I think, crucial in understanding how these ministers acted upon their beliefs about slavery, which was to restrict the role slaves played within the southwestern congregations.

CHAPTER 5

Slavery and the
Postrevival Clergy

If any one characteristic typified the third generation of south-western ministers, it was their remarkable disinterest in a wide range of issues. Unlike the clergy of the revival, who never seemed to tire of evangelical disputes, the post-revival ministers seemed most at ease when little was happening to disturb the religious calm. The various state and local meetings of the denominations infrequently debated substantive issues. Presbyterians attempted to maintain order, and they still occasionally brought ministers before their meetings accused of some wrongdoing. Usually, however, the charges were not related to theological opinions but to improper behavior. The North Alabama Presbytery reflected this new timidity when it barred only those members who did "not keep a house of entertainment" from "retailing spirituous liquors"; unfortunately, the presbytery did not state how many were therefore allowed to continue to do so.[1] Vague appeals issued from the churches for proper Christian behavior, but such pleas, by their lack of specificity, rang hollow.[2] Moreover, clergy began to share some of the values of the society in which they lived. Many engaged in speculation. All of the denominations demanded more money from their members, and in 1826 the Tennessee Methodists set up a system of class collectors of increase contributions.[3]

1. Minutes, North Alabama Presbytery (1825), HFPC.
2. Minutes, South District Baptist Association, Kentucky (1820), BHS.
3. McFerrin, *History of Methodism in Tennessee*, 3:319-321.

A few ministers expressed a growing sense of the decline of religious feeling in the West: "Folly and amusement, intemperance, gaming and swearing, fraud, falsehood and violence are still amongst us; and they appear the more incurable in some places on account of a gross disregard of the Sabbath day, and the precious ordinances of God's house."[4] More often, the unhappiness found expression in less explicit terms. Baptists, for example, tended to pray for order, implying that disorder was the rule: "Discipline means rule, order, good government. . . . How important is it, that we should maintain good discipline."[5]

Benevolent activity stimulated little enthusiasm in the hearts of southwestern ministers after the revival. Presbyterians retained the more interest, especially in their push to establish seminaries.[6] Of course, the proper education of clergy was of only marginal benefit to society. More specific benevolent activities such as Sunday schools and education societies attracted almost no attention from southwestern ministers until late in the 1820s.[7] Baptists almost never mentioned such goals. Their meetings usually consisted of the roll call of the ministers followed by minor bureaucratic business.[8] This reticence to extend church activities much beyond the tending of the flock indicates a beginning of the strain in southwestern religious life of profound social conservatism that later reappeared in the fundamentalist era. Only the most noncontroversial social reform could gain support, voluntary missions to Indians, for example, could bring forth mild enthusiasm.[9] But antislavery was clearly doomed.

Attitudes on Slavery after the Great Revival

A very few abolitionists remained in the Presbyterian and Methodist churches of the Old Southwest after the revival ended.

4. *Christian Register* 1 (August 1822):433.

5. Minutes, Long Run Baptist Association, Kentucky (1827), BHS; see also Minutes, West Fork Baptist Meeting House, Kentucky (April 1813), HCSBC.

6. Minutes, Alabama Presbytery, p. 107, HFPC.

7. Minutes, Kentucky Presbytery, (1823); Presbyterian Theological Seminary, Louisville; see also James McChord, Letters (typed copy), p. 81, Presbyterian Historical Society, Philadelphia.

8. Leavell and Bailey, *Complete History of Mississippi Baptists*, p. 133.

9. *Christian Register* 1 (August 1822):132–133.

Yet even among these few survivors of the abolitionist tradition the vigor of argument was missing. A long series of articles in the *Western Luminary* called for the emancipation of all slaves but insisted that clear class distinctions between whites and blacks should be preserved at all costs.[10] The internal slave trade should certainly end but not primarily because of its immorality; instead, the writer worried about the potential problem of intermarriage.[11] This increasing stress upon the social rather than moral implications of slavery reflected the severely restricted support abolitionism could muster. By the 1820s, antislavery feeling among southwestern clergymen was limited to a small group of Quakers in the eastern sections of Kentucky and Tennessee and to some of the better-educated clergymen in the cities.[12] It fared no better among southwestern laity. Symbolically, Benjamin Lundy moved his *Genius of Universal Emancipation* to Baltimore in 1823.

The last stand of antislavery forces in the southwestern churches may have taken place at the 1819 meeting of the Tennessee Methodist Conference. In 1812 the conference had voted that any preacher or lay member who bought or sold a slave and did not do so for reasons of "justice and mercy" could be expelled. In 1815 the conference decided that members could not engage in the slave trade for gain but that they could buy or sell slaves to keep families together. In 1817 the Tennessee ministers established a rule requiring slaveholding Methodists gradually to manumit their slaves. At the meeting of 1818, the "justice and mercy" rule was formally reestablished, and the conference thereby backed off from the stronger 1817 stand. Ministers would still be expected to free their slaves but only if the law of the state permitted them to do so.[13]

It was with full knowledge of such vacillation and confusion that the Tennessee Conference met in 1819. The Shoal circuit had recommended that appointment of Gilbert D. Taylor as a travel-

10. *Western Liminary* 4 (August 23, 1827):58–59.

11. Ibid. 5 (September 24, 1828): 97; see also Redford, *Methodism in Kentucky*, 3.324.

12. See Asa Martin, "The Antislavery Societies of Tennessee," *Tennessee Historical Magazine* 1 (1915):261–281.

13. McFerrin, *Methodism in Tennessee*, 2:260-268; Redford, *Methodism in Kentucky*, 2:500-505.

ing preacher. Taylor was a member of a wealthy family, and he had inherited a number of slaves. As a young man, he became a physician and served on Andrew Jackson's staff during the War of 1812. According to at least one account, after his conversion in 1816, Taylor experimented with emancipation, freeing two of his slaves, but when both "fell into bad habits" he regretted his decision and ended the experiment. Along with two other candidates for the ministry in 1819, Taylor was told he would not be permitted into the traveling fellowship "in consequence of his owning slaves." The antislavery majority expressed a willingness to employ him if he would promise to free the slaves "when practicable," but Taylor apparently would not or felt he could not agree to that condition. The conference rejected his application by five votes. The victory could not be savored for long; a few years later Taylor was admitted as a full member of the traveling connection, and the antislavery rule in the Tennessee Conference died a quiet death.[14]

The meeting of 1819 is less interesting for its antislavery slant than for its promotion of the idea that the antislavery rule was profoundly misguided and impracticable. That meeting represents the coming of age of opposition to antislavery, which had remained vague and unfocused even during the revival. Sixteen of the thirty-seven members of the 1819 meeting signed a protest rejecting the action taken against Taylor, which they called "oppressively severe in itself." Their protest suggested that the times required Christian moderation. Significantly, the protesters worried that the decision of the conference would be "ruinous in its consequences." They implied that any stiff application of an antislavery rule would limit the number of future ministers and would, as well, decrease the influence of the denomination in the Southwest. Finally, the protesters stated, without developing the argument, that the decision was both "contrary to, and in violation of, the order and discipline of our Church." This assertion makes sense only if order and discipline are understood in broad, social terms. The General Conference had empowered local conferences with the right to determine their own rules on slavery. Far from

14. McFerrin, *Methodism in Tennessee*, 3:161-166.

violating Methodist discipline, the Tennessee Conference had simply restated Wesley's antislavery views. Therefore, the protest must have been directed at a more general interpretation of discipline: the need to bring into the Methodist denomination all members of southwestern society—to bring slaves and free citizens, slaveholders and opponents of slavery, under the church's umbrella. The antislavery rule, the protesters seemed to argue, would artificially and foolishly restrict the church's power and authority.[15]

The failure of antislavery forces in this third generation of southwestern clergymen can most clearly be seen in the increasing prominence of slaveholding ministers by the 1820s. Gideon Blackburn, a leading Presbyterian cleric, became the minister of the Louisville church in 1823. He owned several slaves, for whose "temporal and spiritual welfare" he "always manifested a deep concern."[16] John Bond became a Baptist minister in Tennessee in 1820, and he soon became a leader of Baptists who stood in the center between the Hard-shell and Free-will factions. Bond was "well to do in material things, owning at one time 1,300 acres of rich land with a number of slaves." Eli Cleveland also preached as a Baptist in Tennessee, while at the same time building up a sizable estate worked by a number of slaves. He built the Sweetwater Church in Tennessee, "boarding the hands and furnishing teams, and negroes to drive them, as well as to do other work in connection with the building."[17] Richard Bibb, a Methodist preacher in Kentucky, left thirty slaves in his estate.[18] By the 1820s all of these ministers apparently viewed the peculiar institution as a fact of life. If they did not see the slave system as a positive aspect of southwestern society, neither did it give them much concern or anxiety. Certainly none viewed slavery as fundamentally at odds with Christianity.

A powerful and controversial speech before the General Conference in 1820 by a Virginia-born Mississippi Methodist minister named Thomas Griffin reflected this new, passively proslavery

15. Ibid., 3:160-161.

16. Sprague, *Annals of the American Pulpit*, 4:51.

17. J. J. Burnett, *Sketches of Tennessee's Pioneer Baptist Preachers* (Nashville, 1919), pp. 60-63, 110-114.

18. McFerrin, *Methodism in Tennessee*, 3:264-265.

attitude. Griffin began his remarks by condemning northern antislavery Methodists for their harsh, unchristian rhetoric. He sneered at the hypocritical northerners who came south full of pity for slaves and scorn for slaveholders, but who insisted that slaves be included in the dowry of any southern woman one of them might wish to marry. His aggressiveness and antagonistic tone were unconventional for such meetings, and if Griffin wished to capture the attention of his audience, he could not have been more successful.

Following these statements Griffin switched both the tone and the substance of his address. He provided a brief, slightly indirect biblical defense of slavery, noting that both Christ and the Apostles had failed to condemn slavery. He added, "And if it be offensive and sinful to own slaves, I wish someone would just put his finger on the place in Holy Writ." Not only does the Bible fail to condemn slavery, it is overflowing with rules for the regulation of the institution. The Bible directs true Christians to accept the secular institution of slavery and, instead of wasting precious energy condemning slaveholders, to protect the slave from unchristain treatment. Griffin exclaimed, "What has the Church or ministry done to Christianize the negro? Almost nothing!" Clergy should take the lead in evangelizing the slave population.[19] Although Griffin did not carry the biblical argument past a quick debater's thrust and did not present a full and reasoned argument for the mission to the slaves, his speech contains the embryos of both crucial aspects of southwestern clerical attitudes toward slavery in decades to come.

Much more comprehensive in its development of the evangelical strain in Griffin's argument was the Mississippi Baptist Association's circular letter in 1819 entitled "Duty of Masters and Servants." It treated the relation as part of the "order of Divine providence" and argued that God required certain actions of both parties. Masters should be just, exercising wisdom and prudence as well as kindliness and patience. In particular, the master should carefully guard the welfare of his servant, paying close attention to the quality of his food, clothing, and religion.

19. Jones, *Complete History of Methodism*, pp. 187-190.

140

The Mississippi letter also outlined the duties of slaves. They should be aware that their state was ordained by God: "However dark, mysterious and unpleasant those dispensations may appear to you, we have no doubt that they are founded in wisdom and goodness." Members of the postrevival generation were here unwilling to promote the "positive good" argument for slavery which would later dominate southern clerical discussion. Instead, the Mississippi Baptists counseled forbearance and faith and refused to enter into the debate over the value or role of slavery in a grander scheme. Slaves should be "industrious, honest, faithful, submissive and humble. . . . You must obey your earthly masters with fear and trembling, whether they are perverse and wicked, or pious and gentle."[20]

Postrevival clergymen, moving gradually toward a proslavery position but still reluctant to take the necessary final step away from the traditions of their churches, tended to support two movements for the amelioration of the slaves' situation. Unwilling to leave slaves in the potentially unmerciful grasp of unchristian masters, third-generation southwestern ministers promoted forms of relief. All of the denominations encouraged the religious education of slaves. In 1822 the Pearly River Baptist Association objected to the restrictions some masters placed upon evangelizing slaves. Three years later the Kentucky Synod encouraged its members to instruct their slaves in the basics of Christianity. David McAnnally, a Methodist preacher, occasionally instructed slaves on plantations; he was a pioneer in the extension of circuit riding to southwestern plantations. Such activity, however, was random. The carefully organized mission to the slaves would be a feature of southwestern churches only after a variety of changes took place in the hearts, minds, and composition of the clergy.[21]

Much more often, the churches supported the work of the American Colonization Society. John Bryce, a lawyer turned Baptist preacher, actively worked for the colonization cause. He liberated forty of his own slaves and sent them to Liberia.[22] The

20. Minutes, Mississippi Baptist Association (1819), BHS.
21. For a full discussion of the mission, see Chapter 8.
22. *The Baptist Cyclopedia* (New York, 1881), p. 43.

141

Western Luminary, the journal of southwestern Presbyterians, regularly published news of the society. A group of dedicated agents traveled throughout the region, including the future Methodist bishop Henry Bascom. Of the slaves freed by Gideon Blackburn, all but one were sent to Africa.[23]

Colonization was, for many southwestern clergymen, a godsend. Much of the support for it came from the laity. For example, James Birney, a member of the Alabama elite, actively promoted colonization throughout the 1820s.[24] One of the greatest supporters of the society was Kentucky's favorite son, Henry Clay. Feeling pressed by the need to establish strong links to the laity in this period of decline, clergy produced a complex set of reasons for supporting the society.

Colonization appealed to southwestern ministers because it was perceived as politically neutral, so long as it did not contain any explicit antislavery elements. It was not promoted as an emancipation project. One Alabama supporter warned that if antislavery elements should take over the society, it would appeal to only a very few members of his church. Such a prospect "could plunge us all into the miseries that would result from an indiscriminant emancipation of slaves."[25] As long as ministers avoided any suggestion that colonization might be linked to abolition, they could count on the support of slaveholders.

This is not to say that advocates of colonization universally took the stand that antislavery was incompatible with the society's goals. Some advocates wanted to walk a thin line between advocacy of abolition and expressions of distaste for slavery. Many continued to worry that slavery was fundamentally immoral. In 1828 a southwestern Presbyterian argued in favor of the work of the society because "slavery is our public disgrace."[26] But he was not willing to take the next step and suggest that the work of the society could solve that disgrace. The colonization movement provided ministers with a safety valve, a means of draining off

23. Sprague, *Annals of the American Pulpit,* 4:51.
24. William Birney, *James G. Birney and His Times* (New York, 1890), p. 56.
25. *African Repository* 3 (June 1827):116.
26. *Western Luminary* 5 (September 24, 1828):97.

some of the internal pressure brought on by doubts about the morality of the peculiar institution, and it was valuable largely because advocates only rarely suggested that it would end slavery. Indeed, ministers who opposed abolition gladly joined the cause.[27] Instead of suggesting the value of colonization as a means of dealing with the large slave population, advocates in the Southwest stressed its critical role in solving the problem of the free black population. The existence of freedmen in the population, according to the second annual report of the society, "is unquestionably a great evil. Probably no enlightened and benevolent mind could be found among us but would be rejoiced to see carried into effect a just and proper mode of removing this population to the land from which it came."[28]

Southwestern supporters vigorously followed this line. Stephen Foster of Knoxville argued that the society should deal only with "such people of colour as are already free," for they were given to "every form of indolence, degredation and vice" and consisted of a "redundant population of 250,000." Another southwestern supporter argued that free blacks were pathetically caught between two ranks of society, "the citizen and the slave," and that, as a consequence, they encountered "every positive evil incident to each condition [yet] share none of the benefits peculiar to either."[29] Although these arguments could be found nationwide, nowhere did they receive as devoted an audience as among the southwestern ministers. In other regions, indeed, the antislavery aspects implicit in these ideas were readily articulated. Especially in western new England, colonizationists frequently argued that their program was a means toward gradual abolition.[30] But in the Southwest clergy wanted to stick to that thin line between antislavery and proslavery, between the traditional and still vaguely

27. See Henkle, *Life of Henry Bascom*, p. 205.

28. *Western Review* 1 (October 1819):142; see also P. J. Staudenraus, *The African Colonization Movement* (New York, 1961).

29. *African Repository* 3 (February 1828):373-375; ibid. 5 (March 1829):390; see also A. H. Redford, *Western Cavaliers: Embracing the History of the Methodist Episcopal Church in Kentucky from 1832 to 1844* (Nashville, 1876), pp. 71-72.

30. See Staudenraus, *African Colonization*, p. 121; Bodo, *Protestant Clergy*, pp. 128-129.

present antislavery sentiment in the churches and the secular demands increasingly evident within the broad regional culture.

More than politically neutral, colonization was also theologically neutral. Antimission Baptists, who normally refused to join any benevolent organizations, found colonization acceptable because it contained no coercive element. The movement was, to be sure, begun with the strong support of the same New England ministers who had created the other elements of the "benevolent empire." But in the Southwest colonization was not promoted fundamentally as a religious program but as a practical reform. Its most prominent supporters were social and political leaders and not representatives of one particular faith. Ministers of the postrevival generation, fearful of more disruptive controversies, embraced colonization as an opportunity to take a noncontroversial stand.

Colonization was also attractive to many southwestern ministers because it included a subtle evangelical aspect. This aspect, of course, was little emphasized in the presence of antimission ministers, but moderate southwestern clergymen hoped that if slaveholders were converted, they might free their slaves and send them to Africa, where, as Christians, they could help convert their heathen brethren. Ministers could exercise their revival talents in a small way by converting and training the future emigrants. "Will it not be a source of great national congratulation," one Presbyterian journal asked, "if we should be able to repay our enormous debt [to Africa] by giving to her, the noblest political institutions, the arts, the sciences, and all the lights of life, and above all, the inestimable gift received by us from God: the knowledge of the Lord our savior."[31]

Clearly several of these motives were in potential conflict. Promotion of colonization as a means of opposing slavery ran counter to the notion that the movement was fundamentally apolitical. The sense that colonization might promote evangelical activities ran counter to the notion that it was fundamentally nontheological in origin and approach. These opposing interests may explain why churches in the region seldom discussed the merits of colonization, but rather simply supported its goals. As

31. *Western Luminary* 4 (January 3, 1827):327.

with slavery in general, for the postrevival ministers less was indeed more.

Postrevival Constraints: Internal Upheavals

Of course, this account begs the crucial question: why did antislavery virtually disappear from southwestern clerical discourse? No single answer jumps out of the documents. At least part of the answer resides in the development of the clerical profession. Ministers had begun to tire of constant controversy. They had been tumbled about in debate during and immediately following the revival, and they had little desire to seek out any more. The line of least resistance, therefore, struck many ministers as the only psychologically tolerable path to pursue. Within a context that showed everywhere the effects of two decades of controversy and schism, ministers little desired the uproar which a frank discussion of the issue of slavery most assuredly offered.

For Presbyterians, schism and disruption had become a normal part of life. The revival had torn the church into pieces. The first disruption came when the radical revivalists, led by Barton W. Stone, left the church to form the Christian, or New Light, denomination. The 1803 Kentucky Synod suspended two of Stone's followers, McNemar and Thompson, for promoting doctrine "contrary to the constitution of the church."[32] Between synod meetings the radical revivalists campaigned against this ruling with the result that "scarcely a congregation escaped unhurt—and many were altogether annihilated." Stonites then formed the Springfield Presbytery and published a summary of their beliefs, which included a denial of absolute decrees, belief in the general atonement, and the rejection of all creeds and confessions.[33] Soon thereafter the members of the prebytery decided they should start their own denomination so they could "pray more and dispute

32. Bishop, *Outline of the History of the Church in the State of Kentucky*, pp. 130-131; Minutes, Kentucky Synod, p. 131, Presbyterian Theological Seminary, Louisville.

33. Bishop, *Outline of the History of the Church in the State of Kentucky*, pp. 131, 134-135.

less."[34] The prebytery dissolved itself and proposed communion on the simplest of principles: faith in one God, with Jesus Christ as Savior, and a belief in the teachings of the Bible.[35] Unfortunately, such a simple basis provided insufficient grounds for unity, and dissension soon arose. Peter Cartwright recalled that soon after the founding of the new denomination, "a diversity of opinion sprang up, and they got into a Babel of confusion, Some preached Arian, some Socinian, and some Universalist doctrines; so that in a few years you could not tell what was harped or what was danced."[36] A few defected to the Shakers, and two of the movement's founders returned to the Presbyterian church. Eventually only Stone remained from the group of founders. He continued to gather disciples throughout the period until his church united in the 1830s with the followers of Alexander Campbell.[37]

Into this confusion three Shakers arrived in Kentucky in 1805. They received a friendly reception from the New Lights and established two villages.[38] Stone was initially impressed,[39] but soon he began to complain about the "wild enthusiasm of Shakerism," which consisted, in his opinion of little more than "an old woman's fables."[40] An endless series of tracts both for and against the sect rolled off the presses. One writer argued that Shakerism was most pernicious because it attacked the family: "It prevents propagation...and perhaps murders infants (but this I cannot prove)."[41] More moderate but no less determined to prove the dangers of Shakerism, Christopher Clark attacked Shaker doctrine with a mixture of scorn and ridicule.[42] Such critics missed the

34. Rogers, *Biography of Barton Stone*, p. 52.
35. Davidson, *History of the Presbyterian Church in the State of Kentucky*, p. 198.
36. Head, *A Reply to Arguments*, p. 32.
37. Davidson, *History of the Presbyterian Church in the State of Kentucky*, p, 211.
38. Ibid., p. 208; see also Thomas A Morris, *Miscellany: Consisting of Essays, Biographical Sketches and Notes of Travel* (Cincinnati, 1852), pp. 176-177.
39. Rogers, *Biography of Barton Stone*, p. 62.
40. Stone, *Reply to Campbell's Strictures*, pp. 66-67; see also Carr, *Early Times in Middle Tennessee*, p. 86.
41. Davidson, *History of the Presbyterian Church in the State of Kentucky*, p. 235; Smith, *Shakerism Detected*, p. 15, 35; Smith, *Remarkable Occurrences*, p. 7.
42. Christopher Clark, *A Shock to Shakerism*...(Richmond, Ky., 1812), pp. ii, 20, 33, 44.

appeal of Shakerism. It provided a secure and self-contained community, free of all the problems of living a Christian life in a non-Christian society. Neither orthodoxy nor Arminianism provided guarantees of salvation; the elect might be deluded, and those who chose Christ might have self-interest at heart. Shakers solved this dilemma through their simple faith in Ann Lee, and they provided certainty in a very uncertain world.

The radical revivalists separated for doctrinal reasons, and many Shakers left the church for emotional reasons. Another division in the Presbyterian church resulted from practical considerations. In the first years of the revival, the Kentucky Synod relaxed conventional rules for ordination so as to provide a sufficient supply of clergymen for work in the further reaches of the wilderness. When the Cumberland Presbytery was formed in 1803, its members enthusiastically supported the revival.[43] John Lyle, a moderate revivalist, learned from a friend that the Cumberland Presbytery filled its vacancies with "illiterate exhorters and licentiates who are chiefly Arminians in sentiment and who ride in circuits after the manner of the Methodists."[44] Even Methodists commented on connections between their customs and beliefs and those of the Cumberland Presbyterians: "They advocated union with the Methodists and preached so much like them, and spoke so freely against Calvin's notions of decrees and in favor of salvation for all men that many supposed they had renounced their old system of doctrines."[45] Illiterate exhorters multiplied, although the official historian of the denomination argued that they lacked only a classical education.[46] The exhorters probably would not have received much attention had they not achieved such success. Their combination of revivalism, curcuit riding, and Arminianism did much to promote the Presbyterian church in the

43. Bishop, *Outline of the History of the Church in the State of Kentucky*, p. 118; Davidson, *History of the Presbyterian Church in the State of Kentucky*, p. 235.

44. Lyle, "Diary and Journal," p. 3; see also Garrett, *Recollections of the West*, p. 42.

45. Paine, *William M'Kendree*, 2:353.

46. B. W. McDonnold, *History of the Cumberland Presbyterian Church* (Nashville, 1893), p. 58; on the ministers, see Richard Bond, *Brief Biographical Sketches of Some of the Early Ministers of the Cumberland Presbyterian Church* (Nashville, 1867).

most primitive regions of the West.[47] By 1804 leaders of the Kentucky Synod began to argue that these exhorters had distorted the doctrine of the denomination.[48] The synod appointed an investigatory commission,[49] which reached several conclusions. First, many preachers had been appointed without sufficient examination of their credentials. The commission singled out the case of James Haw, who had been received into the ministry by the Cumberland Presbytery "without examining him upon Divinity, or requiring him to adopt the Confession of Faith of the Presbyterian Church."[50] Second, the commission objected to the lack of respect it had received from many Cumberland ministers. Third, the report of the commission cited several clergymen who had rejected basic tenets of the denomination. One preacher testified that "the Confession of Faith was human composition and fallible."[51] The synod expelled all of the exhorters,[52] and the Cumberland ministers rebelled. Members continued to preach; when the synod suspended two of the leaders and finally dissolved the Cumberland Presbytery,[53] the exhorters formed their own presbytery and synod. The new denomination, the Cumberland Presbyterian church, provided something of a halfway house between Presbyterian government and Methodist preaching.

Two other disturbances hit the Presbyterian church in the wake of the revival, both minor but nevertheless painful. Thomas Craighead, an unusually enthusiastic controversialist, promoted a radical free-will doctrine. John P. Campbell attacked hm as a "Semi-Pelagian," who "groups himself among Pelagians and Socinians

---

47. Posey, *Presbyterian Church*, p. 37; see also Lowry, *Life and Labors of the Late Rev. Robert Donnell*, p. 29.

48. Davidson, *History of the Presbyterian Church in the State of Kentucky*, p. 230.

49. Bishop, *Outline of the History of the Church in the State of Kentucky*, p. 57.

50. Minutes, Kentucky Presbytery (1805), Presbyterian Theological Seminary, Louisville.

51. Bishop *Outline of the History of the Church in the State of Kentucky*, p. 122.

52. Davidson, *History of the Presbyterian Church in the State of Kentucky*, pp. 238-239.

53. Lyle, "Diary and Journal," 16, HFPC; Minutes, Kentucky Presbytery (1806), Presbyterian Theological Seminary, Louisville; Davidson, *History of the Presbyterian Church in the State of Kentucky*, pp. 243-244; Minutes, Transylvania Presbytery (1809), HFPC.

and with a look fiercer than his fellows, sounds a louder blast from the horn of battle."[54] Craighead and his followers soon seceded from the church.

Presbyterians also fought over the fate of Transylvania University. Horace Holley, president in the late 1810s and early 1820s, held views which probably tended toward Universalism or Unitarianism. The synod feared his effect on the minds of the youth of Kentucky: "We see in colleges, and institutions of learning, in miniature, what future society is to be. . . . These principles which they imbibe, they will carry with them into public life. If those principles are correct, they will have a salutary influence on society; if false, they will contaminate it."[55] Holley lost his position, but only after serious disruption of the university and the church.[56]

Divisions among the Baptists had none of the drama of the schisms in the Presbyterian church. The critical split, as we have seen, came over the question of missions. Hard-shell or Primitive Baptists tended to disapprove not only of organized benevolent activity but also of both education and systematic theology[57] and therefore attempted to disrupt the Baptist church in several ways. Antimission leaders effectively prevented any state organization from forming in the Southwest before the early 1830s. Moveover, national societies made little headway in Baptist-dominated regions. Indeed, churches tended to discuss few issues, and passive pietism dominated their meetings. In particular, the Hard-shells caused difficulty in Mississippi and Alabama, for the movement against missions arose at approximately the same time as the migration into the new territories. Churches therefore faced disruption almost as soon as they gathered.[58]

Of the three evangelical denominations, only the Methodists

54. John P. Campbell, *The Pelagian Detected*. . . (Lexington, 1811), p. 19; see also Robert Marshall to Francis Mortfort, February 28, 1811, Marshall Papers, Shane Collection, Presbyterian Historical Society, Philadelphia.

55. *Kentucky Reporter*, January 13, 1819.

56. Townsend, *Kentucky in American Letters*, pp. 52-53; see also Sonne, *Liberal Kentucky*, pp. 160-161.

57. Ewell, *Life of Rev. William Keele*, p. 82.

58. For a discussion of the Disciples of Christ, who disrupted the Baptist church in the late 1820s, see Chapter 6.

faced a major division on a national scale. Several issues had troubled the church in the early nineteenth century. Preachers who no longer traveled the circuits but had located as ministers of one church had consequently lost all say in church affairs. Similarly, laity had no formal power in the church. Laymen and preachers claimed that bishops retained too much power from the days of the Methodist origins within the Church of England. In 1820 the General Conference discussed each of these issues, although few reforms resulted.[59] Dissidents, particularly in Virginia and Maryland, began to organize support for a major reform effort at the next General Conference. In 1824 a group of local clergy met in Baltimore and started publication of a major reform journal, *Mutual Rights of the Ministers and Members of the Methodist Episcopal Church*, which attacked such notions as "the divine right of travelling preachers to govern the church."[60] They also formed a series of union societies.[61] In 1828 the Baltimore Conference expelled one of the reformers,[62] and a large contingent of reformers immediately seceded from the church. They held a constitutional convention in 1830, which officially formed the Methodist Republican church.[63]

The Methodist Republican movement probably received as much support in the Southwest as in any section of the country.[64] The reason may have been partly because the distances between settlements tended to isolate settled preachers, and they felt left out of the functions of the church. One Tennessee writer for *Mutual Rights* argued that depriving these men of their voting rights was immoral: "That man, rendered venerable by age,

---

59. John Paris, *History of the Methodist Protestant Church* (Baltimore, 1849), pp. 15-16; Bassett, *Concise History of the Methodist Protestant Church*, pp. 35-36.

60. *The Mutual Rights of the Ministers and Members of the Methodist Episcopal Church* (1825), p. 367; Bassett, *Concise History of the Methodist Protestant Church*, p. 42.

61. Paris, *History of the Methodist Protestant Church*, pp. 47-50.

62. Bassett, *Concise History of the Methodist Protestant Church*, p. 44; Paris, *History of the Methodist Protestant Church*, p. 167.

63. Edward J. Drinkhouse, *History of Methodist Reform* (Norwood, Mass., 1899), 1:452-478.

64. Miller, *History of North Mississippi Methodism*, p. 59.

talents, influence and experience should be excluded from the councils of the church, merely because they find it impracticable to travel, appears to be an anomaly in ecclesiastical polity, unknown perhaps in any age or any branch of Christ's church but that of our own." Another Tennessee preacher hoped that he would see "the shackles of autocracy fall; and love, union, vital piety, apostolic equality and reciprocal rights, firmly built upon the ruins thereof."[65] Reform conventions met in 1828 and 1829 in each of the four states of the region,[66] although their strength was probably concentrated in Tennessee and Alabama. The size of the movement was hardly impressive. Nineteen ministers attended the 1830 Alabama Conference; the Tennessee Conference the same year reported 346 members.[67] Nevertheless, the split in the church caused great worry for the more conservative ministers. For the first time in the West, the Methodist denomination had lost more members than it had gained, and a church that valued discipline had undergone ten years of rebellion and disorder.

These examples would be little more than minor episodes in the development of the region's religion were they to stand on their own. But they are important because they serve to underline the increased sense of shock that appeared in the southwestern churches after the revival. Emotionally exhausted clergymen had little need for other disruptions. Antislavery, however, was always an explosive topic wherever slaves existed. As we have seen, even as late as 1819 it caused a remarkable explosion within the Tennessee Methodist Conference. It would have been much simpler to have avoided the issue, perhaps postponed it for a time, and thereby avoided the direct political and social meaning of the institution. The limited movement to provide slaves with religious training served, at least for ministers of the 1820s, to finesse the question of slave rights, yet at the same time allowed these ministers the opportunity to treat one of the symptoms of slavery. The colonization movement, profoundly conscious of the need to avoid

65. *Mutual Rights* 1 (1825):419.
66. Paris, *History of the Methodist Protestant Church*, pp. 87-88, 114-115; Miller, *History of North Mississippi Methodism*, p. 60.
67. Drinkhouse, *History of Methodist Reform*, 2:246.

controversy, provided the postrevival generation with the simplest escape from the frightening possibilities of divisiveness. Most important, the ability of postrevival ministers, with very few exceptions, to avoid issuing manifestos on either side of the slavery issue reveals, by way of absence, a great deal about the needs of this generation of clergymen to avoid any further disruption.

In this respect, southwestern ministers most clearly resembled the slightly later group of ministers in the Connecticut River valley, who tried to reassemble their churches in the 1850s after the profound disruptions of the antislavery years.[68] Yet as the ministers of western New England moved toward greater professionalization, those of the postrevival Southwest tended to fall into a state of apathy. By the 1820s enthusiasm for any benevolent activity was increasingly hard to generate. Sermons became perfunctory. In short, antislavery, or more precisely the lack of any such movement, is symptomatic of a profound malaise among southwestern ministers in the wake of upheaval.

Postrevival Constraints: Society

Although the professional development of the ministry after the revival is probably the crucial element in the clergymen's growing apathy, one other complex set of elements is crucial to understanding why they acted (or, indeed, failed to act) the way they did. Clerical apathy may have reflected the relation of ministers to the general southwestern culture, which saw itself undergoing a period of transition between about 1815 and 1830. The panic of 1819 shocked the Old Southwest. The boom that arrived during the war continued until the middle of 1819, when the bottom suddenly fell out. Westerners reacted with a combination of anger and disbelief. "Never within the recollection of our oldest citizens has the aspect of the times as it respects property and money been so alarming," declared the *Argus of Western America*. All must join together, the writer continued, to "avert the calamities which threaten to cover our once happy state with bankrupts and beggars."[69]

68. Scott, *From Office to Profession*, pp. 95-111.
69. *Argus of Western America*, April 16, 1819.

A writer for the *Kentucky Reporter* at first reacted with caution: "An estimate will be made of the advantages and disadvantages of the various expedients, which might be adopted to relieve our difficulties." Within a few weeks, however, the same writer began to consider secession by southwestern states from the Union: "When it becomes their interest to separate, the plausible arguments and motives by which it may be enforced, are numerous and powerful, and will render its influence irresistible."[70] Anxious citizens hoarded specie, creditors called in loans, businesses failed. The feeling of optimism and the attendant speculative spirit gave way to an atmosphere of worry and caution. Richard Johnson of Kentucky led the fight for national relief in the Senate; John Crowell of Alabama introduced matching bills in the House. Representative Thomas Metcalf claimed that debtors had been "beguiled" into error by the federal government. After some debate, a relief bill overwhelmingly passed the Senate, and, with the almost unanimous support of southwestern congressmen, received a sizable majority of votes in the House.[71] In each state of the Southwest, legislatures and newspapers debated various forms of relief, including stays of debt execution, suspension of specie payments, and numerous schemes for the extension of credit.[72] "Franklin," a correspondent for the *Kentucky Reporter,* spoke for the region when he described the situation as "this new state of things."[73]

The panic symbolized a change in the way the region looked at itself. It served as the third unifying event in the history of the Old Southwest, along with the opening of the frontier and the revival. Unlike either of these, however, the panic reflected as much as it produced change. The panic forced southwesterners to realize that they no longer lived in a frontier of limitless possibilities but in a relatively developed society. They could act effectively in their own interests at the national level. They had to develop some clear sense of economic priorities. Most important, they had to examine their society and consider where their best interests

70. *Kentucky Reporter,* May 12, 1819.
71. Ibid., June 16, 1819.
72. Murray N. Rothbard, *The Panic of 1819* (New York, 1962), pp. 25-30, 47-51, 57-59, 91-92.
73. *Kentucky Reporter,* May 12, 1819.

lay. All of this was, for cleric or layman alike, cause for anxiety, especially when, in such times as that of the panic, plans did not work out.

The Old Southwest had even begun to show a few signs of eastern-oriented, genteel culture. Architects occasionally took pains to follow Greek revival standards, as in the Frankfort capitol building.[74] William Gibbs Hunt, a Harvard-educated migrant from Boston, founded a literary magazine in Lexington, the *Western Review*, in 1819.[75] He included reviews of the lives of Haydn and Wesley but appears to have been most taken with Lord Byron. A review of *Don Juan* at once praised Byron for his "genius and independence" and condemned him for failing "to inquire into consequences." On Madame de Stael's German essays, the reviewer proclaimed that he "never read a book where I found myself so lost in reflection.[76] Southwesterners began to pay some slight attention to education; the state legislature of Alabama, in one of its first acts, established a university.[77] Some fashionable life existed in towns like Nashville, with its coffeehouses and theaters,[78] or Lexington, the "Athens of the West," with the Lexington Lyceum, a debating society.[79] One critical visitor to Lexington viewed such attempts at high culture as laughable failures: "Every ediface, saving the college, seems filthy, neglected and in ruins, particularly the court house, the temple of justice, in the best square, which, with its broken windows, rotten window frames, rotten broken doors, all ruined and spoiled for lack of paint, looks like an old abandoned bagnio, not fit to be compared with any workhouse in England." Another visitor deplored the general violence in a region that seemed to be starving for

74. F. Garvin Davenport, *Antebellum Kentucky* (Oxford, Ohio, 1943), p. 161.

75. Ralph L. Rusk, *The Literature of the Middle West Frontier* (New York, 1925), 2:21.

76. *Western Review and Miscellaneous Magazine* 2 (February 1820):1;1 (September 1819):24.

77. Willis G. Clark, *History of Education of Alabama, 1762-1889* (Washington, 1889), pp. 31-36.

78. Thomas P. Abernethy, *From Frontier to Plantation in Tennessee* (1932; reprint Tuscaloosa, 1967), p. 282.

79. Ranck, *History of Lexington*, p. 303.

respectability.[80] Anne Royall showed perhaps the shrewdest judgment when she proclaimed that "this country exhibits man in all his varieties and in all his gradations, from country boor to the most polished gentleman."[81] It was a region so unsure of its place in the nation yet certain of its importance, however vaguely defined, that the laughable pretensions of some of its residents barely masked a profound sense of anxiety.

Indeed, the few attempts at establishing eastern cultural roots in western soil did not last. Hunt's *Western Review* survived for barely three years. By 1827 the once impressive Transylvania University collapsed from lack of public support.[82] The region in which postrevival ministers tried to survive would clearly not be a copy of the East. Nor would it remain the simple, backward region of the revival years, in which ministers could easily become cultural leaders. Instead, the culture seemed increasingly to be dominated by economic, agrarian concerns. Two of the dominant national politicians, Clay and Jackson, represented this aspect of the culture. Despite the shock of 1819, the economy of the Southwest grew at a prodigious rate. Between 1815 and 1830, for example, Alabama's cotton production increased more than tenfold.[83] Travelers who tried to make sense of the special regional character of southwesterns found an extraordinarily pragmatically minded populace, even considering the United State's reputation for practicality. Paul Wilhelm, duke of Württemberg, found in Kentucky a group of people who were "proud, bold and combative, frequently given to fighting," yet "characterized by industry and extraordinary endurance in tedious tasks." Henry Knight recognized that although "this is not yet a country of books, these are a people of enterprise and bravery."[84] Such vague generalizations would be or

80. William Faux, *Memorable Days in America* (London, 1823), p. 188; James Flint, *Letters from America* (Edinburgh, 1822), p. 138.

81. Anne Royall, *Letters from Alabama on Various Subjects* (Washington, 1839), p. 100.

82. Sonne, *Liberal Kentucky*, pp. 254–255.

83. Theodore Jack, *Sectionalism and Party Politics in Alabama, 1819-1842* (Menasha, Wisc., 1919), p. 15.

84. See Paul Wilhelm, Duke of Württemberg, *Travels in North America* (Norman, Okla., 1973); Clark, *Rampaging Frontier*; Lawrence S. Thompson, *Kentucky Tradition* (Hampden, Conn., 1956); Faux, *Memorable Days in America*, p. 193.

relatively little importance, however, were it not that ministers had to work within the context of a society trying to make sense of itself, one that during the 1820s was pulled increasingly toward a purely practical, economically oriented *mentalité*.

Most crucially, this economic spirit assumed that the peculiar institution would provide much of its labor force, particularly in the many prosperous subregions of the Old Southwest. In the Kentucky bluegrass, where most of the farmers had large holdings, the cash crop tended to be hemp, and masters owned an average of fifteen to twenty slaves per farm. In central Tennessee, the Tennessee River valley, and the cultural plains of both Mississippi and Alabama, most of the land was in cotton, with large plantations and significantly greater numbers of slaves per plantation than in Kentucky. In some of the counties of the so-called black belt, slaves outnumbered whites by a substantial margin.

In a region increasingly dominated by the products of slave labor and undergoing a crisis of spirit, attacks on slavery were remarkably only for their absence. An occasional passing reference to the drawbacks of slavery, such as Mississippi Governor Gerard Brandon's comment that "slavery is an evil at best,"[85] did not provoke great alarm. But any concerted effort to deny the validity or the future of the peculiar institution in any concrete terms would clearly have met stiff resistance. Ministers who wished to regain their revival-period prominence had little motivation to rock the boat for the sake of a dubious cause.

In the more recently settled states of Mississippi and Alabama, a few internal tensions on north-south lines began to emerge by the 1820s. The plantation owners in the deep South demanded relief in the form of direct aid in the wake of the panic.[86] In contrast, the less developed northern areas of the region promoted internal improvements.[87] They also began to demand greater democratic reforms and greater access to the political process as

---

85. Charles Sydnor, *Slavery in Mississippi* (New York, 1933), p. 239.
86. Abernethy, *From Frontier to Plantation*, p. 225.
87. Ibid., pp. 229-230; Edwin A. Miles, *Jacksonian Democracy in Mississippi* (Chapel Hill, 1958), pp. 21-23.

the southern areas became increasingly conservative.[88] Alabama and Mississippi had been settled at a much later date than Kentucky and Tennessee, and consequently development occurred much more quickly in the southern status. Analogous to this division was that between the older areas of the Northwest (Ohio, Indiana, and Illinois) and the relatively later to develop state of Michigan. In both cases, conditions of the frontier such as distance between settlements, problems with wild animals, lawlessness, and disputes with Indians prevailed in the more recently settled regions after they had largely disappeared from the older areas. The frontier spirit and experiences of eighteenth-century ministers in Kentucky and Tennessee were replicated in Mississippi and Alabama well into the 1820s. Reuben Davis recalled that his father, a Baptist minister in Mississippi, "never doubted that it was part of his Christian duty to knock down any rascal who happened to deserve such discipline."[89] At the same time, however, the continual movement of people north and south within the region meant that new ideas and developments in Nashville or Louisville had an important effect upon life in the towns of the southern half of the Old Southwest. Such important figures as Joseph Davis, whose younger brother Jefferson would make so great an impact upon southern life, moved from Kentucky to settle in Mississippi, bringing with him many Kentucky ideas and ideals.[90] Alabama politics, at least in the earliest years, were dominated by migrants from Tennessee, who successfully beat back the claims to political hegemony made by migrants from Georgia.[91] In short, the two halves of the region shared much: religion, politics, families. The new states of Mississippi and Alabama were, as a consequence, both within and outside the regional culture of the Old Southwest. They shared many of the same concerns as inhabitants of Kentucky and Tennessee, and a

88. Theodore Jack, *Sectionalism and Party Politics in Alabama* (Menosha, Wisc., 1919), p. 32.

89. Reuben Davis, *Recollections of Mississippi and Mississippians* (Boston, 1891), p. 19.

90. Janet S. Herman, *The Pursuit of a Dream* (New York, 1981).

91. J. Mills Thornton, *Politics and Power in a Slave Society, Alabama, 1800-1860* (Baton Rouge, 1978).

web of leadership linked the four states. At the same time, the greater dependence upon the plantation system, and therefore upon slavery, coupled with the newness of settlements, created interregional tensions.

These tensions would not flare up with sufficient force to produce severe and lasting divisions in the region until the 1850s. But for clergymen of the postrevival generation, they meant that forthright attacks upon slavery would threaten the stability to the regional networks of ministers. Thomas Griffin, in his speech before the General Conference, left no doubt that Mississippi clergymen would have little patience with abolitionism. If ministers in Kentucky and Tennessee wished to disagree—to propound vigorous antislavery views—they would have to do so at the risk of a division of the region's clergy on north-south lines. The more clergymen integrated themselves into the regional culture of the Old Southwest, the less likely they would be willing to pay that price.

The transformation of the antislavery argument into a muted discussion of mild reforms was, then, the product of a variety of developments. The internal transformation of the clerical profession in the region combined with external forces emanating from a changing regional culture to end the self-confident expression of antislavery views. In their attitudes toward slavery, the third generation of southern ministers expressed a variety of anxieties by lapsing into passive social conservatism which was atypical of the spirit of southwestern religion.

CHAPTER 6

The Disciples of Christ and Slavery

American religious thinkers have seldom celebrated diversity except as a short-term solution to overwhelming problems. Instead, mainstream religious figures have usually sought an end to schism and sectarianism; Jonathan Edwards, for one, warned that "a contentious people will be a miserable people."[1] Yet American religion has never been able to avoid the paradox of schism in the garb of union. Never did this paradox so clearly manifest itself as in the reform movement in the Old Southwest which resulted in the creation of the Disciples of Christ. In a period of tremendous disruption in the southwestern churches, the Disciples, seeking Christian unity, fostered the most painful dislocation produced by any of the religious controversies in the region.

Moreover, the Disciples exemplify the spirit and inclinations of ministers in the postrevival generation, carrying some of its views to an extreme that could not have been envisioned by members of the established evangelical denominations. Because Disciples adopted the peculiar stance that antagonism to controversy was best expressed through the use of controversy, an apparent paradox, ministers of the new denomination were viewed by more conventional clergymen as renegades and dangerous influences upon the spirit of the region. But the opponents of the reforms which the Disciples

1. Clarence Faust and Thomas Johnson, eds., *Jonathan Edwards* (New York, 1962), p. 198.

wished to bring to southwestern religion missed a crucial fact. An anxiety about controversy and an inability to channel that anxiety were the most characteristic features of postrevival southwestern churches. In this sense, the Disciples were not renegades; to the contrary, they were the quintessential representatives of the third generation of southwestern clerical thought. The new denomination maintained these characteristics long after they began to disappear in the other churches and thus became a fossil of postrevivalism.

To determine how this denomination addressed the myriad issues surrounding the institution of slavery, I must first explain precisely how it understood its role in the region and why ministers were attracted to it. This story will uncover a complicated set of themes. In both its thought and church structure, the new denomination stressed Enlightenment principles of common sense and republicanism. Although most southwesterners had some taste for both concepts, the Disciples provided a crucial link between the Enlightenment assumptions and the less carefully articulated world view current in the West. In addition, the new denomination breathed life into moribund southwestern religion. Vigorous controversalists who embraced Disciple thought forced other southwesterners to reexamine their assumptions, which explains some changes in the older denominations by the 1830s. It is important to realize that this reform movement possessed a particularly western character. The debates and diatribes that resulted from Disciple sermons and writings harked back twenty years to the heyday of the revival. Once more, the spirit of Daniel Boone was resurrected, and debates over religion often resembled the dirk and fist fights of primitive southwestern society.

Origins and Ideas of the Disciples of Christ

The leader of the Disciples, Alexander Campbell, was one of the more vigorous controversialists of his age. His father, Thomas Campbell, participated in attempts to restore the Scottish kirk in Ireland to primitive Christian purity. This struggle, unfortunately, produced endless sectarian splits, and in despair Thomas Campbell left his family and moved to America. He settled in western Pennsylvania, where he soon began a movement to purify the local Presbyterian churches. After this reform program also failed, he and his followers seceded to found a new sect, the Christian Association, in Washington, Pennsylvania.[2] In their 1809 *Declaration and Address*, the founders outlined four major features of the new association. First, all Christians could join who professed faith in and obedience to Christ and permitted "no uncharitable divisions among them." Second, members would be required to restrict their beliefs and actions to those "expressly taught and enjoined upon them in the word of God." Third, members must believe that the New Testament gave the soul complete account of Christian "worship, discipline and government"; the Old Testament was important but was not the foundation of faith. Fourth, the churches should adhere strictly to scriptural regulations, avoiding "any additions whatsoever of human opinions or inventions of man."[3] Soon after the organization of his sect, Thomas Campbell brought his family to America, and the new church almost immediately ordained his son Alexander. After a few years, father and son adopted the view that only true converts should receive baptism and that this sacrament must be administered by immersion. The reformers consequently began to hold fellowship with Baptists. The Campbells soon moved to western Virginia, and Alexander gradually gained a reputation in the West as a preacher and theologian. He also founded a reform periodical, the *Christian Baptist*, in which he promoted return to primitive Christianity. Although he lived in Virginia, Alexander Campbell attracted most of his support from Kentucky and Tennessee. He gathered around him some of the most effective local Baptist preachers, who joined him in arguing the need for a simpler, purer church. By the late 1820s, these reformers began to call themselves the Disciples of Christ.[4]

Campbell and his followers developed a complex theology for a

2. Lester McAllister and William Tucker, *Journey in Faith* (St. Louis, 1975); Benjamin Smith, *Alexander Campbell* (St. Louis, 1930), pp. 23-54.
3. Alexander Campbell, *Memoirs of Elder Thomas Campbell* (Cincinnati, 1861), pp. 52-53.
4. McAllister and Tucker, *Journey in Faith*, pp. 115-128.

movement that claimed to be simple. First, they believed in the ultimate rationality of Christianity. Campbell had been raised in the more didactic part of the Scottish Enlightenment, created when a group of Scottish philosophers reacted against the cosmology of the skeptical Enlightenment and the politics of the radical Enlightenment. In place of these views, such figures as Thomas Reid, James Beattie, and Dugald Stewart stressed common sense and moderation. They inherited much from Locke and the early moderate phase of the Enlightenment, especially its optimism about man's capability of understanding himself and his environment.[5] Campbell constantly studied Locke and read *An Essay Concerning Human Understanding* at the age of seventeen.[6] His understanding of Locke came through the Scots, who insisted on the unity of mental ideas and external reality. "The representations of truth," Campbell argued, "are the exact pictures of all the realities about which we are conversant, or in which we are interested."[7] Campbell had little interest in Locke's hazy notion of substance, an epistemological compromise which Locke termed "something, I know not what"; instead, Campbell saw no room for doubt. Unfortunately, this Scottish common-sense perception of the world, which seemed to explain the nature of material objects with precision, created problems when applied to faith. A Christian, and a primitive Christian at that, Campbell struggled to reconcile common sense with such puzzling doctrines as the Trinity. He ultimately felt forced to conclude that faith comes from experience. Logic, therefore, has no part in producing Christians.[8] But he still wished to phrase this conclusion in rational terms. After complicated intellectual gymnastics, he divided natural from supernatural knowledge. He then argued that Christians use one kind of common sense to guide them in the natural world and another kind for supernatural affairs.

The rationality of the Disciples was more apparent in their style than in the substance of their arguments. Many of the Disciple

5. May, *The Enlightenment in America*, pp. 111, 341–349.
6. Smith, *Alexander Campbell*, p. 231.
7. *Christian Baptist* 5 (1828):461-462
8. *Millennial Harbinger* 5 (1834):76–78; *Christian Baptist* (1823): 58–59; Alexander Campbell, *The Christian System* (St. Louis, 1839), p. 56.

clergy had little training in theology or philosophy, so their arguments lacked both skill and subtlety. Nevertheless, numerous sermons began with comments that mimicked philosophical language, such as, "If there be such a science as moral philosophy its length and breadth, depth and height, are all involved in the Cross of Jesus Christ. Believing that its principles are as fixed and indestructible as those of the natural sciences or chemistry, I propose to show, from evidences wholly undeniable, that the Cross was not arbitrary, but a necessary antecedent to the pardon of our sins."[9] In their effort to maintain a rational style, the Disciples resembled such moral philosophers in the East as Francis Wayland. Both groups attempted to avoid the anti-intellectual quality of the religion of the revival.

A second general tenet of the reform movement was the simplicity and clarity of the New Testament, its divine nature, and its pivotal place in the faith of all Christians. Phillip Fall, one of Campbell's earliest supporters in the Southwest, believed that all Christians should attempt "to ascertain simply what the divine word ways, and why it is said."[10] The Old Testament, Campbell argued, had great importance in its time and could now be appreciated for "its figurative and prospective character."[11] Purely supernatural matters, he explained, constitute "a very small portion of both Testament."[12] The New Testament was written explicitly for Christians, and Campbell thought that the Old Testament was, in many ways, outdated. Many injunctions in the Jewish law were no longer needed, including those "to urge the disciples of Christ to baptize their infants; to observe holy days;... to sanctify the seventh day; to enter into national covenants; to establish any form of religion by law."[13] The Disciples failed to separate the foolish and useless laws from those still applicable. This task they apparently left to common sense.

9. B. C. Goodpasture and W. T. Moore, *Biographies and Sermons of Pioneer Preachers* (Nashville, 1954), p. 87.

10. Phillip Fall, "Memoirs," Phillip S. Fall Collection, Disciples of Christ Historical Society, Nashville.

11. Campbell, *Christian System*, pp. 149-150.

12. *Christian Baptist* 5 (1828):499.

13. Goodpasture and Moore, *Biographies*, p. 32.

Third, the Disciples adamantly maintained the importance of two sacraments: baptism of converts by immersion and regular, weekly celebration of the Lord's Supper. Although Campbell warned against overemphasizing these sacraments, he argued that each was necessary. Each rite had symbolic value and served to reassert community among Christians. But the Disciples either ignored or muted any mystical implications of baptism or communion. Again, the church revealed its Enlightenment roots through its discomfort with experimental, personal religion.[14]

The fourth fundamental aspect of Disciple thought rose, in part, from the battles between Campbell's father and the clerical leaders of the Irish and Pennsylvania Presbyterians. To avoid such troubles, the Disciples argued for independent churches that would choose their own officers. Campbell repudiated the notions of apostolic succession and clerical supremacy in the church.[15] He wrote, "The community, the church, the multitude of the faithful, are the fountain of official power. This power descends from the body itself—not from its servants."[16] Campbell proposed that the laity should share many of the powers traditionally reserved to the clergy, including the right to preach, to baptize, and to administer communion.[17] The clergy should provide leadership, of course, but ministers should never attempt to exercise control.

The fifth, and most important, element of the Disciple program was the promotion of Christian union. "A plain, unostentatious family arrangement is what we aim at," one early Disciple declared.[18] Somewhat later, another member predicted that the millennium would begin if only the churches could eliminate all qualifications for membership except "faith in Jesus Christ and submission to his authority."[19] Of course, Campbell and his followers realized

14. *Christian Baptist* 3 (1825):175; *Millennial Harbinger* 22 (1851): 325; Alexander Campbell, *Debate on Christian Baptism* (Pittsburgh, 1822); Campbell, *Christian System*, p. 332.

15. Robert Richardson, *Memoirs of Alexander Campbell*, 2 vols. (Cincinnati, 1913), 1:384-387.

16. Campbell, *Christian System*, p. 89.

17. Ibid., p. 87.

18. P. S. Fall, *A Discourse* (Frankfort, 1842), p. 32.

19. Goodpasture and Moore, *Biographies*, p. 368.

that disruptions did occur, and the Disciples blamed schisms and heresies on the sinfulness of man.[20] Moreover, the Disciples understood that too much zeal in chasing down heretics could backfire, as Campbell's father had learned in Ireland. To prevent such problems, Campbell recommended an attitude of toleration and modesty: "A Christian man has a right to express a private opinion when asked for it; but he has no right to obtrude it upon any one unasked; and much less to gain a party to it contrary to the desire of the church or community to which he belongs."[21]

Unfortunately, neither Campbell nor his followers paid much attention to this advice. Their vigor in promoting Christian union was surpassed only by their enthusiasm for condemning other denominations. Campbell debated leading members of several churches, and in his discussion with Bishop Purcell, a Roman Catholic, Campbell called the Catholic church the "Babylon of John, the Man of Sin of Paul, and the Empire of the Youngest Horn of Daniel's Sea Monster."[22] He hoped that the Disciples of Christ would not become a "sectarian name [such] as Lutheran, Methodist or Presbyterian."[23] One group of Disciples attacked the work of Theodore Parker and others as "this heathenish and fabulous system."[24] A leading Disciple journal predicted that "the great contest will soon be between pure Christianity on the one hand, and Popery, Monkery and Infidelity on the other."[25] These combative words do not seem to promote benevolent and peaceful union but instead sound like the propaganda of a denomination on the make.

The greatest manifestation of the disruptive influence of the Disciples was in their raids on the Baptist churches of the West. Campbell's followers drew most of their support from Baptists, primarily because both denominations objected to the baptism of infants. Further, the congregational form of the Baptist church

20. Campbell, *Christian System*, pp. 89, 100.
21. *Millennial Harbinger* 15 (1844):470–471.
22. Smith, *Alexander Campbell*, p. 198.
23. Richardson, *Memoirs of Alexander Campbell*, 2:204.
24. *History and True Position of the Church of Christ in Nashville* (Nashville, 1854), p. 41.
25. *Bible Advocate* 2 (1843):2.

appealed to Campbell. By the late 1820s, no Baptist association in the Southwest remained untouched by the reform movement, and in 1829 three of the largest associations came under Campbellite control.[26] The reformers succeeded in part because the Baptist churches had already divided over the issue of missions, and Campbell's radical congregationalism made him popular among antimission Baptists. In addition, the rise of the reform movement coincided with a revival, and Disciple ministers showed special enthusiasm for gaining new converts.[27]

The division of the First Baptist Church in Nashville typified the results of Disciple tactics. Phillip Fall had arrived in America from England in 1817, and he settled in Adair County, Kentucky. The next year he joined the Baptist church and began to teach school; two years later he became a Baptist minister, starting his preaching in Louisville. In 1823, after reading several issues of the *Christian Baptist*, he joined the reform movement, forming a committee to lead Baptists back to the ways of the primitive church. The Nashville church, at that point a struggling congregation without a preacher, called him in 1826, and he took the reform movement south. He instituted weekly communion, promoted strict adherence to the New Testament, and in other ways altered the normal activities of the church.[28] In 1827 he led a revolt against the Concord Baptist Association, from which the Nashville church soon withdrew. Fall proposed to his congregation a set of reform principles, which were adopted as the new church regulations. The church declared, as a general guide, "that we take the New Testament as the rule of our faith and practice, and will form such rules from it for our worship and government as may consist with its spirit and meaning; and with the peace and

26. Errett Gates, *The Early Relation and Separation of the Baptists and Disciples* (Chicago, 1904), p. 69.

27. Spencer, *History of Kentucky Baptists*, 1:616, 598.

28. Herman Norton, "Life Story of Phillip Fall," MS, Disciples of Christ Historical Society, pp. 14-51; *History and True Position of the Church in Nashville*, pp. 4-5; Herman Norton, *Tennessee Christians: A History of the Christian Church (Disciples of Christ) in Tennessee* (Nashville, 1971), pp. 19-30; *History of the Ohio Falls Cities and Their Counties*, pp. 386-387; Kendall, *History of Tennessee Baptist Convention*, pp. 44-56.

good order of the church." Fewer than five members objected.[29] In 1830 five dissenters withdrew and reorganized the First Baptist Church on orthodox lines, but this remnant of the church took many years to gain any following of its own.[30]

Of course, orthodox Baptists reacted with anger and dismay to such humiliations. The leader of the opposition, Silas Noel, was a well-educated former judge and editor,[31] and he had substantial support among the Baptist clergy. The church establishment took immediate action when it could, expelling supporters of Campbell from associations and churches. One Campbellite recalled this period as "worse than the Spanish Inquisition."[32] The counterattack stressed four major points. First, the orthodox leaders condemned the general disruption: "Before Alexander Campbell visited Kentucky, you were in harmony and peace; you heard but the one gospel, and knew only the one Lord, one faith and one baptism.... Have not these happy times gone by?"[33] This criticism, of course, echoed a major charge against the radical revivalists twenty years before. Second, Campbell's opponents condemned the divisions forced upon churches: "If you would protect yourselves as churches make no compromises with errors—mark them who cause divisions, and divest yourselves of the last vestige of Campbellism."[34] Third, a few ministers attacked the theology which the Disciples promoted. One association stated that if a member church should "maintain the propriety and expediency of uniting upon a bare profession of belief of the Scriptures, that such an individual is at war, not only with the association, and the word of God declares that a house divided against itself cannot stand."[35] Another association listed the errors of Campbellism: the belief in "no promise of salvation

---

29. Norton, "Story of Fall," pp. 47-49.

30. Clayton, *History of Davidson County*, p. 318; Norton, "Story of Fall," pp. 50-51.

31. Spencer, *History of Kentucky Baptists*, 1:202.

32. P. Donan, *Memoir of Jacob Creath, Jr., to Which Is Appended the Biography of Elder Jacob Creath, Sr.* (Cincinnati, 1877), p. 90.

33. Minutes, Franklin Baptist Association, Kentucky (1830), BHS.

34. Minutes, Green River Baptist Association, Tennessee (1831), BHS; Minutes, Long Run Baptist Association, Kentucky (1830), BHS.

35. Minutes, Russell Creek Baptist Association, Kentucky (1830), BHS.

without baptism"; the requirement that all must be baptized who "believe that Jesus Christ is the Son of God, without examination of any other point"; the failure to stress the importance of the Holy Spirit; the notice that "no creed is necessary for the church but the Scriptures as they stand"; and several other, less central, points.[36] Fourth, several Baptists accused the Disciples of general impiety. One association argued that Campbell was guilty of "apeing of Thomas Paine and Voltaire."[37] Another thought reform appealed to the simple-minded and the Disciples had "spoken perverse things, God-dishonoring, self-exalting and soul-destroying things."[38] A third termed Campbell's doctrines "anti-christian" and said "they should be discontenanced by all the lovers of the Holy Scriptures."[39] Almost all the Baptist associations produced general condemnations of the reform movement.[40]

Presbyterians and Methodists soon joined in the attack. One Presbyterian journal, the *Western Luminary,* published a series of articles against the reformers, including "Alexander against Campbell," which repudiated Campbell's views on the Trinity.[41] In a letter to Campbell, Joseph Stiles, a Kentucky Presbyterian, wrote that Campbell seemed "to have studied out and treasured up everything that should be said against every text and argument which stands for the truth; and every ingenious gloss and sophism that promises currency to error." A Methodist, William Phillips, composed a doggerel poem against Campbell, "Alexander the Great; or the Learned Camel."[42]

The counterattack against the reform movement revealed much

36. Bond, *History of the Baptist Concord Association*, p. 45.

37. Minutes, Franklin Baptist Association, Kentucky (1830), BHS.

38. Minutes, Long Run Baptist Association, Kentucky (1831), BHS.

39. Minutes, Goshen Baptist Association, Kentucky (1830), BHS.

40. Norton, "Story of Fall," p. 44; Minutes, South District Baptist Association, Kentucky (1830); Minutes, South Concord Baptist Association, Kentucky (1830); Minutes, Gasper River Baptist Association, Kentucky (1831); Minutes, Franklin Baptist Association, Kentucky (1827); Minutes, Concord Baptist Association, Kentucky (1831); Minutes, Bracken Baptist Association Kentucky (1830); Minutes, Anderson Baptist Association, Kentucky (1830), all in BHS.

41. *Western Luminary* 10 (1834):28.

42. Walter B. Posey, *Religious Strife on the Southern Frontier* (Baton Rouge, 1965), pp. 52, 64.

about the religious atmosphere of the 1820s and early 1830s. Campbell's attacks on the power of the clergy could hardly sit well with ministers who had only recently secured positions of leadership in their churches. The clergy had no interest in unity. Each denomination represented a strikingly different constituency. Baptists controlled the older, wealthier rural areas. Methodists dominated in the poorer, less densely settled sections, and Presbyterians drew their support from the better-educated residents of villages and towns. Each denomination distrusted the others, and each depended, to some extent, on contributions from the laity. Thus a movement that would unite the populace into a new church, and thereby take away membership and financial support, could hardly have won the hearts of very much southwestern preachers.

In addition to undermining the three denominations by his own actions, Campbell united forces, in 1834, with the bête noire of many western clergymen, Barton W. Stone. Stone had continued, with limited success, to promote his New Light church throughout the 1820s. Many of his followers had left to pursue their own, occasionally even more eccentric, ways. Stone, however, started to publish a periodical, the *Christian Messenger,* to promote his sect. He founded the journal, he wrote, because religion, "for centuries past, had fallen far below the excellency and glory of primitive christianity." He decried "partyism and divisions" which brought "shame and confusion [to] the professing world." Stone listed five basic truths that should guide any true Christian: all men are fallible; one should be willing to be rejected by other men for what one believes; one should be willing to sacrifice fame and wealth; a true believer avoids manmade dogma; and the Bible is rational. The journal included frequent attacks on orthodoxy and other denominations.[43] Stone's small sect, however, differed from the Campbellites on some issues. The Stonites provided for a more powerful clergy, attacked the other denominations less vigorously, underplayed baptism and communion, and stressed experience as against reason. Nevertheless, both Stone and Campbell

43. *Christian Messenger* 1 (1826):1; 1 (1827:38; 1 (1826):2–5; 4 (1930):29, for example.

saw the advantages of a union and minimized their differences.[44] It was appropriate that the two most enthusiastic controversialists in the West should join forces to create a denomination that emphasized peace, unity, and brotherhood among Christians.

Disciples and Organized Benevolence

The Campbellites' opposition to benevolent societies, stemming from their distrust of clerical power, was not necessarily a sign of social conservatism. Campbell encouraged philanthropy, which "takes away the dross of selfishness,"[45] but he feared the disruption which organized benevolent activity might bring to his church.[46] He optimistically assessed the future of America: "The United States of America as they grow in learning, in the arts and sciences, and in all the elements of human wealth and power, can extend blessings to many nations; and, indeed, to the four quarters of the world."[47] Yet he wished to tread a line between individual responsibility and benevolent organization: "Christians ought to be industrious, frugal, economical in order to have more than they want for themselves. That they may be rich in good works, liberal, and communicative to the necessities of saints and to the exigencies of society."[48]

When it was ten years old, the denomination began to realize that it needed some means of organizing cooperative effort. Many preachers sensed that the evangelical spirit of the early years could not continue indefinitely. Further, many understood that individual responsibility was an unreliable basis for a large and complex denomination. Campbell gradually began to stress organization to provide fellowship and communication, especially among clergy. "A church," Campbell wrote, "can do what an individual disciple

44. McAllister and Tucker, *Journey in Faith*, pp. 148-149; Posey, *Religious Strife*, p. 49.

45. *Millennial Harbinger* 3 (1832):116.

46. Posey, *Religious Strife*, p. 51.

47. Alexander Campbell, *Popular Lectures and Addresses* (Philadelphia, 1866), p. 185.

48. *Millennial Harbinger* 6 (1835):682.

cannot, and so can a district of churches do what a single congregation cannot."[49] Most Disciples enthusiastically supported the cooperation movement, fearing that individual churches, left to their own devices, would backslide and fail. "Brethren, it is time that we should be up and doing," one periodical proclaimed. "Without some regular plan of contribution, we never can keep evangelists in the field, particularly such as we need now." At the same time, the churches began to promote benevolent reforms, especially temperance. "The constant, habitual, regular dram-drinker, whether he drink to excess of not, will not, we most awfully fear, see the everlasting Kingdom of God."[50]

The Disciples moved toward benevolent activity with a growing postmillennial spirit, an optimistic belief that Christian society would move toward perfection with the approach of the Day of Judgment. Campbell began to comment on the nature of the millennium only in the 1840s, although the journal he edited had included the word in its title for ten years. The millennium, he declared in 1843, would be "a state of greatly enlarged and continuous prosperity, in which the Lord will be exalted, and his divine spirit enjoyed in an unprecedented measure." The arrival of the new age, he felt, would come "at no very distant day."[51] Other Disciples saw their activities as the fulfillment of Revelation: "This coming of the Lord, in vengeance to destroy his enemies, cannot now, at the furthest, be very far off, and may be much nearer than we anticipate. The 'signs of the times' and the approach of the close of the prophetic spirit plainly indicate it. And should you not be found among his true people—his genuine disciples—but arrayed in opposition against them, he will destroy you."[52]

Disciples and Slavery

The Campbellite attitude toward slavery can be explained only in the context of the complicated developments of the denomina-

49. Ibid. 2 (1831):31.
50. *Bible Advocate* 1 (1843):28; 1 (1842):3.
51. *Millennial Harbinger* 14 (1843):9, 74.
52. *Bible Advocate* 1 (1843):81-82.

tions and the special notion of internal cooperation upon matters of benevolence. The seemingly paradoxical desire of the Disciples to destroy controversy by using extreme, controversial techniques was clearly in evidence in their discussion of slavery in the 1820s. Barton W. Stone, who had taken the most radical (and least practical) stance against slavery during the Great Revival, continued to oppose the ownership of slaves until he died. The Stonite faction, consequently, remained the antislavery conscience of the church; the coeditor of Stone's *Christian Messenger,* John Johnson, was an uncompromising enemy of slavery and a friend of the abolitionist James Birney.[53] In the 1820s Stone had become an advocate of immediate abolition followed by colonization, writing, "It is our wish to awaken the attention of the West and to engage all in the laudable work," which he later termed the "holy cause." By the 1830s, Stone began to promote the views of the abolitionists, while remaining a somewhat less enthusiastic colonizationist. "Let the freedmen of America blush to be the last in this great cause of removing oppression from the poor Africans, and of restoring them to that liberty which [has] been unjustly wrested from them by superior power." In 1835 Stone moved to Illinois. Once out of the slave states, he joined wholeheartedly in the abolition cause.[54]

The majority of the members of the denomination underwent a different transformation. Few had either Stone's intellectual powers or his tendency toward extremes. Two of the earliest leaders of the reform movement had taken strong positions against slavery. Fanning Tolbert, the son of an Alabama planter, preached against slavery as late as 1831. He was arrested after one antislavery sermon and accused of using inflammatory language to incite slaves.[55] The father of "Raccoon" John Smith had refused to own slaves because he feared their presence would make his sons lazy. Smith became a close friend of David Barrow, the leader of Baptist

53. Robert Fife, "Alexander Campbell and the Christian Church in the Slavery Controversy" (Ph.D. dissertation, Indiana University, 1960), pp. 20-23.

54. *Christian Messenger* 1 (1827):95; 3 (1829):198; 5 (1831):238; 9 (1835):82-88, for example.

55. James Wilburn, *The Hazard of the Die: Tolbert Fanning and the Restoration Movement* (Austin, 1969), pp. 11, 24.

antislavery during the revival, and remained opposed to the peculiar institution throughout his life.[56]

Early in their careers, the Campbells had also opposed slavery. After he was warned not to preach to slaves, Thomas Campbell asked, "Is it possible for me to remain in a place where, under any circumstances, I am forbidden to preach a crucified Savior to my fellow beings?" Alexander Campbell was converted to antislavery in South Carolina, where he saw what he considered to be overwhelming brutality.[57] Through the 1820s he advocated gradual emancipation, and he actively participated in the debate over slavery in the Virginia Constitutional Convention of 1829–30. He condemned as "Barbarous" a Georgia law banning the education of slaves or free blacks: "This is the year 1830, if I mistake not, and yet, even now, the person who will dare, male or female, to give the knowledge of letters to a slave, shall pay for it as a crime to be punished by the judge." He suggested that the Nat Turner rebellion, "this unexpected and appalling visitation," might force Virginia to end slavery.[58]

Behind Campbell's antislavery position lay several of the contradictory elements of his theological program. The common-sense notion of self-evidence, abounding in his theological writing, remained in evidence in his random, almost careless, condemnations of the institution. The "tyrannical, unjust and impious" quality of slavery struck him as self-evident.[59] Campbell's sometimes maddening self-confidence is nowhere in better evidence than in his inability, or perhaps more precisely, unwillingness, to spell out the commonsensical objections he felt emerged from a study of slavery. More, he failed in any of his early decisions of slavery to test the institution against Scripture, whether read in his commonsensical way or in any other manner.

Just as he failed to detail the moral (in his terms "supernatural") shortcomings of slavery, Campbell held true to his faith in the

56. John A. Williams, *Life of Elder John Smith* . . . (St. Louis, 1879), pp. 14-15, 179-180.
57. Richardson, *Memoirs of Alexander Campbell*, 1:495; 2:189.
58. *Millennial Harbinger* 1 (1830):47; 3 (1832):14-15.
59. David E. Harrell, *Quest for a Christian America: The Disciples of Christ and American Society to 1866* (Nashville, 1966), p. 102.

congregational nature of his new denomination. The church therefore never insisted upon opposition to slavery as a precondition for
admission. Campbell did list among the many goals of his newspaper,
the *Millennial Harbinger,* that he wished to undertake a study of
American slaves "as preparatory to their emancipation and exalta-
tion from their present degraded condition."[60] Yet never did he go
so far as to demand an end to slaveholding by all members of the
Disciples. Indeed, in 1830, he was willing to concede that slavery
would probably never cease to exist until Judgment Day. Campbell
could not easily adopt a harsh antislavery position at least in part
because he himself had become a slaveholder, buying two brothers
from a Methodist minister. Campbell intended to free the two
slaves when they reached age twenty-eight, and when he carried
out his promise he could be considered to have demonstrated the
viability of gradual emancipation. His participation in the internal
slave trade, however, meant that the antislavery faction of the
Disciples of Christ had little hope of promoting a more radical and
activist denominational position on the issue.

Campbell did not disregard the possibility that his denomination might make a concerted effort to deal with slavery. Reform, as
explained above, meant that some premillennial united spirit
should be stimulated. In keeping with this constrained notion of
the limits of reform, Campbell recommended that Disciples support the American Colonization Society. The society's careful
rejection of strong-arm tactics and its equally careful avoidance of
direct denominational ties fit well with Campbell's rejection of
coercion but also with his interest in Christian unity. As a
consequence, Campbell recommended Henry Clay's colonization
views to the readers of the *Millennial Harbinger,* reprinting in the
first issue Clay's speech before the American Colonization Society.
Campbell had considered recommending to the Virginia State
Constitutional Convention that the government surplus of the late
1820s be used to buy slaves and send them to Africa.[61] In 1835 he
proposed a complex emancipation/colonization plan which includ-

60. *Millennial Harbinger* 1 (1830):31.
61. Harrell, *Quest for a Christian America,* p. 103; see also Robert West,
Alexander Campbell and Natural Religion (New Haven, 1948), p. 202.

ed creating a black colony in the Western Hemisphere: "Let, then, a territory on this continent, or on the African, be obtained or purchased, to which all the young Negroes, especially, which can be purchased annually from those who will not manumit, be deported, and to which those that are now, or shall hereafter, be made free, shall be invited to withdraw in the prospect of a comfortable settlement."[62] Implicit in this solution is a strong belief in the unworkability of a biracial society. Campbell was never a simple-minded racist, but he did admit, "Much as I may sympathize with a black man, I love the white man more."[63]

Alexander Campbell's attitude toward slavery contained the potential for a variety of developments, clarifications, and changes of course. To be sure, the most straightforward, obvious possibility was that he would abandon his moderate, carefully restricted abolitionism, and by the mid-1830s he did just that. He began to argue that he should direct his energies against sin, "the root of the problem," rather than against slavery, "only one branch of the evil."[64] As gradualists and colonizationists increasingly found themselves under attack by both the proslavery and radical antislavery forces, Campbell began to return the attack, condemning immediate abolitionists as antisouthern extremists. To defend himself against these attacks, Campbell began to promote a mission to the slaves by the end of the 1830s. He castigated masters for their failure to care for their servants and to show slavery in its best light: "What will you say for yourselves when the wretched fate of your own household shall be traced to your neglect of duty?" Campbell had worried for several decades about the material welfare and spiritual needs of slaves, but by 1840 his sense of the "patriarchal character of the institution"[65] permitted a more positive view of the peculiar institution to creep into his writing.

Campbell's final break from his moderately antislavery past came in 1845, when he published an extensive analysis of slavery in the *Millennial Harbinger*. Here the dominant elements of his thought once again appeared, but he reached the opposite conclu-

---

62. *Millennial Harbinger* 6 (1835):589.
63. McAllister and Tucker, *Journey in Faith*, p. 193.
64. *Millennial Harbinger* 7 (1836):182-183.
65. Ibid. 10 (1839):313.

sion from two decades before. He applied his common sense to the issue, and his analysis yielded a result that was typical of his thought. No longer constrained by his antislavery views to ignore Scripture, Campbell offered a close analysis of the text, leading to the conclusion that both of the Testaments support the morality of slavery. Slaveholding was, therefore, not "necessarily and essentially immoral and unchristian."[66] His fundamental belief in the independence of each congregation no longer had to be given short shrift. In his judgment, slaveholding could not be a "term of Christian Fellowship or a subject of discipline," and, therefore, no church would have to struggle between its loyalty to Campbell and the presence of slaveholders in its pews; that potential conflict simply disappeared. Indeed, Campbell concluded that the issue of slavery had best be left to the political process; it should not break up the unity of Christians, which he fervently desired. He hoped and trusted that the issue of slavery could be dropped from religious discussion.

Of course, Campbell was mistaken if he believed he would have the last word. John Fee, a Kentucky minister, objected heartily to what he viewed as Campbell's backsliding.[67] Such criticisms of Campbell fundamentally misunderstood the place slavery held in his view of the emerging millennium. If he allowed that issue to divide his church, north against south, the denomination would be destroyed. For Campbell, Christian unity should not be sacrificed for mere worldly concerns. Within the system of thought which he tried to advocate, slavery was a minor matter, and when it got in the way of major issues, it had to be eliminated as a subject of concern.

Other, more social developments within the Disciples of Christ contributed to Campbell's change of course. The habit of slaveholding had, by the 1840s, become firmly entrenched within the denomination. Not only did Campbell own slaves, but so did several other leading preachers. Thomas B. Caskey, for one, became one of the more significant ministers in the denomination. In at least one attempt to quantify slaveholding along denominational lines,

66. Ibid. 16 (1845):195-196.
67. Ibid., pp. 197-200.

the American and Foreign Antislavery Society found that, by 1850, the Disciples owned more slaves per capita than members of any other denomination.[68]

Equally important, by the 1840s this reform movement had matured into a functioning denomination, with a rudimentary government and a strong leader. In 1857 the Disciples claimed more than two hundred thousand members.[69] Such a substantial group could hardly be expected to accept a single set of social standards. As long as the Disciples claimed to adhere to only a brief and simple statement of faith, they could hardly require that their members subscribe to antislavery principles, or indeed proslavery ones. Moreover, Campbell had learned a lesson from the three other evangelical denominations: unless carefully avoided, the issue of slavery necessarily would bring about denominational fission. His hope for unity dictated the route he took. In this sense, as in so many others, the Disciples of Christ remained fixed in the social attitudes of the postrevival generation long after the conventional churches had begun to move into a new phase of development. The odd combination of a faith in unity and a tendency toward controversy, along with the ambivalent attitude toward reform, which characterized the Disciples and the other evangelical denominations in the 1820s, stayed with the Campbellites at least until the beginning of the Civil War. In this way, their seeming shift from antislavery to proslavery was truly only a change in the balance of the various forces at work on the minds of many members of this generation. Just as members of other denominations in the 1820s found great difficulty in expressing either strong support for or disapproval of the peculiar institution, so Disciples, in the main, pronounced on slavery without much conviction, whichever side of the fence they chose. Indeed, with most of the postrevival ministers, the sense that seems to underlie most Campbellite comments upon slavery is a wish that the issue would leave them alone.

---

68. Wilfred Garrison and Alfred DeGroot, *The Disciples of Christ, a History* (St. Louis, 1948), p. 468.

69. McAllister and Tucker, *Journey in Faith*, p. 188.

CHAPTER 7

Slaves in
Southwestern Churches

The reevaluation of slavery, begun in earnest with the publication of Kenneth M. Stampp's *The Peculiar Institution*, has produced impressive analyses of slave religion. Ulrich B. Phillips had briefly treated the subject of religion in *American Negro Slavery*, and but for some understanding of the separation of the races in religion, he saw in much of the slave religious experience that "the negroes merely followed and enlarged upon the example of some of the whites."[1] Stampp's revision of this picture suggested both that whites attempted to use religion as a means of social control and that the private religion of slaves, always conducted out of the master's sight, was a complex of African roots and Christian messages.[2] This private religion, which Albert Raboteau calls the "invisible institution," has brought out the best of historical analysis: studies of folklore, of the African heritage, and of the complexity of slave theology have made slave religion one of the most studied and best understood of nineteenth-century American religions.[3] The other half of Stampp's analysis, his extension of

1. Ulrich B. Phillips, *American Negro Slavery: A Survey of the Supply, Employment, and Control of Negro Labor as Determined by the Plantation Regime* (1918; reprint, Baton Rouge, 1956), p. 318.
2. Stampp, *Peculiar Institution*, pp. 156-162, 371-377.
3. Albert J. Raboteau, *Slave Religion: The "Invisible Institution" in the Antebellum South* (New York, 1978); John W. Blassingame, *The Slave Community: Plantation Life in the Ante-bellum South* (New York, 1972), pp. 61–75; Lawrence W.

Elie Halevy's thesis to the antebellum South, has been investigated with equal enthusiasm, stressing such subtopics as the biblical defense of slavery, the mission to the slaves, and ministers' attitudes toward their enterprise in the slave South.[4] Scholars have also recognized that many slaves were not impressed with the vision of religious propriety preached at them by white ministers and that blacks chose to create a separate church at least in part as a form of rebellion.

This separation of the slave religious experience into two discrete categories is both attractive and, I think, correct for the immediate pre–civil War period. As Donald Mathews argues, although blacks and whites may have shared some religious forms and practices, "their religious experience and ultimate hopes differed as radically as their social position."[5] The issue I raise in this chapter is whether the last years of the peculiar institution might have significantly differed from earlier, less well-organized, less theoretical religious situations in the Old Southwest.

The transappalachian South in the first three decades of the nineteenth century was as active in the development of evangelical religion in America as any other region in the nation. In Kentucky, Tennessee, Mississippi, Alabama, and the peripheral sections of bordering states, the Great Revival so greatly shaped the culture that later visitors continually saw its lingering effects. The development of the camp meeting, the promulgation of a simple, conversion-oriented faith, and the use of many important techniques of revivalism either originated or gained special prominence in the region. Unlike the more rigid, traditional, intellectualized churches of much of the seaboard South, and Old Southwest was a great pot of religious ferment in the first decades of the nineteenth century, with much in common with the burned-over district of New York in the 1830s and 1840s. It is this special, regional religious character that makes the Southwest a particularly interesting object for the study of black-white relations within the churches.

Levine, *Black Culture and Black Consciousness: Afro-American Thought from Slavery to Freedom* (New York, 1977).

4. Mathews, *Religion in the Old South*, pp. 136-184; Genovese, *Roll, Jordan, Roll*, pp. 202-209.

5. Mathews, *Religion in the Old South*, p. 185.

Black Experiences in White Churches

Interesting subjects are not always productive, unfortunately. Information on black-white relations in this period in the Old Southwest is in remarkably short supply. The voice of the slave, which is crucial to any full understanding of the black experience in white churches, is almost altogether silent on the early nineteenth-century Southwest. The Works Progress Administration slave narrative series includes the recollections of few survivors from the period before 1830; such former slaves would have had to have been well over one hundred years old when interviewed. The other large body of black testimony on slavery, slave memoirs, autobiographies, and letters, offers little on the subject of early nineteenth-century religion in the Old Southwest. Of the nine autobiographers who lived in the Southwest before 1830, one declared that slaves had no religion, a second claimed that the only religion that mattered was the meetings "gotten up by some of the blacks on the place," and a third, Josiah Henson, stressed only his personal religious commitment and provided no information on the early sociology of white-black religious relations.[6]

Works written by whites are somewhat more helpful, although clerical memoirs are also curiously lacking in much direct information on the experience of slaves in the churches of the Old Southwest. The surviving records of early southwestern ministers tend to be those of the most important and influential members of the clergy, and hence they tend to concentrate on broader issues such as the morality of slavery but fail to account for the week-by-week religious experience of the faithful, black or white. They are, that is, better sources for intellectual than for social history. Specific church records are the richest sources on the subject of white-black relations in churches before 1830. These are especially difficult sources to use because they are full of the trivia of church activity. Seldom the work of well-educated church clerks, they are often desultory and illegible. Nevertheless, they tell a

6. Henry Bibb, *Life in Slavery* (N.p., 1849), p. 68; Elisha Green, *Life of the Rev. Elisha Green* (Nashville, 1888), p. 2; Josiah Henson, *Life of Josiah Henson* (N.p., 1849), pp. 27-31.

story which is of remarkable importance to the subject of religion and slavery, for they reveal that consistently in southwestern churches before about 1830 blacks were in many ways on an equal standing with whites in the day-to-day activities of the congregations. Although this equality had very clear limits, it was nonetheless real.

In the parts of the Southwest with significant black populations, sizable numbers of slaves joined churches. When the Salem Baptist Church of Mississippi recorded its membership in 1821, the list included eight white men, ten black men, twenty white women, and six black women.[7] The May 25, 1828, church census of the Tuscaloosa Presbyterian Church in Alabama listed fifty-five white members and twenty-five blacks.[8] George Brush, a Methodist itinerant minister, reported that fifty-eight whites and twenty-eight blacks attended a Kentucky meeting in 1828.[9] Although the list seldom used the term "slave," they conventionally appended a master's name to that of the black man or woman. Such cryptic references as "black man belong bentley" sufficed to define the social status of a member.[10] Especially before 1830, slaves regularly joined whites in southwestern churches. The implications of this remarkable fact are, at once, complicated and elusive.

Of course, in the areas where few slaves resided (eastern Kentucky and Tennessee, upland Mississippi and Alabama), the church records included few mentions of slaves.[11] In areas with

7. Minutes, Salem Baptist Church, Jefferson County, Mississippi (1821), HCSBC.

8. Minutes, Tuscaloosa First Presbyterian Church, Alabama (May 25, 1858), HFPC.

9. Redford, *Western Cavaliers*, pp. 95-102.

10. Minutes, Bethlehem Baptist Church, Kentucky (1810), HCSBC; see also Minutes, Wilson Creek Primitive Baptist Church (1821), HCSBC; Minutes, Louisville First Presbyterian Church, Kentucky (1826), HFPC. The churches also frequently used such terms as "a man of colour." See Minutes, First Presbyterian Church, Bardstown, Kentucky (1813), University of Kentucky; Minutes, Concord Presbyterian Church, Nicholas County, Kentucky (1828), University of Kentucky.

11. See, for example, Minutes, Bethel Presbyterian Church, Fayette County, Kentucky, p. 480, HFPC; Minutes, Philadelphus Presbyterian Church, Mississippi (1821-52) HFPC; Minutes, Murfreesboro Presbyterian Church, Tennessee (1812-60), HFPC; Minutes, Unity Presbyterian Church, Amite County, Mississippi (1832-60), HFPC; Minutes, Walnut Hill Presbyterian Church, Kentucky (1818-60), HFPC.

significant slave populations, however, just the opposite was true. "The negro came so easily into the ranks of the church," one Methodist minister recalled, "that no particular program of missionary work was considered necessary before 1829."[12] In fact, many western churches could claim slaves among their founders. The Dumplin Creek Baptist Church listed the "Black Brother" and "Black Lyah" as original members; the slave Polly helped found the New Providence Presbyterian Church in Kentucky. When Peter Cartwright visited a relatively "wicked" section of Tennessee, he organized a Methodist class of six, including an elderly slave who contributed twenty-five cents to Cartwright's work. Blacks were carefully screened for membership, asked to give a full account of their religious experiences, and apparently taken as seriously as whites in the important business of extending fellowship. In the West Fork Meeting House "A negro woman belonging to bro. Tandy came forward and told her experience, which not giving general satisfaction to the church, it was recommended to her to wait till the next meeting." Membership was a precious gift, and that these early churches considered blacks worthy of it is significant.[13]

Once members, slaves in the southwestern churches before about 1830 participated in much that churches had to offer on an equal footing with all other members. They could expect courtesy for as long as they remained full members of the church. At the very least, slaves found, at each important stage of their membership in the church, that the formalities they met would be the same as those for whites, and if any problem arose, slaves received as much attention as did whites. For example, in 1812 the Old Salem Baptist Church "appointed Brethren Joyner, Champion and

---

12. Posey, "Development of Methodism," p. 98; see also Minutes, Pisgah Baptist Church, Somersett, Kentucky (1820), HCSBC.

13. Minutes, Dumplin Creek Baptist Church, Jefferson County, Tennessee (1816), HCSBC; Minutes, New Providence Presbyterian Church, Kentucky (1814), HFPC; Minutes, West Fork Meeting House, Christian County, Kentucky (May 8, 1813), HCSBC; Cartwright, *Autobiography*, p. 173. Two accounts which make great claims to equality than I have found justified by the sources are Miller, *History of North Mississippi Methodism*, p. 62; and Wendell Rone, *A History of the Daviess-McLean Baptist Association in Kentucky* (N.p., n.d), p. 19.

Watson to visit Black Sister Hannah."[14] A formal meeting would be held to notify the slave member of charges leveled against him or her. Committees called on slaves or whites who had failed to attend recent meetings, thereby often providing visits to sick members. Proper form also obtained when a slave member wished to leave the church because he or she had been sold. The West Fork Meeting House appointed a committee to decide whether a slave deserved the official papers of dismissal. "The report of the committee to inquire into the conduct of Black Sister Judy, being favorable, ordered that the Clerk furnish her with a letter of dismission."[15] Most important, slaves could expect a fair and courteous hearing when they applied for membership. One Baptist church received a slave "into their membership by experience, against the judgment of their venerable pastor, Elder Robert Elkin."[16]

Church records most frequently show that slave and white life in the church joined together in the exercise of church discipline. Most church business meetings focused on the sins and misdeeds of members. In fact, these Saturday or Sunday afternoon sessions included little else in their discussions. After such opening business as a report on the number of members, the reading of the minutes, and the admission of new members, the meeting would entertain charges against church members brought by fellow churchgoers or as a result of civil arrests or common rumor. On occasion, a member might confess a set of sins and ask the church's pardon. If the offender showed sufficient repentance, he or she would receive a reprimand and retain membership in the church. More often, the offending member failed to attend the meeting, and the church then appointed a committee to bring him or her to the next meeting. In extraordinarily complicated situations, the church meeting would conduct a trial, occasionally taking several weeks to reach a conclusion. Finally, the meeting would decide whether the accusation had merit and, if so, whether the

14. Minutes, Old Salem Baptist Church, Livingston County, Kentucky (June 1812), HCSBC.

15. Minutes, West Fork Baptist Meeting House, Christian County, Kentucky (July 8, 1809), HCSC.

16. Conkwright, *Churches in Boone's Creek Baptist Association*, p. 26.

violator had repented of the sin. At this point, the church retained, reprimanded, suspended, or excluded the member. If the last, the person could not join another church of that denomination, for he or she needed a letter of dismissal showing that his or her reason for leaving the church had nothing to do with the violation of morality. The original church covenants always mandated these disciplinary activities. The Old Salem Baptist Church, for example, required its members "to pray for each other, to watch over each other, and if need be, in the most tender and affectionate manner to reprove one another."[17]

Slaves received particular attention from their fellow churchgoers, which seems natural because slaves worked harder, had fewer amusements, and in general led a much more difficult life than most whites. Moreover, most slaves had little incentive to practice the virtues prescribed by white society, at least when dealing with that part of their lives. It is little wonder, then, that rebellion against the pressures and unfairness of the peculiar institution manifested themselves in actions which the churches might see as sinful.[18] Occasionally, the church stated the charge in general terms: "Rindah, a black woman, belonging to Mr. Turner, was debarred from church privileges for improper conduct."[19] More often, a member would accuse a slave of a long series of misdeeds. Joseph Graves, a member of the Sand Run Baptist Church of Kentucky, "brought in a complaint against Joseph, a black member belonging to Sister Fanny Demlaney for taking from several circumstances a parcel of Tobacco and when interrogated about it stating falsehoods also for raising a riot at Bro. Ferrilson the Sabboth and making use of Unsavory language." It took the church a week to digest all this, and at the next meeting it

17. Minutes, Old Salem Baptist Church, Livingston County, Kentucky, (1805), HCSBC.

18. See Kenneth M. Stampp, "Rebels and Sambos: The Search for the Negro's Personality in Slavery," *Journal of Southern History* 37 (1971):367-392; Raymond A. Bauer and Alice Bauer, "Day to Day Resistance to Slavery," *Journal of Negro History* 27 (1943):388–419.

19. Minutes, Monroe Presbyterian Church, Hebron, Mississippi (June 1823), HFPC; Minutes, Bethel Presbyterian Church, Fayette County, Kentucky (1834), University of Kentucky.

excluded Joseph.[20] At one meeting of the same church members accused four different slaves of such varied offenses as adultery, quarreling, breaking and entering, drunkenness, and fighting.[21]

Whites also occasionally misbehaved, but they were often disciplined for activities which slaves, given the constraints of southern law and society, could not possibly have engaged in. Most obvious of these are various disputes over property. Church after church heard long and complicated testimony over whether members had swindled one another. Nevertheless, slaves committed most of the same offenses as did their white brethren, and the most common of these was certainly drunkenness. Whites appeared more frequently accused of both intoxication and selling alcohol. Blacks tended, however, to face accusations of simple drunkenness far more times than the proportion of slave members in the churches might suggest would be likely. The New Providence Presbyterian Church in Kentucky accused Polly, a slave, of "intemperate use of ardent spirits." She repented and was admonished. The frequency of this charge against blacks, as opposed to a number of times churches disciplined whites for the same offense, had its root in a variety of factors. Slaves had less opportunity to get their hands on alcohol; masters watched over that aspect of their morality very carefully. The slaves therefore had much less opportunity to develop a tolerance for the often very low-quality local drink they could find. Slaves also had more difficult lives than their masters, working harder, longer hours, fearing the breakup of their families, often being separated from loved ones by some distance, and experiencing corporal punishment. Alcohol provided a brief interlude from the pressures of life, relief with which even religion could not always compete. Whites could drink in the privacy of their homes, a luxury few slaves could enjoy. Thus drunken whites were not as likely to be detected and accused of their sin. Masters had little use for drunken workers and possibly were afraid of them. Therefore, slaveholders used the pressure of

20. Minutes, Sand Run Baptist Church, Hebron, Kentucky (May 1821), HCSBC; see also D. P. Browning, *One Hundred Years of Church History* (N.p., 1922), on the Mt. Pleasant Church.

21. Minutes, Sand Run Baptist Church, Hebron, Kentucky (December 1826), HCSB, see also Minutes, Pisgah Presbyterian Church, Mississippi (1831), HFPC.

church opinion to accomplish personal reforms when other discipline failed.[22]

Other offenses appeared somewhat less frequently in the church records. Both whites and blacks faced discipline for oral misdeeds. Churches disciplined black members in various ways for swearing, often at masters.[23] Apparently more offensive, because more frequently raised in meetings, was lying. The Mt. Pleasant Baptist Church entertained an accusation against "Sister Amy, a woman of colour, for abrupt language and Lying. She is found to have made contradictory statements and is excluded." Of course, masters eagerly supported such discipline. They wanted to be able to trust slaves to report the misdeeds of their fellows when asked. For example, when Brother Gris of the Red River Baptist Church reported that his slave had lied and refused to obey orders, the congregation immediately expelled the slave. Of course, slaves were not alone in facing church pressure to avoid prevarication. Several whites in different churches were accused of engaging in fraud in their dealings with fellow members.[24]

Slaves came before church committees accused of stealing much more often than whites. At the Unity Baptist Church, "Sister Moore laid in a complaint against a black brother pompey, a slave of her own, for the crime of theft."[25] One slave was accused simply of "coniving at a theft."[26] Churches frequently heard accusations against slaves for thievery plus another offense. That is, usually the slave stole for a reason. For example, the Dandridge Baptist Church cited Black Rebeccah "with stealing money and

22. Minutes, New Providence Presbyterian Church, Kentucky (April 1823), HFPC; see also Minutes, Turnbull Primitive Baptist Church, Paris, Kentucky (July 1817), HCSBC; Browning, *One Hundred Years of Church History*, p. 13.

23. Minutes, Old Salem Baptist Church, Jefferson County, Mississippi (September 1819), HCSBC; Minutes, Davis Presbyterian Church, Paris, Kentucky (January 1824), HFPC; Minutes, Severns Valley Baptist Church, Elizabethtown, Kentucky (October 1802), HCSBC.

24. Browning, *One Hundred Years of Church History*, p. 13.

25. Otto Rothert, *A History of Unity Baptist Church, Muhlenberg County, Kentucky* (Louisville, 1914), p. 18.

26. Minutes, Concord Presbyterian Church, Alabama (December 11, 1829), HFPC; Minutes, Red River Baptist Church, Adams, Tennessee (December 14, 1822), HCSBC.

going to a ball."[27] Theft was the one sin over which most contacts with the civil authorities took place. The Sand Run Baptist Church excluded a slave who had struck someone with a stone and stolen a turkey. The church excluded him, however, only after he had been tried by civil authorities and publicly whipped.[28] These churches seldom tried slaves for more serious crimes than assault and theft, which may indicate that slave members had moral standards in keeping with church views, or at least that they had developed extremely subtle means of resistance.

The churches only very infrequently accused slaves of failing to attend to religious duties. This failing was much more common among white members; indeed, it was the most frequent accusation against whites in the church records I have examined. In several instances, white members made a great point of their nonattendance. One church called a white member to account for his failure to come to meeting; in his response, he railed against the church for acting "tyrannically in expelling her former Pastor." No black could have dared to make such an accusation. Black failure to attend to religious duties never took the form of rebellion but always appeared to be the result of negligence. Occasionally this neglect had to do with religious observances outside the church. The Paris, Tennessee, Presbyterian Church disciplined "Scipio, a negro slave of Dr. Andre Todd . . . because he did not attend family worship in his master's home."[29] After members of the West Fork Meeting House met with "Black Brother Davey," he agreed that he had "neglected his duty in not attending meetings that it was not for want of support but proceded from his negligence yet he at the same time confessed his anxiety to attend meetings in the future."[30] It is reasonable to assume that the infrequency of this accusation may indicate the importance slaves

27. Minutes, Dandridge Baptist Church, Jefferson County, Kentucky (January 1825), HSCBC.

28. Minutes, Sand Run Baptist Church, Hebron, Kentucky (January 1825), HCSBC.

29. Robert S. Sanders, *Presbyterianism in Paris and Bourbon County, Kentucky 1786-1961*, (Louisville, 1961), p. 21.

30. Minutes, West Fork Baptist Meeting House, Christian County, Kentucky (March 1810), HCSBC.

placed on church membership. Without sufficient black testimony on this subject, however, just how much it indicates about the balance in their minds between spiritual and temporal benefits cannot be known. It is doubtless true, however, that some slaves understood that only in the churches might they find some small measure of equality with their masters.

Discipline and the Slave Family

With some reluctance, churches had to consider the occasional irregularities in the sexual practices of slave members. In their regulation of white sexual activities, churches faced most complaints regarding day-to-day marriage squabbles. A few racier items did occasionally appear: one member was accused of "whoredome." Much more frequently, the churches disciplined slaves for loose sexual activities, especially adultery. The Yelvington Baptist Church accused Brother Charles of abandoning his wife to sleep with his mistress. He apologized, and the church admonished him to return to his wife.[31] Church members did not single out men, however; several churches disciplined women for the same offense.[32] Accusations of engaging in premarital sex also regularly appeared in the records. The Old Salem Baptist Church excluded a slave for "going to bed with a woman"; the Severns Valley Baptist Church excluded a female slave for fornication.[33] Occasionally, the churches could not decide whether to accuse the slave of fornication or adultery. Instead, slave women would be excluded simply for "having a little one."[34]

31. Minutes, Yelvington Baptist Church, Owensboro, Kentucky (October 1829), HCSBC; see also Minutes, Severns Valley Baptist Church, Elizabethtown, kentucky (August 1806), HCSBC; Minutes, Sand Run Baptist Church, Hebron, Kentucky (May 1820), HCSBC.

32. Minutes, Monroe Presbyterian Church, Mississippi (August 1828), HFPC; Minutes, Wilson Creek Primitive Baptist Church, Kentucky (July 1823), HCSBC.

33. Minutes, Old Salem Baptist Church, Livingston County, Kentucky (April 1813), HCSBC; Minutes, Severns Valley Baptist Church, Elizabethtown, Kentucky (April 1827), HCSBC.

34. Posey, "Watch-Care," p. 314; the regulation of the sex lives of slaves

The problem of definition is related to a second general way in which the churches involved themselves in the sex lives of slaves. States refused, for a variety of reasons, to treat slaves as legally equal to whites. Consequently, the marriage of slaves had no legal sanction. Masters could sell wives and husbands separately without fear of reprisals, and slaveholders gave little protection to slave marriages, so it is little wonder that the nature of the marriage relation between slaves occasionally blurred. The churches faced the problem of sorting out sin from tragedy. The Red River Baptist Church initially accused Brother Luke of marrying a free woman, which was considered a dangerous alliance for a slave; soon the church decided "he has committed Fornication for he had copulation with a Girl which we do not conceive he had any right to claim as his wife, even agreeable to the customs of slaves."[35] Another church excluded a slave for "leaving his wife, living in adultery with a woman and afterwards marrying her and living with her as his wife."[36] A third church forced "Black Win" to withdraw his membership "on account of some of the members being dissatisfied with her Manner of living with a Black man."[37] The opposite problem also presented itself. "Jane (a woman of colour) belonging to Brother French, was excluded for refusing to live with Simm as her husband. Simm was excluded for disagreeing with his wife."[38]

The problem these churches faced was broader than simply the misdeeds of their slave members. The real issue was whether ultimate control over the institution of marriage rested with churches or masters. The Red River Baptist Church, at three separate points, had to face direct abuses of the marriage institu-

---

remained a great concern in these churches up until the Civil War. See Minutes, Bethany Presbyterian Church, Gloster, Mississippi (May 3, 1846, October 1, 1848), HFPC.

35. Minutes, Red River Baptist Church, Adams, Tennessee (July 14, 1821), HCSBC.

36. Minutes, Sand Run Baptist Church, Hebron, Kentucky (June 1824), HCSBC.

37. Minutes, Sinking Creek Baptist Church, Johnson City, Tennessee (April 19, 1816), HCSBC.

38. Conkwright, *Churches in Boone's Creek Baptist Association*, pp. 71-72.

tion by slavery. The members acted in a manner typical of the congregations in the Old Southwest by deciding in favor of the peculiar institution or by failing to decide at all. They refused to answer the question of "whether a Negroe that was sold from his wife in some of the Eastern States and brought to this country and has taken another wife can be received into fellowship or not." Five years later they suspended a slave for "marrying a man against his master's wish and living in a disorderly way before marrying him." In 1821 the congregation decided it was wrong for "a Slave member of the Baptist church to marry a free woman."[39] Each of these choices served to put the master before God, slavery before the church. Moreover, no church in the West ever argued the converse. The marriage relation was sacred, the congregations felt, but the slave-master relation had precedence. To be sure, many laity and clergy owned slaves; slavery was taken for granted by whites. Nevertheless, this vacuum of moral leadership on the importance of slave marriages seems extraordinary.

The issue of slave marriages underlines the precarious nature of slave equality within the churches. As members, slaves could expect many different indications of a special status in a society that mandated their abasement. Yet this was a fragile equality, which slaves seldom allowed themselves the luxury of insisting upon. A very few did, however. Black members of the Red River Baptist Church protested when they were told by one white member to leave their seats. Unfortunately, their loss was not merely an immediate one; the church, reacting harshly to the unseemly nature of the protest, voted to establish as a rule "that Black people are hereafter to give place or go out of the Meeting House, when called upon or requested to do so."[40]

39. Minutes, Red River Baptist Church, Adams, Tennessee (September 19, 1801, May 3, 1806, July 18, 1821), HCSBC. As we have seen, the churches seldom addressed the problem of the internal slave trade. For three rare instances of churches that did mention this problem, see Minutes, Boiling Fork Baptist Church, Lincoln County, Kentucky (February 1826), HCSBC; Minutes, Concord Presbyterian Church, Nicholas County, Kentucky (1827), University of Kentucky; Minutes, First Presbyterian Church, Bardstown, Kentucky (1822), University of Kentucky.

40. Minutes, Red River Baptist Church, Adams, Tennessee (August 1820), HCSBC.

Slaves never truly entered into the important parts of church life. Neither blacks nor women could vote for the various officers of the church, nor could they assume any of these offices. To be sure, blacks occasionally preached in white churches, most notably "old Captain," who had come west with the so-called "travelling church."[41] But few black preachers lasted long. Brother James, a member of the Bethlehem Baptist Church of Kentucky, preached for a trial period before the congregation and was then advised to restrict his activities to the betterment of his own race.[42] In addition to their control of church offices, white males held the exclusive right of proposing motions in church meetings, although church rules never explicitly required this. As both a right and a duty, only white men were required to pay for the upkeep of the church.[43] Slaves, in short, enjoyed only partial equality, which allowed them remarkable access to the day-to-day activities of the church but constricted their role.

Change in the 1820s

Slaves' tenuous hold on this limited equality is in no way better demonstrated than by its passing in most of the churches of the Old Southwest sometime after 1830. Slaves continued to be disciplined with whites in some churches up until the Civil War, but in the vast majority of church records I have examined, such discipline became increasingly rare, especially in churches located in areas with large slave populations. From a survey of forty southwestern church records, or about 10 percent of those existing in archives, I can provide a very limited statistical basis for this generalization. In the year 1815, 42.1 percent of the acts of discipline in these churches concerned blacks. By 1850, this

41. Leo Crimson, ed., *Baptists in Kentucky, 1776-1976* (Middletown, 1977), p. 67.

42. Minutes, Bethlehem Baptist Church, Kentucky (July 2, 1820–August 11, 1821), HCSBC; see also Minutes, West Fork Baptist Meeting House, Christian County, Kentucky, (April 12, 1806), HCSBC.

43. Minutes, Red River Baptist Church, Adams, Tennessee (1815), HCSBC; Minutes, Sand Run Baptist Church, Hebron, Kentucky (1820), HCSBC.

proportion had dropped to 9.7 percent. Almost all of these churches were in Alabama and Mississippi, in regions settled somewhat later than the rest of the Southwest. Therefore, as suggested earlier, many developments of the region as a whole happened with a lag in these more recently settled subregions. Many churches began to formalize the separate consideration of slave sins. A few at first gave other slaves the right to watch-care. In 1816 the Red River Baptist Church took up the readmittance of a slave named Sarah: "The church met. Sarah's case was then considered the Black Brethren being present who appeared to be satisfied with her acknowledgements." After further consideration, the church decided to readmit her.[44] The Wilson Creek Baptist Church formalized the separate consideration of slave affairs. In August 1825 the members decided that "there should be a committee appointed of the black members whose duty it should be to take note of all disorderly conduct among the black members of the church."[45] Such independent scrutiny of slave affairs might be considered liberating; slaves now had control over their own lives. More important, however, whites had begun to separate slaves from the congregations, reflecting the segregation of the society.

The second indication of this trend was the physical separation of blacks and whites in the churches. Little evidence remains today of special galleries or slave sections in the pre-1820 churches. In the 1820s, many of the churches constructed new church buildings, and the members frequently made provision for slaves. In 1829 one Baptist church added a "shed" for its black members, separated from the white section by a high partition.[46] The Sand Run Baptist Church built a new meeting house in 1821 and heard the "motion of Bro. W. Montegue to take into consideration the propriety of the provisions made by the church in alloting the Black members and friends the northeast end and the ajoining front of the galery to the partition." At the next meeting the

44. Minutes, Red River Baptist Church, Adams, Tennessee (September 1816), HCSBC.

45. Minutes, Wilson Creek Primitive Baptist Church, Kentucky (August 1825), HCSBC.

46. Leavell and Bailey, *Complete History of Mississippi Baptists*, p. 77.

church approved the separation. Some of the slave members objected, a committee tried to convince them of their error, and the church eventually excluded two black women who refused to accept the plan. Some churches closed off white meetings to blacks altogether, and the slaves had to attend separate afternoon sessions. By the 1840s the Coldwater Association of Baptists in Mississippi announced separate services for black members, the better to suit their comprehension and needs.[47] Blacks and whites were also segregated at other church functions. For example, the Concord Presbyterian Church in Alabama had a separate table for blacks at baptisms.[48] Less frequently, slaves formed completely separate congregations, although these were still associated with the mother church.[49]

Paradoxically, this transition was often accompanied by a growing number of slaves in the church rolls. One Presbyterian congregation had fifty-four slave members and forty-six white members in 1857. Another, in 1858, had fifteen blacks and nineteen whites.[50] The numbers are deceptive however. These slave members had no function in the church, they participated in few activities with whites, and they often attended a separate service. The segregation of the churches made blacks into shadow members.

Part of the reason for the disappearance of some measure of equal treatment of blacks and whites may have been the development of the Southwest itself. As churches grew from frontier outposts to rural centers, they could afford to build more permanent structures. They no longer needed every member to maintain a reasonably sizable congregation, and so blacks were to some

---

47. Darnell, *Forks of Elkhorn Church*, p. 35; Leavell and Bailey, *Complete History of Mississippi Baptists*, p. 605.

48. Minutes, Concord Presbyterian Church, Alabama (October 26, 1815), HFPC.

49. Minutes, First Presbyterian Church, Nashville, Tennessee (1828), HFPC.

50. See annual lists of members, Minutes, Centre Ridge Presbyterian Church, Alabama (1857), HFPC; Minutes, Unity Presbyterian Church, Amite County, Mississippi (1858), HFPC. See also Minutes, Bethsalem Presbyterian Church, Alabama (1859), HFPC; Minutes, Mesopotamia Presbyterian Church, Alabama (1850), HFPC.

extent expendable. Although this surely can explain some support for segregation and separation, it understates greatly, I think, the true concern on the part of many whites for black souls.

The development of antislavery thought north of the Ohio put many ministers in the Southwest on the defensive, and perhaps blacks were the unfortunate objects of displaced anger. Numerous historians have noted the stiffening of proslavery sentiment throughout the South after the coincidence of Nat Turner's rebellion, William Lloyd Garrison's rise to antislavery prominence, and the debate over slavery in Virginia, all happening in the early 1830s. To be sure, these events are all reflected in the experience of blacks in white churches. Increasingly, southwestern intellectuals within the churches began to see the mission to the slaves, in which slaves would be trained as Christians only on the plantation, as both the most intelligent and the safest means of dealing with the problem. Indeed, one Baptist convention argued that slave religion was primarily not the church's but the master's true responsibility.[51]

A somewhat more complex explanation depends upon an understanding of the history of southwestern clergy. The churches of the Old Southwest faced hard times after the revival began to ebb, leadership began to take a timid approach to most issues, and the controversy created by the attacks of the Disciples of Christ seemed further to fatigue the church leaders. During the late 1820s, a group of eastern ministers, generally more highly educated than their western colleagues, migrated to the Old Southwest, and soon these immigrants controlled many of the major pulpits, church organizations, and denominational periodicals. Ministers such as R. B. C. Howell, the new leader of Nashville Baptists, campaigned for attention by attacking abolition and undue equality of the races. They provided most of the support for the mission to the slaves, began to promulgate proslavery theories (previously extremely rare in the region), and enthusiastically called for the special and separate training of slaves as Christians. In short, although the southwestern churches had begun to move away from their measure of racial equality, the new leadership, bringing many

51. Proceedings, Baptist Denomination of the State of Mississippi, p. 34.

ideas from the East, provided the necessary intellectual justification.[52]

To this group of explanations of the change might be added one more: blacks perhaps preferred the separation. The richness and vitality of slave religion, as practiced in the dark, in the woods, or through the code words of spirituals, may well have been more rewarding than the severely restricted equality that slaves could find in white churches. Unlike Mrs. Stowe's Uncle Tom, many blacks doubtless preferred their own brand of Christianity to the compromises demanded by the white church. Slaves, to be sure, could find some degree of equality within church bodies, but it usually caused them some anguish. Just as their white brethren,when slaves transgressed, they were expelled or chastised. Those who found satisfaction in equal treatment were, doubtless, true, humble, and obedient Christians. That more slaves did not rush to embrace this opportunity for equal treatment is hardly surprising given the continual opportunities for other forms of discipline available in the plantation system. The shortage of "posititve" equality in the churches and lack of opportunities for slaves to take responsibility are perhaps the most understandable reasons, from the black point of view, for the gradual segregation of churches in the Old Southwest.

It is crucial to remember, however, that these church records reveal very little of the black perspective. Many blacks who joined southwestern churches in the early nineteenth century may have been motivated in a variety of ways, seeking a complex set of goals which the white-run churches might satisfy. They could have been the southern black equivalent of "rice Christians" or they may have been true and devout followers of Jesus. From the sources that exist, no definitive personality portrait can be drawn. What we can understand, though, is that some churches, for a brief period of time, saw fit to make a limited commitment to the equality of the races.[53] Much as was the case with Doctor Johnson's

52. See Chapter 8.

53. One of the best and most thoughtful recent studies of the issues involved in this chapter is John Boles, *Religion in Antebellum Kentucky* (Lexington, 1978), pp. 80-100. Although not committed as I am to portraying a specific change in black-white relations, Boles provides much evidence of a general transition in the history of Kentucky churches on this issue, especially stressing a growing

little dog, however, the remarkable fact was not that this development remained incomplete and inadequate but that it happened at all. This fact, indeed, forces a serious reevaluation of the development of religion within the regional culture of the Old Southwest.

---

sentiment among blacks "to escape the religious supervision of whites" (p. 93). More than in any other historical account of blacks in white churches, Boles has understood that some measure of equal treatment did exist there, especially regarding discipline. See also Raboteau, *Slave Religion*, pp. 180-210.

PART FOUR

THE GENERATION OF
MORAL REFORMERS

By the end of the 1820s, a new group of ministers began to emerge in positions of leadership in the churches of the Old Southwest. This fourth cohort in the history of southwestern religion is demographically the most complex. For the first time in the region, a majority (57.4 percent) of the members were born and raised in the Southwest; the third cohort had been only 31.3 percent native-born. Moreover, western-born ministers achieved positions of authority in the churches in almost direct proportion to their numbers: 55.7 percent of the important posts in the churches (educators, presiding elders, editors, bishops, association moderators, and domestic missionaries) went to native-born preachers. Although their predominance obviously reflects the sheer size of the population of native-born preachers, it also suggests that the churches were finding in these ministers the qualities necessary for leadership.

This new group of western-born leaders worked in close alliance with a fourth wave of eastern-trained migrants. Such migrations occurred regularly in the history of American religion; the infusion of Yankees into the burned-over district is but one of many dramatic examples. What combination of factors stimulated the migration is almost impossible to pinpoint. One possibility is that western-born ministers encouraged the migration to provide intellectual backing for the reforms they desired to promulgate; in numerous instances eastern ministers were called west to lead an urban congregation or to build up a school's reputation.

The fourth-generation migration was by far the most diverse in the history of religion in the region. Only 26.8 percent of the new wave of migrants came from Virginia, a drop from 43.6 percent in the third cohort, 49.7 percent in the second, and 56.9 percent in the first. Of the Virginia ministers who moved to Kentucky, a remarkably increased percentage came from the sophisticated tidewater region (23.9 percent) than had been the case since the pioneer generation. Of the migrants 39.2 percent came from other states of the South, especially moving west into Alabama and Mississippi. South Carolina and Georgia. contributed 42.3 percent of Alabama's new ministers and 37.8 percent of Mississippi's. More than a quarter (27.3 percent) of the new ministers came from the North or from Europe. Indeed. 7.9 percent came from the states of New England. In short, a substantial proportion of the new migrants came from parts of the East which had provided only limited simulation to the Southwest in previous phases of its development. They formed a real and palpable new wave.

The transformation of southwestern churches by this alliance of easterners and westerners occasionally forced civil wars upon churches and associations. In 1840 the Sulphur Fork Baptist Association met to discuss the leadership of its moderator, R. W. Ricketts. Rabidly antimission, Ricketts described benevolent agencies as "the abominations of the great mother of harlots."[1] The association, in an unprecedented move, impeached and deposed Ricketts, and his followers left in shock to form their own association.[2] The transformation in some bodies involved virtual purges; the Flint River Association condemned an old member of the ministry, Ezekiel Craft, quoting a Methodist who said that "Mr. Craft cannot preach, nor can he be considered an orderly man."[3]

This cohort of ministers shared a variety of characteristics. A

1. Minutes, Sulphur Fork Baptist Association, Kentucky (1840), p. 12, BHS.
2. See also the detailed account of the turmoil in the Yalobasha Baptist Association in Leavell and Bailey, *Complete History of Mississippi Baptists*, pp. 567-571.
3. Hosea Holcombe, *A History of the Rise and Progress of the Baptists in Alabama* (Philadelphia, 1840), p. 110.

remarkable number (29.2 percent) had received college educations, well above the percentage of all western clergymen between the founding of settlements and the beginning of the Civil War (15.9 percent) and almost triple the percentage of the third cohort (10.9 percent). Examples of the variety of college education received by these ministers show that education cut across denominational bounds. Martin Ruter, a Methodist preacher from Massachusetts and New York, graduated from Transylvania University in 1822 while in charge of the Western Book Concern. In 1828 he took over the presidency of Augusta College in Tennessee.[4] Ryland Dylard, a Baptist minister, had attended the best schools in Virginia, and he practiced law before accepting a call to the pulpit. By 1843 he was the superintendent of public education in Kentucky.[5] Presbyterians, of course, had always been the most highly educated members of the southwestern clergy. Those in the fourth cohort had broad backgrounds. J. R. Hutchison, for example, was a graduate of Jefferson College in Pennsylvania.[6] Most of the western-born clergy, whatever their denomination, took their degrees at the denominational colleges established in the Southwest in the 1820s and after; here they were taught, for the most part, by the new migrants from the East.

To go with their greater learning, these ministers had strong and forceful personalities, and they showed notable skill in developing and maintaining personal followings. Robert Boyte Crawford Howell came to Nashville in 1834 as minister of the First Baptist Church, recently reorganized after its division over Campbellism. After a short time he had rebuilt it to respectability, combating antimission and Campbellite influences and founding a major denominational journal.[7] John Maffitt, an Irish immigrant, came west as a Methodist preacher in 1833 to work on the *Western*

4. Redford, *History of Methodism in Kentucky*, 3:427-431.

5. Spencer, *History of Kentucky Baptists*, 1:447.

6. J. R. Hutchison, *Reminiscences, Sketches and Addresses* (Houston, 1874), p. 15; see also L. S. Foster, *Mississippi Baptist Preachers* (St. Louis, 1895), p. 213, on Eleazer Eager.

7. Linwood Horne, "A Study of the Life and Work of R. B. C. Howell" (Ph.D. dissertation, Southern Baptist Theological Seminary, 1958); P. E. Burroughs, *The Spiritual Conquest of the Second Frontier: The Biography of an Achieving Church, 1820-1942* (Nashville, 1943), pp. 55-60; Lynn May, *The First Baptist Church of*

Methodist. He gained fame as a great orator and debater in promoting education for the Methodist clergy. Men such as Maffitt and Howell willingly and eagerly promoted themselves along with their reforms. They envisioned a church led and dominated by clergymen such as themselves; in a region where laity had always assumed an important role in all church matters, this was a striking view. It is little wonder such occasionally arrogant and headstrong preachers annoyed the remnants of the third cohort. In these characteristics the fourth generation resembled the men of the revival.

Part of the reason for the self-confidence exuded by these ministers may have been related to their age. Members of the first cohort had been disproportionately older: 44 percent were over the age of thirty. Members of both the second and third cohorts had tended to fall into two groups: over thirty or under twenty-five. In short, before 1830, most ministers in the West had either arrived when they were already well established in their careers, or they became ministers as young men, fresh and enthusiastic. The fourth cohort represents a striking change in this demographic characteristic. The largest single age group in the generation that dominated the Southwest after 1830 was that between twenty-five and thirty (36.8 percent). Thus the largest single group in the cohort was several years past college and indeed several years past the age when most young men in America had already begun to establish themselves in their life's work. The pent-up energy and desire of members of this age group made them extraordinarily willing to engage in terrific bursts of hard work. William C. Buck was probably the most tireless promoter of Baptist goals in the nation. He led the church in Louisville, edited the *Baptist Banner,* gave regular reports on the state of religion to the General Association of Baptists and became its missionary agent, wrote a treatise on the philosophy of religion, fought Campbellism and antimissionary, and promoted every element of benevolent reform in the region.[8] James Pendleton was nearly Buck's peer, leading

---

Nashville, Tennessee, 1820-1970 (Nashville, 1970), pp. 44-58; Kendall, *History of the Tennessee Baptist Convention,* p. 52.

8. Spencer, *History of Kentucky Baptists,* 2:171.

the fight to form a general association for Baptists in Kentucky and fighting intra-and interdenominational struggles of all description.[9] The enthusiasm of this young group of ministers stood in striking contrast to the quiescence and torpor of the previous leaders of southwestern religion.

The most interesting and complicated fact about this cohort is its relation to churches in the East. Although this was the cohort with the largest percentage of western-born ministers, it was also the one that began to promote most of the benevolent reforms popular in the East, in a sense thereby eroding the specialness and separateness of southwestern religion. Migrants from the East consciously maintained their ties with their intellectual homes. John Armstrong, a Mississippi Baptist leader, was born in Philadelphia and educated in Washington, D.C. He taught at Wake Forest and in 1837 took a tour of France and Italy. In 1841 he came to Mississippi to lead the reform movement in Columbus.[10] John Dagg, a Baptist professor at the University of Alabama and later president of Mercer University, had led the temperance and mission movements in Philadelphia.[11] Henry Bascom, one of the first bishops of the Methodist Episcopal church, South, fit comfortably into this cohort although he had been in the South throughout the postrevival period. Bascom was born in New York, became a preacher in Kentucky, and traveled back and forth between the East and Southwest for most of his career.[12] Young western ministers, taught by such men and hearing stories of the grandeur of East Coast colleges, found themselves increasingly separated from their own culture. Fresh with eastern enthusiasms, imbibed directly or indirectly, members of the fourth cohort could ignore the complicated situation of most western churches and instead promote the eastern package of reforms, temperance, Sunday schools, tracts, and missions. Although perhaps a western flavor was lost in the process, the fourth cohort began the inevitable process of integrating southwestern religion into the national one.

9. J. M. Pendleton, *Reminiscences of a Long Life* (Louisville, 1891).
10. Leavell and Bailey, *Complete History of Mississippi Baptists*, p. 580.
11. John L. Dagg, *Autobiography* (Rome, Ga., 1886), pp. 29-38.
12. Henkle, *Life of Henry Bascom*.

CHAPTER 8

Moral Reform
Moves Southwest

A period of confidence and cultural development followed the economic and spiritual depression of the 1820s in the Southwest. In 1833 Daniel Drake announced to the Literary Convention of Kentucky that the future of the nation depended upon westerners from both sides of the Ohio: "The palladium of the Constitution is committed to them by nature, and they should faithfully preserve it." They should unite, welcome immigrants, "foster western genius, encourage western writers, patronize western publishers, augment the number of western readers, and create a western heart."[1] Another writer remarked on "that transformation, as if of magic, which had converted the wilderness to fields and orchards."[2] Both writers hoped their section might avoid a battle over slavery. Otherwise, the West would not assume its rightful role, leading the nation toward the American destiny, and they felt such an outcome would be a disaster not just for the region but for the nation as a whole. Unity of the northern and southern sections of the region remained elusive, however, because the Southwest would not abandon its peculiar institution and the Northwest, primarily Ohio, contained substantial pockets of antislavery sentiment.

1. Shapiro and Miller, eds., *Physician to the West*, pp. 233, 238; see also *Baptist Banner* 2 (1835):4.
2. Timothy Flint, *The History and Geography of the Mississippi Valley* (Cincinnati, 1832), p. x.

Although these visions of a transappalachian Israel were doomed, the Southwest reached a degree of cultural self-awareness in the 1830s and 1840s. Although never self-consciously sophisticated in comparison with the easterners, southwesterners did begin to take pride in their culture and its achievements. Education underwent a striking transformation. In 1838, for example, Kentucky instituted a public school system, and at least four colleges began operation in the state between 1829 and 1850.[3] By the 1830s all four states of the Southwest had active and thriving political systems. Some of the most important leaders of the nation, including Jackson, Clay, James K. Polk and George Poindexter, lived in the Southwest, and several major figures of the Civil War, most notably Andrew Johnson and Jefferson Davis, grew up in the region during this period. Even the economic troubles of the late 1830s revealed a changed spirit; instead of creating reaction and retrenchment, the crash of 1837 produced a major agricultural reform movement.[4] In 1827 the Southwest could even claim its own epic poet, Richard Emmons, author of *The Fredoniad: or, Independence Preserved, An Epic Poem on the Late War of 1812.*[5]

Within the context of these strong signs of cultural self-consciousness, ministers of the fourth generation began to promote a variety of moral reforms within southwestern society. The early nineteenth-century push for moral reforms developed first in the Northeast during the carefully controlled and organized Second Great Awakening. During the first two decades of the century, New England, New York, and Pennsylvania preachers developed what Gilbert Barnes termed a "benevolent empire."[6] A bureaucracy, typified by the American Tract Association and the American Bible Society, directed the movements of benevolence. The imperial capital was probably New Haven, Connecticut, and the "empire' extended as far as western New York and the Western Reserve of

3. Alvin Lewis, *History of Higher Education in Kentucky* (Washington, 1899), p. 18.

4. John Hebron Moore, *Agriculture in Antebellum Mississippi* (New York, 1958), pp. 69-92.

5. Rusk, *Literature of the Middle West Frontier,* 1:328-332.

6. Gilbert Barnes, *The Antislavery Impulse* (1938; reprint, New York, 1964), p. 17.

Ohio. Directors of the societies expressed little interest in extending their work into the Old Southwest, however; few representatives made the arduous journey down the Ohio. Consequently, relatively few tracts and Bibles from the benevolent societies found their way west before about 1830. Similarly, other notions popular in the Northeast, including temperance, missions, and improved financial backing for ministerial education, found scant support in the region. By 1830, when the eastern benevolent empire began its steady decline in national religious affairs, southwesterners began to take up the cause of moral reform.[7]

Ideas of benevolent reform did not come directly from new England, but traveled first to the seaboard South and then west in the custody of the migrants who helped make up the fourth generation of southwestern ministers. The reforms of the benevolent empire were slow to take root in the Southeast, emerging there only after the War of 1812. In the first decade and a half of the century, the Great Revival in the Southeast was not the organizing and organized phenomenon such as had existed in relatively settled and sedate Connecticut. Rather, the southeastern revival was much less intellectual, much less controlled, and much more diffuse. It was not nearly as disruptive as the Great Revival experience in the Southwest, however, and it was not followed by a period of recovery. The peculiar revival experience of the Southeast therefore prevented much development of benevolent reform during the peaks of revival feeling but produced no powerful, long-run barriers to moral reform after the awakening had begun to lose its force.[8]

Another element of southeastern religious life which helps explain the relative weakness of sentiment for moral reform in the region was that only a very few southeastern ministers had transatlantic connections that could stimulate benevolent organization. The New England enthusiasts for a benevolent empire looked to the example of the British benevolent societies in creating such

7. For further analysis of the benevolent empire, see Bodo, *Protestant Clergy;* Charles I. Foster, *An Errand of Mercy: The Evangelical United Front, 1790-1837* (Chapel Hill, 1960); Clifford S. Griffin, *Their Brothers' Keepers: Moral Stewardship in the United States, 1800-1865* (New Brunswick, 1960).

8. Boles, *Great Revival in the South*, pp. 223-254.

organizations as the American Board of Commissioners for Foreign Missions. Even the briefest review of southeastern religious thought in the early years of the nineteenth century reveals that this international perspective was not available to the region's clerics. As a consequence, southeastern ministers did not begin to promote moral reforms until after northeastern clergymen had began to absorb British thought and to apply those concepts to the American experience.[9]

Donald Mathews has argued that the attention of southeastern ministers to matters of moral reform may have been the result of generational change such as I have delineated in the Southwest. After the War of 1812, a more worldly, more politically self-conscious generation of ministers came to dominate the seaboard South and began to absorb some of the notions of benevolence issuing from the Connecticut River valley. Typical of these clergymen, John Holt Rice began his career in Virginia as a Presbyterian minister in 1803 but after the War of 1812 became one of the great advocates of a variety of benevolent activity. He established a weekly religious journal in Richmond, went to New York as one of the founders of the American Bible Association, and promoted many of the key components of the benevolence movement, especially education and missions. By the 1820s, then, most of the elements of the benevolence movement had reached the Southeast, and the stage was set for a subsequent expansion into the Southwest.[10]

Benevolent Reform in the Southwest

Within the context of this enthusiasm for various forms of moral regeneration the members of the fourth generation who were migrants from the East brought with them a wide range of reform projects, including their means of coping with the peculiar institution.

9. On the international Quaker network, see David B. Davis, *The Problem of Slavery in the Age of Revolution* (Ithaca, 1975), pp. 213-254; see also Frank Thistlethwaite, *The Anglo-American Connection in the Early Nineteenth Century* (Philadelphia, 1959).

10. Mathews, *Religion in the Old South*, pp. 87ff.; Holifield, *Gentlemen Theologians*, p. 33.

A clear sense of this new-found, self-confident trust in a set of clerically led reforms must, therefore, precede any discussion of fourth-generation attitudes toward slavery.

The 1832 Methodist Conference in Kentucky opposed the use of alcohol, supported the Bible and tract societies, and proposed a system of education and support for preachers.[11] The Presbyterian Synod of Mississippi and South Alabama noted in 1832 that the "greater benevolent institutions of the day, the Bible, Tract, Sunday School, Missionary, Education and Temperance Societies, have received some attention pretty generally throughout our Churches."[12] The West Union Baptist Association asked in 1835 which of the many benevolent institutions deserved support. After some discussion, the members decided they should advocate "all objects and institutions which have a tendency to ameliorate the condition of man."[13] In 1844 the Long Run Baptist Association decided to "give voluntarily and systematically" to support Sunday schools, clerical education, Home, Indian and Foreign missions and the Bible Society.[14] A circular letter in 1841 from the Laurel River Baptist Association succinctly stated the aims of the benevolence movement: "Finally, brethren, strengthen the weak and feeble—assist the needy—be gentle to the wayward and violent—reclaim the backslidden—establish the wavery—cultivate friendship with all the world, and as much as lieth in you live in peace with all men.[15]

Of the several reforms that came west in the late 1820s and early 1830s, the most important was the mission movement. Methodists, of course, saw nothing novel in missions; circuit preaching was essentially a domestic mission system. Presbyterians, however, warmly embraced the notion of missions to the Indians and unchurched whites. Presbyteries had engaged a few missionaries in the frontier period, but this practice had lapsed in the early nineteenth century. By 1830, however, complacency turned into

11. Redford, *Western Cavaliers*, pp. 27-28.
12. Minutes, Synod of Mississippi and South Alabama (1832), p. 22, HFPC.
13. Minutes, West Union Baptist Association, Kentucky (1835); see also Minutes, Long Run Baptist Association, Kentucky (1838), both in BHS.
14. Minutes, Long Run Baptist Association, Kentuky (1844), BHS.
15. Minutes, Laurel River Baptist Association, Kentucky (1851), p. 8, BHS.

enthusiasm. The 1833 Transylvania Presbytery meeting recommended the "hearty cooperation of our pastors" in missionary work and lamented insufficient funding and manpower.[16] In 1836 the Ebenezer Presbytery published a "Plan of the Missionary Society," "for the purpose of furnishing the destitute churches within its own bounds with a state ministry."[17] Most presbyteries earmarked funds for domestic missions, and a few preachers volunteered for duty. These decisions indicated a turnabout for the denomination that had forced its original mission enthusiasts, the Cumberland Presbyterians, to secede.

Baptists did not join in the enthusiasm for missions until somewhat later than the other two denominations. Although the *Baptist Banner* proclaimed in 1835 that "the revival of missions in modern times, and the formation of societies for their promotion, if we except some incipient movements among the Moravians, had their origin with the Baptists,"[18] this statement was premature in the 1830s. The decade witnessed the final struggle between powerful forces on both sides of the issue.

Antimission preachers did not limit their attention to the question of missions. The fiercely congregational tendency of antimission Baptists, combined with the radical Calvinism of their beliefs, caused them to oppose all associated actions of Baptist churches, save an occasional friendly meeting to discuss mutual problems. Individualistic in the extreme, they saw no need for complicated organizational structures within their church. Instead, they viewed religion as a terrible personal struggle to reach salvation. Churches served two functions: they provided arenas in which Christians might help other Christians toward self-knowledge, and they provided converts with a place to meet and testify to their faith. Antimission Baptists felt that churches had no authority over the nonelect; nor, they argued, should churches extend their functions to education, missions, or reform. Antimissionary, therefore, embraced the radical conservatism always present in extreme Calvinism and, unlike the American Puritanism of the seventeenth

16. Minutes, Transylvania Presbytery (1833), HFPC.
17. Minutes, Ebenezer Presbytery (1836), FHPC.
18. *Baptist Banner* 1 (1835):17.

century, had no covenant theology to bring religion back into the world.

Antimission clergy consequently repudiated any attempt to join national benevolent organizations. In 1834 the Little River Association split over the proper interpretation of the atonement, and the Calvinistic antimission Baptists formed the Original Little River Association. One of their first resolutions stated that "the missionary proceeding, with the Baptist Convention and all the train of benevolent institutions (false so called), we believe to be unscriptural and antichristian, and to belong to the kingdom of darkness."[19] The *Baptist*, the major journal of the denomination in the West, published an imaginary dialogue between two clergymen:

W.—The names church, ambassador, apostle, preacher, pastor and minister are found in the Bible. But the words convention, missionary, bible, tract, temperance, and Sunday School societies, itinerants, etc., are nowhere found in scripture. They ought to be abandoned and their advocates severely reproved by the church.

R.—O! there's where you are, ha! Well, then, I'll ask you a few plain questions. Do you not use the names association, moderator, clerk, trinity, original sin, spiritual death, etc.? If so, as I know you do, are you not as guilty as we are? None of these names exist in the scriptures.[20]

The antimission movement found its strongest support in areas with the fewest towns and cities, such as northern Alabama.[21] Antimission advocates occasionally took a mild, even condescending, attitude toward their opponents: "In answer to the Blue Spring Church concerning mission societies, we believe they are not founded on Gospel authority, and therefore we would advise the Churches, as organized bodies, not to have any connection with them."[22] The Campbell County Association replied to a question from a member church by denying that "we as an association

19. Spencer, *History of Kentucky Baptists*, 2:183-184.
20. *Baptist Banner* 2 (1836):25; see also Minutes, Dumplin Creek Baptist Church, Jefferson County, Tennessee (May 4, 1839), HCSBC.
21. Riley, *History of Baptists in Alabama*, pp. 65-66.
22. Minutes, Green River Baptist Association, Kentucky (1843), BHS.

have, nor have we had, any thing to do with the Missionary question, whether 'home or foreign,' since the meeting at Brush Creek some years since, which time it was agreed to let the matter rest."[23] Somewhat more vigorous attacks did on occasion emerge, however. A. Keaton advised his comrades, "Do not forget the enemy, bear them in mind; the howling, destructive wolves, the ravenous dogs, and the filthy, and their numerous whelps."[24] The Green River Association underwent a small revolution over the issue, and mission forces seceded to form the Liberty Association. They stated that they undertook their rebellion because "we have for several years past witnessed in the Green River Association, a departure from the former usages of that body, and a culpable opposition to the missionary enterprise—an enterprise not only authorized, but made obligatory by the Savior's last command: 'Go ye into all the world, and preach the gospel to every creature.'"[25] Such counterattacks proliferated, especially in promission strongholds such as the denominational journals. The *Baptist Banner*, for example, stated, "The truth is, that most of our violent opposing brethren are supremely ignorant of every principle which characterized the benevolent institutions for which they feel such horror and of which they speak with such clamor."[26] By the late 1830s and through the 1840s, several antimission churches withdrew from promission associations;[27] a few promission churches seceded from antimission associations as well.[28] Most Baptist associations began to debate resolutions such as that submitted to the Russell Creek Association, "to take into consideration the propriety of forming a society, or societies, for the purpose of promoting preaching of the gospel."[29] One Baptist association, which had experienced painful division over the question of

23. Minutes, Campbell County Baptist Association, Kentucky (1830), BHS.
24. Holcombe, *History of the Rise and Progress of the Baptists in Alabama*, p. 91.
25. Minutes, Green River Baptist Association, Kentucky (1840), BHS.
26. *Baptist Banner* 2 (1836):96.
27. Leavell and Bailey, *Complete History of Mississippi Baptists*, p. 324; Grimes, *History of Middle Tennessee Baptists*, p. 18; Riley, *History of Baptist in Alabama*, pp. 110-112.
28. Mattie Crow, *Asheville Baptist Church and Its Beginnings* (Birmingham, 1965), p. 17.
29. Minutes, Russell Creek Baptist Association, Kentucky (1832), BHS.

missions, celebrated peace in an 1842 circular letter: "The schism and division which have to long marred the prosperity of our denomination, are fast giving way to the genial influences of Gospel truth. The rancor and party spirit is dying away, and the spirit of philanthropy and love is springing up in its stead. One great principle animates every breast and fires every heart—it is a desire to give the everlasting Gospel, to the perishing millions of the earth."[30] By the mid-1840s almost every Baptist association in the Southwest had formed a missionary agency.[31]

A second element of the benevolent reform movement, temperance, received enthusiastic support from all the denominations, usually expressed in general moral injunctions against the use of alcohol. The Baptist Convention of Mississippi declared that "we believe the grand object to the Temperance enterprise is prevention; and that it is the imperious duty of every patriotic citizen, every judicious parent, and every consistent church member, to plead the cause of Temperance by the sweeping eloquence of precept and example."[32] In 1834 the Tennessee Methodist Conference resolved itself "into a Temperance Society, on the broad principle of total abstinence from the use of ardent or intoxicating spirits, except as medicine.[33] The program for promoting temperance stressed three methods. First, the temperance societies asked every

30. Minutes, Boone's Creek Baptist Association, Kentucky (1842), BHS.

31. Minutes, Little Bethel Baptist Association, Kentucky (1837); Minutes, Middle District Baptist Association, Kentucky (1840); Minutes, Cumberland River Baptist Association, Tennessee (1840); Minutes, West Union Baptist Association, Kentucky (1839); Minutes, South District Baptist Association, Kentucky (1837); Minutes, Russell Creek Baptist Association, Kentucky (1840); Minutes, Long Run Baptist Association, Kentucky (1841); Minutes, Goshen Baptist Association, Kentucky (1841); Minutes, Gasper River Baptist Association, Kentucky (1839); Minutes, Franklin Baptist Association, Kentucky (1840); Minutes, Campbell County Baptist Association, Kentucky (1844), all in BHS.

32. Proceedings, Convention of the Baptist Denomination of the State of Mississippi (1838); see also Minutes Dumplin Creek Baptist Church, Jefferson County, Tennessee (September 19, 1845), HCSBC; Leavell and Bailey, *Complete History of Mississippi Baptists*, pp. 138-139; Minutes, Gasper River Baptist Association, Kentucky (1840), p. 6, BHS; Mary Weaver, *One Hundred Years—A Story of the First Baptist Church, Clinton, Tennessee* (Clinton, 1940), p. 10; Minutes, Elkhorn Baptist Association, Kentucky (1831), p. 8, BHS.

33. McFerrin, *History of Methodism in Tennessee*, 3:438-439.

minister to preach sermons on the evils of drink.[34] Second, temperance enthusiasts occasionally made abstinence a condition of membership. The Dixon Creek Baptist Church proposed a requirement that "when any individual hereafter shall apply for membership, it shall be the duty of the moderator to enquire if he is in the habit of drinking." If the prospective member confessed that he did occasionally imbibe, the church required him to practice total abstinence. Eventually the regulation passed, but it applied only to deacons and preachers.[35] Third, temperance enthusiasts occasionally addressed comments to distillers. In "A Word to Distillers," the *Baptist Banner* listed seven evils for which they were responsible, including "this year many murders."[36]

A variety of other reforms attracted the attention of these ministers. Many churches enthusiastically supported the American Bible Society and its Baptist offshoot, the American and Foreign Bible Society.[37] Clergy also advocated the formation of Sabbath schools throughout the area. One Baptist association declared that Sabbath school instruction "is second in importance only to the preaching of the gospel."[38] Presbyterians vigorously promoted ministerial and general education,[39] but they also strongly supported the related movements for the distribution of tracts and other religious publications.[40] Baptists focused considerable attention upon creating a working regional and state organization; ministers who promoted benevolent reform also worked to build viable associations and state conventions.[41]

34. Minutes, West Lexington Presbytery, 4:117, HFPC; Minutes, Holston Methodist Conference, Tennessee (1839), Library of Congress.

35. *Baptist Banner* 2 (1836):24.

36. Ibid. 3 (1837):48.

37. Minutes, Gasper River Baptist Association, Kentucky (1836); Minutes, Goshen Baptist Association, Kentucky (1840); Minutes, Laurel River Baptist Association, Kentucky (1840), all in BHS.

38. Proceedings, Convention of the Baptist Denomination of the State of Mississippi (1838), BHS.

39. Minutes, Synod of Mississippi and South Alabama (1832), HFPC.

40. Minutes, Transylvania Presbytery (1841), HFPC; Leavell and Bailey, *Complete History of Mississippi Baptists*, p. 228; Minutes, Salem Baptist Church, Jefferson County, Mississippi (April 1830), HCSBC.

41. Spencer, *History of Kentucky Baptist*, 1:359; Bond, *History of the Baptist*

Behind these specific tasks they set for themselves, the new wave of southwestern ministers had a deeper commitment: they desperately wanted to reshape the characteristic western minister into a new mold. They tried to redesign southwestern religion so that it would follow the leadership of such educated and sophisticated men as themselves. To this end they organized informal meetings of preachers to discuss doctrine. Not that they were fomenting new ideas—indeed, most wanted to find an orthodoxy upon which most preachers could agree and which would lend an air of sophistication to their sermons and discussions with the laity.[42] Weeding out inefficient or ignorant clergymen, as we have seen, become commonplace in the effort to shape up the profession.[43] Numerous journals took similar stands to that stated by the *Baptist*, which proclaimed that it intended to "Unite, harmonize and invigorate the Church in this State."[44] Editors of these journals, many of whom were recent migrants from the East, assumed enormous power and used their periodicals to promote or protest various developments in the Southwest. A few such vehicles had existed before the migration of the fourth generation, but these new clergymen were the first to use the periodicals with brilliant success.[45] Most churches in the Southwest also found that these new ministers regularly and vociferously raised the issue of clerical education. Before the arrival of the fourth generation, churches provided only the most meager support for the improvement of the clergy. The church letter of the Middle District Baptist Association now argued that ministerial education had become a central necessity if the churches of the region expected to succeed. The church should provide for a candidate's "maintenance and education, and encourage him in the exercise of his gifts, until his mind has so far matured, and his intelligence has become so suited

Concord Convention, p. 64; Minutes, Gasper River Baptist Association, Kentucky (1841), BHS.

42. Kendall, *History of the Tennessee Baptist Convention*, p. 85.

43. Spencer, *History of Kentucky Baptists*, 2:476-477.

44. *Baptist Banner* 1 (1835):2.

45. See Roger Crook, "The Ethical Emphases of the Editors of Baptist journals published in the Southwestern Region of the United States up to 1865" (PhD. dissertation, Southern Baptist Theological Seminary, 1947).

to his station, as to warrant confidence in his future usefulness."[46] To this end, denominations began to build their own seminaries throughout the region, promoting a set of professional standards and a specific clerical education.[47] Closely related was the demand of many ministers that churches provide sufficient financial support for the clergy. One Baptist association now included in its articles of faith a promise that ministers "should be sustained in their labors by the churches—'for the laborer is worthy of his hire.' "[48]

These were not, of course, the first young men to come into an area and attempt to set things straight. At other times, brash young men have been largely responsible for reform movements, indeed to some extent for a revolution. In few instances, however, has the transition from old to new, from one generation to another, been so abrupt and dramatic. These were men with a greal deal on their minds, with fabulous hopes for the Southwest, and of course, for the nation as well. Unlike some other groups of young turks, however, they were unusually capable of using a variety of technical resources to promote their many, complex causes. They were clever politicians as well as brash young men with vision. Like many other groups, the members of this cohort felt impelled to move west because they were still young and could find a place in the Southwest which might provide more satisfaction than would the opportunities in the East. Such men had seldom made large reputations in their home states; instead, they took a chance on the Southwest, and they made of their careers whatever the

46. Minutes, Middle District Baptist Association, Kentucky (1841); Minutes, Little Bethel Baptist Association, Kentucky (1840); Minutes, West Lexington Baptist Association, Kentucky (1842), all in BHS; Holcombe, *History of the Rise and Progress of Baptists in Alabama*, p. 73; *Alabama Baptist* 2 (1844):74.

47. Minutes, Synod of Alabama, p. 6, HFPC: Leavell and Bailey, *Complete History of Mississippi Baptists*, p. 142; Avery H. Reid, *Baptists in Alabama: Their Organization and Witness* (Montgomery, 1967), p. 58; Minutes, Long Run Baptist Association, Kentucky (1841), BHS; W. C. James, "A History of the Western Baptist Theological Institute," *Publications of the Kentucky Baptist Historical Society* 1 (1910):46-47.

48. Minutes, Liberty Baptist Association, Kentucky (1840), BHS; *Baptist Banner* 1 (1835):23-24; Leavell and Bailey, *Complete History of Mississippi Baptists*, p. 321.

area would allow to them. They were, almost to a man, committed professionals, determined to institute standards, modernize professional methods, establish barriers to entry, create means of communication, and in countless other ways professionalize religion in the West. In the process, they breathed new life into a drab and perhaps collapsing set of denominations. They felt they had rescued southwestern religion and returned it to prominence in American Christianity.

The Fate of Southwestern Antislavery Thought

This new wave of southwestern clergy differed from their counterparts in the Northeast in one important respect: their views on slavery. Many religious leaders in other regions, especially the Tappans in New York and Theodore Weld in the burned-over district, had adopted a vigorous stance against slavery by the early 1830s. Although most northeastern preachers remained cool to abolition, a great number found they could not avoid the issue, and especially those in the burned-over district began to articulate a complex antislavery argument.

The leaders of benevolence in the Southwest could not join their northern brethren in this benevolent crusade against slavery, although many of them had deep roots in the Northeast. Omitting even the most moderate antislavery activity from the panoply of benevolent reforms was, for this new generation, unavoidable. It took little imagination to understand that slavery was a respected and important institution in the region; indeed, in the southern-most part of the Old Southwest, it was the central economic institution. The last enthusiastic supporters of abolition among the southwestern clergy, members of the revival generation, had left in despair when their message was either ignored or repudiated in the churches of the Old Southwest. Of the fourth generation, the most forthright in his views on the danger of antislavery to the benevolent cause was that survivor of the postrevival malaise, Henry Bascom. Although he held strong antislavery sentiments, he decided as early as 1814 to avoid the issue at all costs, subscribing, he said, to Bishop McKendree's argument that slavery would ruin evangelical work in the West if it became a central issue.[49] In short, then, any underlying distaste for slavery, any anxieties and moral qualms about it, had to be ignored if the broader enterprise of moral regeneration were to succeed.

This did not mean, initially, that many members of the fourth generation went to the opposite extreme, vigorously arguing that slavery was a positive good. At its most refined, the positive good analysis was used by such southeastern intellectuals as James Hammond, Thomas R. Dew, and, of course, John C. Calhoun, all of whom carefully examined the practical consequences of abolitionism and concluded that such a doctrine was at once dangerous, impracticable, and utterly unnecessary. Moreover, their arguments led them to conclusion that slavery had a variety of strong, albeit utilitarian, benefits which justified its continued existence. Hammond argued in Congress that slavery would best promote the economic development of the nation, and Dew took a more scholarly route to a similar conclusion. Calhoun outdid his cohorts by producing a complicated political theory resting upon the existence of slavery; he argued that the peculiar institution provided myriad benefits to masters, slaves, and society as a whole.[50]

Only a very few members of the south cohort expressed explicit proslavery sentiments. Basil Manley, the leading educator among Baptists in the region, had privately expressed grave doubts about the morality of slavery in the 1820s and 1830s. He had overcome these doubts by the time he wrote Francis Wayland that slavery was a benevolent relationship, saving blacks from much worse slavery in Africa and providing moral and religious training unavailable there: "I had not been in the habit of regarding the fact of slavery as a question of morals at all. I considered that our divine master had not so regarded it, but finding it part of the . . . existing institutions of society thought it was the province

---

49. Henkle, *Life of Henry Bascom*, p. 23.

50. See William S. Jenkins, *Pro-Slavery Thought in the Old South* (Chapel Hill, 1935); a recent study focusing on the rhetoric of a few leading figures in the South is John McCardell, *The Idea of a Southern Nation: Southern Nationalists and Southern Nationalism, 1830-1860* (New York, 1979).

of . . . religion only to prescribe the duties of the relation."[51] James Smylie appears to have experienced none of Manley's initial inner struggle. He was one of the first migrants to the Mississippi territory, where his service spanned three generations, but only in the fourth cohort did he find companions in his enthusiasm for benevolent reform. Smylie also produced the most vigorous defense of slavery written by a southwestern clergyman before 1845. In response to an abolition letter written by the Chillicothe Presbytery of Ohio to the Presbyterians of Mississippi, Smylie wrote *A Review of a Letter . . . on Slavery*. Most of the pamphlet consisted of an outline of the extent of biblical support for the peculiar institution, especially stressing passages from Colossians. Smylie attacked abolitionists as misguided, "never reflecting or dreaming, that slavery, in itself considered, was an innoxious [sic] relation, and that the whole error rested in the neglect of the relative duties of the relation."[52] Such candid comments, although hardly out of line with the general sentiments of southwestern clergy, were nevertheless rare in the 1830s and 1840s and almost always came from Mississipi or Alabama, where citizens were always most sensitive to the issue of slavery.

Equally rare, and even less representative, were the occasional echoes of the antislavery past of the Old Southwest. In 1835 an abolitionist faction briefly took control of the Kentucky Synod, passing strong antislavery resolutions and agitating controversy on the issue.[53] When one of its members inherited slaves, the Kentucky Methodist Conference of 1839 required that he free the children by age twenty-five and "execute a will securing the Emancipation" of the parents.[54] The *Western Luminary*, the principal Presbyterian journal in the Southwest, published a series of articles condemning the insidious nature of slavery; the author proposed a gradual emancipation program as the only rational

51. Manley to Francis Wayland, November 23, 1835, Basil Manley Papers (microfilm copy), BHS.

52. James Smylie, *A Review of a Letter from the Presbytery of Chillicothe to the Presbytery of Mississippi on the Subject of Slavery* (Woodville, Miss., 1836), p. 3.

53. Minutes, Transylvania Presbytery, p. 103, HFPC.

54. Redford, *Western Cavaliers*, pp. 202-203.

solution.[55] Such rare expressions of abolitionist sentiment in the region came exclusively from Kentucky and Tennessee. In the latter state, antislavery advocates found their task all the more difficult after Frances Wright's Nashoba experiment, a utopian community for slaves in Tennessee, which suffered from countless problems, mostly the result of incredibly bad management. Wright gave a great deal of ammunition to opponents of the spread of moderate antislavery views in the state.[56]

Although the fourth generation differed from the third in almost every respect, a majority of both would have preferred to evade the implications of slavery if at all possible. Direct statements in favor of the institution would threaten the unity of the churches at the national level. Direct condemnation of slavery, of course, would alienate a larger percentage of the laity. In 1833, consequently, the Kentucky Presbyterian Synod adopted a resolution to take no position on the issue of slavery. In 1840 the Transylvania Presbytery responded to a series of questions posed by abolitionists in Maine. Although the questions raised most of the issues surrounding slavery, the presbytery took no stance on any of them.[57] The leading Methodist journal in the region, the *Western Christian Advocate*, refused to address the issue because it "assumes more and more the character of a political one."[58]

If the fourth-generation southwestern ministers spoke with one voice about the issue of slavery, it was, in spite of their occasional proclamations of neutrality, to make a harsh attack upon northern antislavery advocates. The enthusiasm and comprehensiveness of the attacks greatly exceeded any issued during the 1820s by the postrevival ministers. Moreover, these attacks did not typically adopt a simple, defensive tone. Instead, the moral reformers desired to reform abolitionism, cleansing it of its mistakes in theology and practice. Several attacks developed the very general proposition that abolitionism was harmful to the peace and tranquility of American religion, echoing the main thrust of earlier

55. *Western Luminary* 7 (1831):27-33.

56. On Frances Wright and Nashoba, see Alice Felt Tyler, *Freedom's Ferment* (1942; reprint, New York, 1962), pp. 206-211.

57. Minutes, Transylvania Presbytery (1839), HFPC.

58. Charles Elliott, *History of the Great Secession . . .*(Cincinnati, 1855).

southwestern opponents of antislavery. The *Protestant and Herald*, a Presbyterian journal, declared abolitionist measures to be injurious and ill-advised.[59] The Tennessee Baptist Convention disapproved of "Abolition Societies and their measures as being wrong and calculated to do evil."[60] The Kentucky Methodist Convention resolved that abolitionists had interfered in southern affairs, "by which the peace and quiet of a large portion of the nation are disturbed."[61] The South Alabama Presbytery felt that the schemes of abolitionists were "ruinous to the peace and happiness of our beloved country."[62] The West Lexington Presbytery warned that if abolition societies were to succeed, the result would "fill the land with blood, and bring on all the horrors of a dreaded civil war."[63] At least one southwestern clergyman meditated upon the reason for abolitionist sentiment. William Winans, the leader of Mississippi Methodists, decided not to "impugn their motives—I infer insanity."[64]

Attacks upon abolitionists also occasionally appeared within biblical analyses of the peculiar institution. If the Bible demonstrated the validity of the slave-master relationship, it was possible to argue that abolitionists were heretics, acting and arguing against scriptural teaching. More often, however, biblical analysis was used to defeat abolitionist arguments rather than to tar abolitionists with the accusation of heresy.[65]

Many southwestern ministers accused the abolition movement of a dangerous, thoroughgoing ignorance of everything southern. In evaluating an antislavery pamphlet by L. G. Goodrich, David McAnnally, a Methodist preacher, wondered "who that had any-

59. *Protestant and Herald* 11 (1842):104; James, "History of the Western Baptist Theological Institute," p. 62.

60. Kendall, *History of the Tennessee Baptist Convention*, pp. 57-58; see also, Northcott, *Biography of Rev. Benjamin Northcott*, p. 90; Redford, *Western Cavaliers*, p. 124; *Baptist Banner* 3 (1837):62; J. Blanchard and N. R. Rice, *A Debate on Slavery*... (Cincinnati, 1846), p. 470; *Alabama Baptist* 1 (1844):198.

61. Redford, *Western Cavaliers*, pp. 148-149.

62. Posey, *Presbyterian Church*, p. 80; see also Elliott, *History of the Great Secession*, p. 131; Riley, *History of the Baptists in Alabama*, p. 71.

63. Redford, *Western Cavaliers*, pp. 148-149.

64. Ray Holder, *William Winans: Methodist Leader in Antebellum Mississippi* (Jackson, 1977), p. 117.

65. Reid, *Baptists in Alabama*, pp. 71-72.

thing like a correct acquaintance with the south, and who had in his possession the facts with regard to the slave as they really exist" could read such a work "without blushing for the character of Mr. Goodrich as an author." According to McAnnally, Goodrich ignored the obvious and well-known fact that thousands of slaves attended church and were "exemplary Christians." McAnnally also condemned the vague and general nature of Goodrich's assertions of the evils of slavery, which, to any fair-minded observer, would be seen to exist only in "a few isolated cases."[66] The *Baptist* argued that "the slaves of the south are fully as competent to legislate for the north, so far as knowledge is concerned, as the northern abolitionists are to judge the condition of southern slaves, and what is best to be done to serve their interests."[67] Kentucky Methodists condemned the work of abolitionists as "officious insolence," which should be stopped by any means necessary. In a debate with Ohio abolitionists, William Winans tried to teach his opponents his version of the facts, and although one report accused Winans of issuing a "flagrant falsehood," he had succeeded in raising the argument that abolitionism stemmed from ignorance and that such ignorance unskillfully masked antisouthern feeling.[68]

Finally, and most tellingly, southwestern clergy accused abolitionists of a misguided benevolence. Considering the broad goals of social and moral reform which the fourth generation had set for itself, it is this issue which was the most important and, as a consequence, most complex. If one evaluated the success of abolitionists strictly upon their own terms, the *Baptist Banner* pointed out, abolition had been a stunning failure, accomplishing none of its stated goals: "On the contrary, they have to no small extent, checked the cause of emancipation which was fast growing in the southwest."[69] That is, northern evangelical abolitionists were incompetent as reformers, and they had given no thought to the situation of slaves after freedom. Abolition, one Presbyterian minister wrote, would

66. David Rice McAnnally, "Diary," pp. 12-13, Methodist Historical Society, Lake Junaluska, N.C.
67. *Baptist Banner* 1 (1835):137.
68. Holder, *William Winans*, pp. 120-121.
69. *Baptist Banner* 3 (1837):210.

only leave slaves open "to the villainy of every white man" they met.[70] Henry Bascom pointed out that free blacks in the North were falling into lives of vice and crime. "Blasphemy, profaneness, drunkenness, Sabbath breaking, dishonesty, lying, and defamation," the very ills which the fourth generation wished to destroy in their region, faced blacks as a product of freedom.[71] Most worrisome of all, southwestern opponents of abolition feared that abolitionists gave false hope to slaves, thereby agitating them and threatening the lives of their masters. Abolitionist writing, one Baptist wrote, was "well calculated to create rebellion in the mind of the servant against the master."[72] One logical outcome might well be that the lives of slaves would become even less pleasant, the institution even harsher.[73] In these arguments fourth-generation ministers exhibited remarkable self-confidence. They were behaving as tacticians, logically analyzing the shortcomings of fellow reformers and raising some of the criticisms of antislavery activists that would be rediscovered by conservative historians of the mid-twentieth century.[74]

The Mission to the Slaves

As a group, fourth-generation ministers found no common ground on the general subject of slavery except in their consensus opposition to antislavery. Of course, broad statements of a political or philosophical nature were never their strength. These clergymen were activists, and their reflective moments were seldom particularly inspiring, whatever the topic. Rather, it was as reformers in action that they most clearly reflected their confident sense of a Christianized Southwest.

70. James Blythe to Samuel Blythe, February 3, 1830, James Blythe papers, Presbyterian Historical Society, Philadelphia.

71. Bascom, *Methodism and Slavery*, pp. 55-56.

72. *Baptist Banner* 2 (1836):89.

73. Holder, *William Winans*, p. 121.

74. The most famous attempt to dismiss abolitionists as transcendental, anti-institutionalist cranks is Stanley Elkins, *Slavery: A Problem in American Institutional and Intellectual Life* (Chicago, 1969), pp. 140-206.

Just as they seldom doubted the need for missions and education societies, so these ministers knew how to deal with slavery as a purely practical matter. They enthusiastically followed the lead of the postrevival ministers in continuing support for the American Colonization Society as the only feasible means of handling troublesome former slaves. Although this benevolent reform had, by the mid-1830s, lost a good deal of its respectability in the Northeast, it remained alive in the Southwest as a relatively controversy-free solution of the troubling aspects of a biracial society. Indeed, by the 1830s, southwestern ministers showed little of the ambivalence and defensiveness that characterized some of the postrevival support for the American Colonization Society. One Methodist preacher believed that it was "so noble a cause" that all Christians would immediately unite behind it.[75] Speaking in the paternalistic rhetoric that came naturally to members of the fourth generation, the *Baptist Banner* celebrated colonization as a project "worthy of the generous support of all friends of the African Race."[76] In 1831 the Kentucky Methodist Conference adopted a resolution in support of colonization which summarized neatly the issue that made the society exciting to fourth-generation clergymen. Liberia would be "an asylum for the free people of color of these United States." It would have nothing directly to do with slavery: "The scheme of African colonization is considered as the most likely means, and well calculated to extend the blessings of civilization and the light of the gospel of the grace of God to the benighted regions of Africa." In effect, colonization would function as an extension of missionary work, using free blacks as stand-ins for clerical missionaries. The society itself, as the virtual model of benevolent institutions, "has manifested a laudable zeal, and spirit of benevolence, and virtuous enterprise in performing

75. John Littlejohn, "Journal," p. 211, Methodist Historical Society, Lake Junaluska, N.C.; see also Northcott, *Biography of Rev. Benjamin Northcott*, p. 86; Mathews, *Slavery and Methodism*, p. 98.

76. *Baptist Banner* 2 (1836):2; Minutes, North Alabama Presbytery, p. 97, HFPC; *Extracts from the Records of the Synod of Mississippi* (New Orleans, 1849), pp. 10-11; Minutes, Synod of Alabama (1843), HFPC; *Western Presbyterian Herald* 6 (1837):201; *Presbyterian Advocate* 1 (1830):114; Minutes, Tuscaloosa First Presbyterian Church, Alabama (March 28, 1833), HFPC, *Baptist* 1 (1835):3.

much with very limited means." The organization, that is, was well structured and efficient.[77]

Colonization received important support from ministers who took the clearest stands against abolition and in favor of the southern peculiar institution. Bascom, much more at ease in the company of fourth-generation ministers than he had been with the third cohort, worked as a general agent of the American Colonization Society throughout the Southwest.[78] William Winans praised Bascom's work in the "most godlike enterprise ever devised by human wisdom or prompted by human benevolence."[79] Even James Smylie proclaimed, "I love it, because I find it so perfectly in accordance with the precepts and example of Jesus Christ and his Apostles."[80] Such support underlines the fact that by the 1840s colonization lacked even the hint of abolitionism in the minds of southwestern clergy.

The care with which colonization advocates avoided direct connections between the society and slavery meant that the Liberian experiment was of little help in coping with the day-to-day issues of slavery. As a consequence, members of the fourth generation had to look elsewhere, and they found one response to antislavery agitation which more than any other dovetailed with their belief in benevolent reform: they advocated a complex and carefully developed mission program for the slaves.[81] The leaders of this movement included several slaveholders. John Lane, a Methodist minister, prominent Vicksburg merchant, and slaveholder, promoted missions to the slaves of Mississippi.[82] In organizing a mission society in Nashville, James Gwin assumed "the members of it will be

77. Redford, *Western Cavaliers*, p. 72.

78. Mathews, *Slavery and Methodism*, p. 95; Henkle, *Life of Henry Bascom*, p. 205.

79. Holder, *William Winanas*, p. 110.

80. Smylie, *Review of a Letter*, p. 60.

81. See Leavell and Bailey, *Complete History of Mississippi Baptists*, p. 288; Minutes, Transylvania Presbytery, p. 205, HFPC; Minutes, North Alabama Presbytery (1829), HFPC; Clayton, *History of the Church Davidson County, Tennessee*, p. 320.

82. Thomas Summers, ed., *Biographical Sketches of Eminent Itinerant Ministers* ...(Nashville, 1859), pp. 245-252.

primarily slaveholders."[83] Basil Manley, who owned several slaves, "delivered a discourse" before the Alabama State Convention of Baptists "on the Oral Religious instruction of our slave population, urging the subject on the convention with pathetic earnestness and great power."[84] It was only natural that the clergy who showed the most interest in missions to slaves would be those most directly affected by the missions. In addition, the participation of slaveholding clergy gave the slaveholding laity some measure of confidence in the enterprise.

A disproportionate percentage of the source material for recent studies of the mission to the slaves has been drawn from materials on the Southeast. Such analyses have been shaped largely by the thought of Charles Colcock Jones, the most articulate and impressive of the advocates of the mission. Jones was steeped in northern notions of benevolence from his days at Andover Academy, and his analysis of the pressing need for a mission to the slaves was subtle and complex. According to Donald Mathews, Jones worried about the threat inadequate socialization of blacks posed for broader southern society and the obligations whites had to themselves and to the blacks to ease the slave's burden. He hoped to end the adversarial relationship between masters and slaves, he wanted Christians to be better managers of the relationship, and he wished to provide a useful cosmic and moral framework for blacks.[85] Others in the East tended to provide a simpler analysis, based primarily upon two related but potentially contradictory motives. Certainly a high percentage of masters, and perhaps a smaller group of southeastern clergymen, openly discussed the importance of the mission as a form of social control which would make slaves calmer and more passive. In an attempt to regain the attention of masters after abolitionist crusades and slave revolts in

83. Elliott, *History of the Great Secession*, p. 87.

84. Minutes, Alabama State Convention (1844).

85. Mathews, *Religion in the Old South*, pp. 138-150; Mathews, "The Methodist Mission to the Slaves, 1829-1884," *Journal of American History* 51 (1965):615-631; Mathews, "Charles Colcock Jones and the Southern Evangelical Crusade to Form a Biracial Community," *Journal of Southern History* 41 (1975):299-320; see also Loveland, *Southern Evangelicals*, pp. 218-256, which presents a factual, if undigested, account.

the 1820s and 1830s had damaged the image of catechizing slaves, such advocates of missions as Charles C. Pinckney suggested that religious training would "render [slaves] more contented with their situation."[86]

This essentially defensive argument appeared only rarely in the rhetoric of mission proponents in the Southwest. It is crucial to remember that the fourth generation of southwestern ministers felt such a profound sense of confidence in their actions and such certainty in the righteousness of their cause that the notion of forcing religion upon slaves for purposes of social control almost never appears in their writings. To be sure, advocates to slaves missions fully realize that they had to work within the confines of a complicated legal and social system. They had to obtain the master's permission to evangelize his slaves, and occasionally they had to cope with masters' fears that missions might be the work of abolitionists in disguise.[87] Nevertheless, churches tried to bring masters to "a sense of their duty with respect to the religious instruction of their servants."[88] Missionaries kept within the restrictions created by slavery, to be sure. In providing spiritual assistance, the Mississippi Baptist Convention noted, "It is not necessary that we should destroy or even attempt to destroy the vital bond that now exists, and that distinguishes one portion of the community from the other."[89] The Mississippi Methodist Conference stated that "it is not our province, and is equally foreign from our disposition, to interfere with the question of civil policy, which discourages or prohibits large meetings of colored people, even for worship, in parts of the country where they are numerous."[90]

The other major component of the mission, juxtaposed to the defensive concept of social control, was the undeniable commit-

86. Elliott, *History of the Great Secession*, p. 278; see also Kendall, *History of the Tennessee Baptist Convention*, p. 81.

87. Lazenby, *History of Methodists in Alabama and West Florida*, p. 255.

88. Minutes, Synod of Mississippi and South Alabama (1835), HFPC; see also Minutes, Synod of Alabama pp. 170-173, HFPC; Elliott, *History of the Great Secession*, p. 135; Proceedings, Convention of the Baptist Denomination in the State of Mississippi, pp. 15-16.

89. Proceedings, Convention of the Baptist Denomination in the State of Mississippi, p. 20.

90. Elliott, *History of the Great Secession*, pp. 278-279.

ment on the part of southeastern ministers to protect the souls of slaves, evangelizing them and bringing them the benefits of gospel religion. For eastern ministers such a commitment had, of course, overtones and undertones. Implicitly, it denied the value of the private religion of the slave cabin and occasionally involved an explicit attack upon slave preachers. Ministers often felt an underlying sense of guilt, or at least of obligation, in their mixed feelings about the peculiar institution.

In the Southwest, any attempt to promote an evangelical commitment to the slaves for their own sake required one prior step. Whereas in the East no strong opposition to missions had developed, and therefore no elegant argument was needed to justify them, fourth-generation southwestern clergy felt impelled to explain that slaves would eagerly receive the word of God: "The sons of Ethiopia, whatever may be said of their natural stupidity, under the influence of proper means, have ever shown a ready disposition to stretch forth their hands unto God."[91] These ministers felt a duty to convert the entire slave population of the Southwest. The Alabama Methodist Conference noted "the evident necessity . . . for special care and pains in the instruction of those who have not the benefit of reading the whole Scripture, that they may be made wise unto salvation."[92] Enthusiasm for promoting the strong black interest in salvation produced caricatures of the good, faithful, Christian slave. When Jacob, a slave overseer, died, for example, his master was said to have declared, "I have lost a friend, whom I loved, in my childhood, hardly less than my father."[93] The *Baptist Banner* extracted a story from Hannah More's memoirs of a slave who drowned after giving up his space on a lifeboat to two children.[94] Another article termed one slave the "Lord's freeman."[95]

The corollary notion of a special obligation, of the necessity of the mission because of the unfortunate state of blacks, received

91. Minutes, Synod of Alabama (1843), HFPC; see also Minutes, Alabama Baptist State Convention (1845).

92. Elliott, *History of the Great Secession*, p. 278; see also Kendall, *History of the Tennessee Baptist State Convention*, p. 81.

93. *Baptist* 1 (1844):75.

94. *Baptist Banner* 2 (1836):81.

95. Ibid. 4 (1838):49.

much less attention in the Southwest than in the Southeast. Perhaps some ministers experienced secret feelings of guilt concerning their participation in the institution, but if they did, they left no such record. A few ministers belabored the obvious, and therefore perhaps suggested some reservations; one writer felt obliged to remind his readers, and himself, that slaves "are not chattels, but human beings, conscious, intelligent, immortal."[96] Yet others, strong supporters of the mission, gave no inkling of such conflicts. Basil Manley early shared the reservations of many other preachers about slavery, but by the time he became a leading figure among Alabama Baptists, his correspondence contained records of his enthusiastic participation in its workings. He wrote, for example, "This day, for repeated and persevering misconduct, I sent my boy Claiborne to the workhouse to be put on the Treadmill and Set in solitary confinement."[97] For Manley and many southwestern preachers of the fourth generation, the mission to the slaves was approximately as important as education or temperance. The only rhetorical outbursts that suggested a special status for the mission came in the face of attacks by northern clergymen.

Missionary activities seem to have varied little from the East to the West. Methodists organized the activity with the most care, Baptist support varied from association to association, and Presbyterian interest depended upon the relative enthusiasm of presbyteries or synods. No specific group of minsiters apparently specialized in mission work; the South Alabama Presbytery reported that virtually all ministers were "devoting a considerable part of their labors to the benefit of the colored population."[98] Richard Cater, a South Carolina—trained Presbyterian minister, divided his time in Selma, Alabama, between his church duties and the "many sons and daughters of Ethiopia."[99] At least some of the enthusiasm for the missions came from the financial benefits missionaries could gain from the work. In Mississippi one slaveholder provided a

96. H. M. McTyeire, *Duties of Christian Masters* (Nashville, 1859), pp. 18-19.
97. Basil Manley, "Diary," July 5, 1833, BHS.
98. Ernest T. Thompson, *Presbyterians in the South*, 2 vols. (Richmond, 1963-68), 1:437.
99. Sprague, *Annals of the American Pulpit*, 4:523.

fifty-dollar fee for work on the souls of his servants; Methodists in Mississippi could be guaranteed the best wages in the state working for masters in the black belt.[100]

Missionaries attempted to outline with some care the relative duties of masters and slaves. Masters should "give unto your servants that which is just and equal, avoid threatening, knowing that you have a master also in heaven, neither is there respect of persons with him."[101] A Christian master should work his slaves a judicious amount, provide proper tools, allow sufficient rest and sleep, respect the Sabbath, and provide proper food and shelter. Moreover, slaves should be well-governed, punished when necessary, but not "for the gratification of revenge."[102] Slave marriages and families must be respected, and elderly slaves must be supported. Most important, masters should provide careful religious instruction for their slaves.

The missions provided slaves with catechisms which the missionaries taught orally. The Synod of Mississippi commissioned John Montgomery and James Smylie to write a catchism for general Presbyterian use,[103] and the Alabama Baptist State Convention chose A. W. Chambliss to do the same for Baptists.[104] Chambliss's *Chatechetical Instructor* gained great popularity and later in the century was used to instruct children. He gave no particular emphasis to the obligations of masters and slaves, although he did cite the oft-used passage in Colossians 3:22, "Servants,obey in all things your masters according to the flesh."[105]

The southwestern variant of the mission differed from its eastern counterpart in a curious lack of enthusiasm. To be sure, a

100. Jones, *Methodism as Connected with the Mississippi Conference*, p. 432; Riley, *Methodism in Alabama*, p. 151.

101. Minutes, Gasper River Baptist Association, Kentucky (1835), p. 7; Minutes, Goshen Baptist Association, Kentucky (1844), p. 5, both in BHS.

102. *The Cumberland Presbyterian Pulpit* (Nashville, 1833), 1:145; Proceedings, Convention of the Baptist Denomination in the State of Mississippi, pp. 15-16; Minutes, Ebenezer Presbytery, Kentucky (1832), Shane Collection, Presbyterian Historical Society, Philadelphia.

103. Minutes, Synod of Mississippi, p. 26, HFPC.

104. A. W. Chambliss, *The Catechetical Instructor* (Montgomery, 1849), p. xv.

105. Minutes, Synod of Mississippi, p. 26, HFPC.

great deal of rhetoric emerged from the churches of the fourth-generation preachers extolling the virtues of this enterprise, but no one with the messianic fervor of Charles Colcock Jones came west to promote the cause. Perhaps this lack reflects the myraid interests of southwestern ministers. but equally likely, and clearly reflected in their reticence to generalize about slavery, fourth-generation clergymen chose the path of cautious activism so as not to disrupt their broader goal of reforming southwestern morality.

CHAPTER 9

Ecclesiastical Divisions
and the Southwest

Each generation of the southwestern evangelical clergy faced some dramatic, dangerous, and potentially disastrous situation, either of its own making or forced upon it from outside. For the first generation, of course, the frontier provided countless troubles and almost as many possibilities. The second generation had to cope with the revival, at times a monster out of control, at times an apparent blessing. Third-generation preachers worked in a region in transition and coped as best they could with real or apparent declension from the heady years of the revival. For a few years, ministers of the fourth generation had to cope only with their own success. As benevolent reformers took control of the southwestern evangelical denominations, they attempted to eliminate remnants of past inattention to benevolent enterprise. Leaders of the fourth generation also had to develop such varying structures for their many enterprises as Bible associations, colleges, and state conventions. The business of benevolent reform provided several special challenges, for which members of the fourth generation appear to have been remarkably well prepared.

Among the many goals of the highly ambitious clergymen in the fourth generation, one that underlay all others was a quest for national prominence. For Presbyterians, publication was a certain route to eastern acclaim. For Baptists, a prominent urban pulpit, such as Howell's in Nashville, or presidency of a university, such as Manley's in Alabama, seemed to convey national status. The simplest route to fame was that open to a few southwestern Methodists: evaluation to the episcopate. In dealing with these ambitions fourth-generation southwestern clergymen faced the most severe test of their faith and mettle. Only a few years after they had wrested control of their denominations from the third generation, this new wave of clergymen was rocked by the national division of their churches.

Presbyterian Division

Members of the Presbyterian church had long worried over a variety of issues, both theological and narrowly institutional, and finally in the 1830s this unshaped debate coalesced into the New School–Old School confrontation. At least in part this crisis occurred because some young, well-trained ministers had begun to ease away from traditional Presbyterian support for covenants and original sin. In addition, some innovative theologians argued that Christ's atonement was at least potentially general, applicable to all, and therefore the traditional Presbyterian commitment to the doctrine of election was, if not outdated, at least subject to considerable rethinking. The great New Haven theologians of the early nineteenth century, Nathanial W. Taylor, Chauncy Goodrich, and Lyman Beecher, provided much of the intellectual background for these revisionist doctrines, increasingly but simplistically lumped together under the label New School.[1]

A second group remained steadfastly orthodox, rejecting any attempts to move away from the Edwardsian tradition; this segment came to be labeled the Old School. Part of the Old School's complaints against the New Haven–based reformers was that, in 1801, early New School ministers had created a Plan of Union between Congregationalists and Presbyterians in order to promote the work of the "benevolent empire." Old School preachers argued

1. For the first-rate analysis of the New School movement, see George M. Marsden, *The Evangelical Mind and the New School Presbyterian Experience* (New Haven, 1970); see also Joseph Haroutunian, *Piety versus Moralism: The Passing of the New England Theology* (New York, 1932); Sidney E. Mead, *Nathanial William Taylor, 1786-1858* (Chicago, 1942).

that this union had corrupted the church, forcing Presbyterians to become little more than mushy-headed revivalists. Regional tensions underlay the moral and practical issues, perhaps turning the balance once and for all. Southern Old School ministers resented the notion that their church should be run by New England theologians who wanted all Presbyterians to adhere to certain New England norms. Indeed, such southerners saw in the Plan of Union a suggestion that it was more important to be a New Englander (especially an inhabitant of Connecticut) than it was to be Presbyterian or Congregationalist.

Especially galling to southern Old School preachers was any hint that the church should take a firmer stance on slavery. Although discussion of that issue did not explicitly cause the division, it did serve as a focus, for the Old School ministers at least, of the dangers inherent in New School thought. For Old School advocates agitation on slavery was anathema, as was every form of modernism and misrule pouring forth from the New School divines. For example, Albert Barnes, the bête noire of the Old School camp, was a firm abolitionist. In the 1835 General Assembly, antislavery members of the New School faction brought forth numerous resolutions and memorials against the peculiar institution; especially inflammatory were the resolutions sent to the meeting by the Chillicothe Presbytery. More important, however, were the fears of southern Old School members that antislavery forces were using the theological innovations of the New School as a smoke screen for an attack on slaveholding.[2]

In response to the factionalism within their church, a vast majority of southeastern ministers supported the Old School. Fourth-generation ministers of the Southwest, full of ambition and heady from their many successes in the region, responded diversely to the crisis and division of the Presbyterian church. By far the majority stayed with the Old School after the ultimate cataclysm of 1837, when the New School forces were finally defeated and

2. See Elwyn A. Smith, "The Role of the South in the Presbyterian Schism of 1837-1838," *Church History* 29 (1960):44-63; C. Bruce Staiger, "Abolitionism and the Presbyterian Schism of 1837-1838," *Mississippi Valley Historical Review* 36 (1949):391-414; Marsden, *Evangelical Mind*, pp. 88-103.

the most outspoken presbyteries expelled. Three of the five southwestern synods contained a majority which enthusiastically followed the General Assembly meeting with a vote of support. A second faction of fourth-generation ministers supported Old School theology but stopped short of supporting the actions taken by the majority at the 1837 General Assembly toward dissenting minorities. Fourteen of the thirty-six members of the Synod of Mississippi and South Alabama voted to reject the Old School actions. The objection of these ministers, as expressed in a written protest, was that the assembly had overstepped its authority and taken on "powers not delegated." Although eighteen churches ultimately joined the New School under the leadership of these dissidents, there is no evidence that their action was motivated by antislavery sentiment.[3]

Still another faction took the controversy as an opportunity to condemn, in the strongest possible terms, the dangerous antislavery tendencies of New School thought. James Smylie led the Old School faction in Alabama, which issued a powerful attack on the abolitionist underpinnings of reform thought: "An overwhelming majority [of the New School] and of those in the North who adhere to it, are hostile to at least one of the domestic institutions of the South. . . . In some churches, abolition sentiments have already been made the test of membership; and where this course will end, the future will determine. We feel bound, therefore, to warn our Churches against all attempts to change their ecclesiastical relations, and to place them under the control of a new, unconstitutional and revolutionary body."[4] The sentiments of Smylie and his Old School cohorts were unmatched in the West for their vigor and thoroughgoing dismissal of antislavery views. In this sense, they reflected eastern rather than western views. By the mid-1830s, southeastern Old School Presbyterians had little trouble linking New Haven theology and the abolotionist menace. In the Southwest, however, few fourth-generation ministers were willing to insist upon such an explicitly drawn connection, in part because of the antislavery tradition of the church in the Southwest

3. Thompson, *Presbyterians in the South*, 1:399-400.
4. *Extracts from the Records of the Synod of Mississippi*, p. 44.

and in part because young ministers on the make did not wish to stir up unneeded trouble.

The strongest New School faction in the Southwest encouraged the fears of such Old School ministers, however. Eastern Tennessee New School clergymen so dominated the Tennessee Synod that only two ministers and six elders voted to support the measures passed by the 1837 General Assembly. As a consequence, Tennessee became a battleground for Presbyterians of both sides,with all shades of belief in between the two demanding a hearing. It is almost impossible to sort out the reasons for such strong New School sentiment in Tennessee. The historian of the Tennessee Synod argues that the most important factor was the influence of the American Home Missionary Society and the American Education Society in the state, two benevolent agencies that had drawn the wrath of Old School Presbyterians.[5] Another influence on Tennessee New School thought was the Hopkinsian theology in the eastern part of the state. A first-generation southwestern minister, Hezekiah Balch, had founded a college in the Holston valley and on a trip north had been strongly influenced by the reform thought of Samuel Hopkins. Returning to the southwestern frontier, Balch taught and preached his variant of new Divinity, much to the irritation of other pioneer Presbyterians, who saw him as an innovator and perhaps a heretic. Charles Coffin, who received New Divinity training as a young man in Massachusetts, joined Balch in his work in Tennessee, and the two men prepared a number of ministers to preach a reformed Presbyterian theology.[6]

How strongly Balch and his Hopkinsian followers opposed slavery is unclear. Neither Balch nor Coffin campaigned against the peculiar institution; the negligible number of slaves in the mountain counties of Tennessee probably placed the issue well down on any list of reform priorities. Nevertheless, some of Balch's followers may have been influenced by the thought of the "Presbyterian bishop" of eastern Tennessee, Samuel Doak. Doak is one of the only southwestern preachers whose career spanned

5. Alexander, *Brief History of the Synod of Tennessee*, pp. 22-23.

6. Sprague, *Annals of the American Pulpit*, 3:309-314; see also Sweet, *Religion on the American Frontier*, 2:34-35.

all four generations. Born in Virginia in 1749, Doak was raised in poverty among the Scotch-Irish migrants of upland Virginia. He attended Princeton, graduating in 1777, and soon headed west among the first settlers of what would become Tennessee. As a pioneer leader of the Presbyterian church, he involved himself in the writing of the Franklin state constitution, and, most important, he founded a local school, which eventually evolved into Washington College. Doak appears to have opposed slavery from early in his life, but his commitment to abolition reached maturity only in 1818, when he freed his slaves, many of whom moved to Brown Country, Ohio. He preached immediate abolition to his students, influencing such divergent men as Sam Houston, the Texas hero, Robert McEwan, Doak's son-in-law, who was an enthusiastic Union man in Nashville during the Civil War, and several important figures in the antislavery movement of the Presbyterian church. Among these, John Rankin briefly preached in the Southwest but by 1822 had become a mainstay of immediate abolitionism in southern Ohio.[7] Indeed, Doak's influence upon antislavery thought appears to have been strongest upon southwestern Ohio, where a number of his students began antislavery work that would prepare the way for the Lane Seminary explosion.[8]

The relationship between Doak's antislavery influence and the New School followers of Balch in eastern Tennessee cannot be determined with any precision. Both men had been close comrades in the founding of Presbyterian churches in eighteenth-century Tennessee, riding together to Philadelphia to report on the sometimes primitive ecclesiastical affairs in the West, standing in for one another in church duties, and consulting on most issues of importance to southwestern religion.[9] It is not clear when the two friends began to follow different paths, but Doak never embraced the Hopkinsian theology which dominated Balch's thought, and it is probable that he was involved in the decision of the Abington Presbytery to suspend and admonish Balch for his

7. Sprague, *Annals of the American Pulpit*, 3:392-397; Birney, *James G. Birney*, pp. 74-76.

8. Lawrence T. Lesick, *The Lane Rebels: Evangelicalism and Antislavery in Antebellum America* (Metuchen, N.J. 1980).

9. Sprauge, *Annals of the American Pulpit*, 3:309-310.

innovations. Doak remained firmly in the orthodox (later Old School) camp within the denomination, and he trained his students in that set of theological beliefs. Any direct connection, then, between the antislavery views of Doak and his followers and the New Divinity of Balch and his students makes little sense in the context of eastern Tennessee Presbyterianism.

In only one faction of the fourth-generation southwestern Presbyterian clergy did antislavery sentiments and attitudes on the crisis in the church coincide, although even here no causal link can be proved. In the fall of 1837 the Kentucky Synod voted thirty-three to fourteen to support the Old School actions of the General Assembly. Much of the unhappiness about New School Presbyterianism in Kentucky came from the perception that most missionaries sent to Kentucky were trying to promote New Haven theology, neglecting their more crucial role as general evangelists. One of the most important steps leading to the ultimate division, the issuance of the Old School "Act and Testimony," had been promoted by Kentucky ministers and mostly written by Robert J. Breckinridge, a leading figure in Kentucky politics and Presbyterian affairs who was temporarily preaching in Baltimore during the mid-1830s.[10] For Breckinridge and others, however, the issues were strictly theological and ecclesiastical. The Old School leadership of Kentucky hoped to stake out a middle ground in the battle, purifying the church but stopping short of a full break. For example, at the same time that the West Lexington Presbytery deplored any General Assembly pronouncements on slavery, it noted that "slavery as it exists among us [is] a great political and social evil."[11] Breckinridge had promoted an antislavery resolution in the Kentucky Synod, but he objected to any national statement by the General Assembly on the issue. Slavery had engaged the attention of the Kentucky Synod for several years. President John C. Young of Centre College became the spokesman in the region for gradual emancipation to which the Kentucky Synod gave its approval in 1835, in which "the full future liberty of the slave [would] be secured against all contingencies, by a recorded deed of

10. Marsden, *Evangelical Mind*, p. 60.
11. Minutes, West Lexington Presbytery (1836), HFPC.

emancipation, to take effect at a specific time."[12] James Birney spoke for the immediate emancipationists when he debated with Young, and in a letter he stated that he was "almost daily contemplating the injury it has done to the cause of emancipation in the Presbyterian Church."[13] Nevertheless, Young and Breckinridge doubtless spoke for a majority of the synod in expressing their distaste for slavery and offering moderate solutions. At least in Kentucky, therefore, many of the major figures in the Old School wanted a weak and conservative General Assembly but also to allow substantial self-determination on the level of synod and presbytery. Indeed, this moderate position became identified with the Kentucky Synod after it issued a statement expressing the hope that some compromise might be reached before the church was forced into a division that would benefit no one.[14]

Because of this moderate position and the moderate antislavery assumptions that were linked to it, Kentucky Presbyterians viewed the events of 1837 with confusion and alarm. Several opponents of New School theology felt forced to reject the actions of the General Assembly on ecclesiastical grounds. The most significant of these was Thomas Cleland, the successor to David Rice as the most respeced Presbyterian minister in the state. The expulsion of antislavery New School synods may have eliminated heresy, but it also crushed "liberty of thought, conscience, speech and trial." Initially these moderates formed an independent synod, but finally they felt compelled to unite with the New School. In no sense were the leaders of this faction explicitly advocating immediate abolition. Insead, they were trying to balance their Old School theological beliefs, their opposition to centralized ecclesiastical commitments, and a set of gradualist antislavery proposals which were popular to neither side in the deeply divided church of the 1830s.[15]

12. A Committee of the Synod of Kentucky, *An Address to the Presbyterian of Kentucky, Proposing a Plan for the Instruction and Emancipation of Their Slaves* (Newburyport, Ky., 1836), p. 31.

13. Dwight Dumond, ed., *The Letters of James G. Birney* (New York, 1936), 1:174.

14. For one example of the status of the Kentucky Synod in the controversy, see *Biblical Repertory and Princeton Review* 9 (1837):146.

15. Thompson, *Presbyterians in the South*, 1:407-408.

Methodist Division

By the 1830s, the Methodist Episcopal church had come a long way from the antislavery views of Wesley, Asbury, and Coke. As a practical matter, the bishops had to hold together a church with numerous regional and subregional factions, each with a slightly different slant on slavery. The two extremes were represented by some southern clergymen, who wished to keep discussion of the peculiar institution out of the business of the denomination as a whole, and a number of New England ministers, who promoted discussion of the moral status of slavery whenever possible. The leading figure in the second group, Orange Scott, used his position as a presiding elder in the New England Conference to encourage the reading of Garrison's *Liberator* and thereby bring a majority around to immediate abolitionism. A debate followed among New England Methodists concerning the biblical and moral status of slavery, and the discussion ultimately reached the General Assembly of 1836, at which a bitter confrontation between antislavery and antiabolitionist clergymen dominated the meeting. Although the members of the conference overwhelmingly approved a resolution condemning "modern abolitionism," the debate continued in the following years, with increased bitterness at each turn of the argument.

In 1842 Scott and other leading antislavery Methodists decided that their church could no longer provide them with the Christian community they desired, and upon their withdrawal, a mass exodus from the Methodist Episcopal church filled the new antislavery Wesleyan Methodist Connection of America. Immediately afterward, the third major division of the church in its brief history, the Methodist General Conference, met in 1844. Here Francis A. Harding, a Maryland minister, and James O. Andrew, a bishop of the church from Georgia, were accused of slaveholding in clear violation of the discipline of the church. Andrew's relationship with the peculiar institution was the central focus of debate at the meeting, and when a mild resolution requesting him to suspend his episcopal activities until he could unburden himself of his slaves was passed, southern ministers exploded in outrage.

Delegates from slaveholding states met the next year in Louisville to organize yet one more child of Wesleyanism, the Methodist Episcopal church, South. All that remained in the old denomination was a group of moderately antislavery ministers who had seen more than half a million members secede.[16]

Almost every southwestern organization of the Methodist Episcopal church stated its opposition to the actions of the General Assembly and its support for a new southern denomination. Only a few members of the fourth generation took the narrow, strictly ecclesiastical interpretation of the events of 1844. The Alabama Conference of 1845 attempted to avoid the broader issue of slavery in its rejection of the actions of the General Conference. In particular, the Alabama Conference deplored the action of the majority toward Bishop Andrew as "unconstitutional. Being but a delegated body, the General Conference has no legitimate right to tamper with the office of a General Superintendent, his amenableness to that body and liability to exclusion by it, having exclusive reference to maladministration, ceasing to travel, and immoral conduct. They are of opinion that Bishop Andrew's connection with slavery can come under none of these heads."[17] This interpretation by the Alabama Conference, with only two references to the peculiar institution, served to reject any attempt at compromise by viewing the debate as legal and constitutional rather than moral or practical. In this sense, it was one of the most wholeheartedly separationist documents coming out of the South in the crisis.

Most southwestern Methodist clergymen tended toward a more complex and maltifaceted interpretation of the 1844 General Assembly and the nature of an appropriate response. Virtually every analysis viewed slavery as the central issue in the debate. More precisely, the issue in the minds of these ministers was reduced to the question of the relationship between the church and the laws of the South. According to the Tennessee Conference, "The simple holding of slaves, or mere ownership of slave property in states or territories where the laws do not admit of emancipation

16. Mathews, *Slavery and Methodism*; see also Shelton Smith, *In His Image, But . . . : Racism in Southern Religion, 1790-1810* (Durham, 1972), pp. 94-114.
17. Lazenby, *History of Methodism in Alabama and West Florida*, pp. 648-649.

and permit the liberated slave to enjoy freedom, constitutes no legal barrier to the election or ordination of ministers."[18] This line of argument led one Alabama quarterly conference to suggest that forcing Methodist ministers to violate the law "is contrary to the teaching of the New Testament."[19] The most fully developed analysis of this and other aspects of the issue came from Henry Bascom, in his book *Methodism and Slavery*.[20] Bascom had been one of the most important spokesmen for the South at the General Assembly, and his book is one of several attempts he made to state a position on the issues which would reflect the attitudes of fourth-generation southwestern ministers. He began his analysis with the assertion that Asbury, McKendree, and other founders and early pioneers of Methodism in America had always intended the slavery rule to be a compromise between the full-fledged antislavery position they desired and the realities of a slaveholding South that had to be evangelized. Bascom appealed to the history of the denomination, the nature of slavery as a legal institution, and his own recollections of early Methodists to support his calm. As a northerner who had made his greatest success as a minister in the South, Bascom felt that he was equipped to speak for what he termed a third force in Methodist politics, neither northern nor southern, which would provide "a bond of mediation and intercourse between the two, and holding both in check."[21] It was precisely this third force which had failed the church in 1844 by forgetting the heritage of compromise.

Of course, other aspects of slavery and antislavery entered into discussion of the crisis. Most significantly, several statements went much further in defense of slavery than fourth-generation ministers had previously wished to go. David McAnnally argued that "all good men must and will favor the continuance of slavery in this country until in the providence of God it can be terminated in strict justice to the master and mercy to the slave. In this sense the

18. Caleb Patterson, *The Negro in Tennessee, 1790-186* (Austin, 1922), p. 120.

19. Lazenby, *History of the Methodism in Alabama and West Florida*, p. 646.

20. For a summary of his role in the dispute, see Henkle, *Life of Henry Bascom*, pp. 393-395; Mathews, *Slavery and Methodism*, pp. 266-267.

21. Bascom, *Methodism and Slavery*, p. 22.

Church South is pro-slavery, ever has been, and it is devotedly hoped ever will be."[22] Bascom blamed the British and northerners for imposing slavery on the South (an increasingly popular charge by the 1840s), arguing that "slavery is, to all intents and purposes, a national arrangement."[23] An abrupt end to slavery would be cruel and would ignore the good work accomplished by southern ministers in the mission to the slaves. McAnnally had little patience with abolitionists who passed petitions but had never gone "to the cotton and rice plantations of the south, passing days and weeks without ever seeing a white face—preaching to the negroes by hundreds and sometimes by thousands—visiting their cabins, praying with them when sick or dying—catechising their children, and laboring day after day, and year after year in a sickly climate—trying to win their souls to Christ and lead them to heaven!"[24] To be sure, this enthusiasm for slavery remained qualified, but it also reflected the scars of too many condemnations from the North.

The slight interest in searching for a middle ground between North and South came from northernmost Kentucky and eastern Tennessee. The Kentucky Annual Conference met on September 11, 1844, and Henry Bascom spoke for five hours, stressing the unconstitutionality of the General Conference's actions. Although the meeting deplored these actions, it hoped that some means "may be suggested and devised by which so great a calamity [as a division] may be averted." Although the conference decided to send delegates to the organizing convention in Louisville, it withheld its decision on whether to participate in a southern organization. The most interesting proposal for compromise came from two writers to the Nashville *Christian Advocate*, who argued that Bishop Andrew should resign, but so also should any abolitionist bishop.[25] These limited expressions of regret and desires for compromise had very little effect in the final analysis. Only a very

22. McAnnally, *Statement of Facts*, p. 44.
23. Bascom, *Methodism and Slavery*, p. 61.
24. McAnnally, *Statement of Facts*, p. 25.
25. Elliott, *History of the Great Secession*, pp. 411-412; see also Martin, *Antislavery Movement in Kentucky*, pp. 80-81.

few southwestern ministers and even fewer churches decided to stay with the northern church.

Baptist Division

In the decentralized Baptist church, a break between North and South was at once more and less to be expected than in the other two churches. Division was more likely because any union among Baptists was very difficult to maintain. But the challenge of organizing the Baptist denomination nationally provided leaders with a conservative, cautious attitude toward proposals that might threaten the delicate balance they had achieved. Leaders of the Board of Foreign Missions had to fend off antislavery proposals from England for fear of causing southern members to turn their backs on missionary activity. Other organizations faced similar threats to their continued existence. As some northern Baptists began to enter into antislavery activities, national Baptist organizations increasingly had to protest that they intended to avoid any discussion of the issue. The American Baptist Home Mission Society issued a circular letter in which it argued that its constitution forbade any consideration of slavery. Such neutrality tended passively to accept the religious validity of slaveholding, and conservative members of the denomination determined as much when the Home Mission Society convention of 1841 declared that no new tests would be allowed to determine the eligibility of Baptists for various positions within the church. In short, slaveholding Baptists would remain on equal footing with all other members of the church.

Although various organizations staved off a crisis as long as possible, antislavery factions in the North continually tried to raise the issue of slavery. In 1845 the Home Mission Society once again faced the question of special tests for internal missionaries. As the debate became more and more heated, it became apparent that antislavery members of the denomination would secede if slaveholding missionaries continued to represent the church in the West. Conservative northern Baptists found themselves facing a horrifying dilemma: they could either allow their comrades in the North, with whom they dealt on a weekly or monthly basis, to secede from this and other denominational organizations, or lose the South and the possibility of converting slaveholders and slaves to Baptism. Ultimately, with infinite regret, conservatives voted against licensing slaveholding missionaries. Soon after, the Foreign Mission Board followed suit. Southern Baptists almost immediately began to call for secession, although only two of the many national Baptist organizations had decided against slavery. On May 8, 1845, southern Baptists met in Augusta, Georgia, to create the Southern Baptist Convention.[26]

Southwestern Presbyterians had, for the most part, regretted the Old School–New School division, but few considered it a true calamity. Even less traumatic for fourth-generation Methodists, the division in their church was embraced with unbridled enthusiasm by many ministers. Southwestern Baptists, however, could not avoid the realization that the division of their denomination directly affected the work they were undertaking in the West. The remnants of antimission, Hard-shell Baptists continued to cause problems for benevolence-minded preachers; they continued to have to justify national, cooperative venures as valid, posing no threat to the independence of southwestern churches. The antislavery agitation was, in effect, making liars of these men, proving to those who needed proof that benevolent agencies were dictatorial organizations which the antimission agitators had warned them about.

Many leaders of southwestern Baptism at first tried to read a positive message from the acts of the various national organizations of the church. After the meeting of the Triannual Convention in 1844, the *Alabama Baptist* expressed its "devout gratitude to God, that we perceive the late memorable meeting of the Convention has terminated without any sundering of the ties which bind together the hearts of brethren, who love the cause of God and the salvation of souls."[27] Moreover, several southwestern writers, put

26. Smith, *In His Image*, pp. 114-128; Mary B. Putnam, *The Baptists and Slavery, 1840-45* (Ann Arbor, 1913).

27. *Alabama Baptist* 2 (May 18, 1844).

the crisis of the Baptist churches in a broad, frightening, yet ultimately promising light. The editor of the *Baptist Banner* argued that "our great political fabric, adheres mainly by the integrity with which the three great religious denominations, in this country, cohere; and if they are once sundered, political combinations will scarcely be sufficient to preserve the union. The Methodists seem to be, hopelessly, divided; the Presbyterians are very much agitated upon the same question; and the Baptist Home Mission Society has taken a very exceptionable course on this question." Any attempt at compromise would preserve not merely the Baptist denomination but the entire nation. The *Banner* published a series of letters pleading for compromise.[28]

Compromisers attempted to hold off the creation of a southern branch of the denomination as long as possible. The Tennessee Baptist Foreign Mission Society, in condemning the antislavery decision of the national Foreign Mission Board, nevertheless opposed the creation of a strictly southern board.[29] The *Baptist Banner* insisted that "it is the policy of the Abolitionists of the North to effect such a State-line separation, in order to compel those who oppose them, in the free States, to unite to their ultra measures." The creation of a southern convention would simply play into the hands of northern antislavery men.[30] R. B. C. Howell, in many regards the exemplar of fourth-generation southwestern Baptists, had no positive words for the mission boards. By refusing to let slaveholders be missionaries, "they unchristianize us all." Yet the creation of a purely southern branch of the denomination, Howell argued, was a gross overreaction. It would credit the action of the missionary boards with too much importance, thereby playing into the hands of the abolitionists. Moreover, such a precipitous southern action would "manifest disrespect for the large number of brethren in the North and East who disapprove the late decision of the [Foreign Missionary] Board."[31] When the division finally seemed inevitable, southwestern Baptists contin-

28. *Baptist Banner* 12 (March 27, 1845, April 17, 1845).
29. *Baptist* 1 (April 12, 1845).
30. *Baptist Banner* 12 (May 1, 1845).
31. *Baptist* 1 (April 26, 1845).

ued to express regret, or, as did the Mississippi Baptist State Convention, "surprise and grief."[32]

No matter how much many fourth-generation leaders regretted the developments of the 1840s, they gave almost no support to the decision of the national organizations to penalize slaveholders. Indeed, the Alabama State Convention had pressed the issue in 1844 by demanding "from the proper authorities in all those bodies to whose funds we have contributed, or with whom we have in any way been connected, the distinct, explicit avowal, that slave-holders are eligible and entitled, equally with non-slave-holders, to all the privileges and immunities of their several unions."[33] Most antiabolitionist comment in the crisis stressed that the northern forces were under the control of a few crazed men: "The hope of Abolition fanatics, of driving slavery from the South by force, is the delusion of madmen. They may, by their reckless course, sunder every religious sect and dissolve all the social ties that bind society in these States—Ah! they may dissolve the Union itself, and drench the whole land in blood."[34]

The Baptist comment on the crisis lacked any of the internal bickering within the Southwest that characterized the other two denominations. Again, the key to understanding fourth-generation Baptist leaders is their unity against the ultraconservative, antimission men. For these advocates of benevolence, more than for any other southwestern religious leaders, the fissures of the antebellum period were profoundly disturbing and potentially disastrous.

Intraregional Tensions

In their attempt to cope with the various fissures and chasms that developed within the three evangelical denominations in the 1830s and 1840s, the fourth-generation southwestern clergy had begun to exhibit some divisions of its own. To be sure, the churches of the Southwest had never been monolithic. Factionalism,

32. *Baptist Banner* 12 (May 8, 1845); see also, *Proceedings of the Convention of the Baptist Denomination of the State of Mississippi* (N.p., 1845), p. 24.
33. *Proceedings, Alabama Baptist State Convention* (N.p., 1844).
34. *Baptist Banner* 12 (May 15, 1845).

especially along denominational lines and over theological issues, had been exhibited in the region from the beginning of settlement. But it was only in the response ministers made to the developments of the 1830s and 1840s that differences began to be increasingly pronounced along subregional lines. Some hint of this divisiveness, as we have seen, could be found as early as the response to the Panic of 1819, but ministers had remained united in fellowship throughout the region, trading pulpits, corresponding in the regional denominational journals, and attending the colleges springing up in the region. Such cooperation was particularly evident at the beginning of the fourth generation in the region and implicit in the benevolent enterprises undertaken by this group of ministers. The members of this generation, more than any other except perhaps the revivalists, felt they had a shared set of beliefs and a consequent need for community.

By the 1840s, contrasts between the subregions of the Old Southwest had become increasingly pronounced, although many of the sources of cultural unity remained. The four states of the Old Southwest experienced significant cross-migration, enjoyed important cultural ties, interacted in politics, could look to a complex web of leaders who traversed the region, and despised the East. Most important, slavery continued to unify the culture. Nevertheless, by the mid-1840s, increasingly serious differences had begun to emerge, creating a wider and wider rift between the northern and southern halves of the Old Southwest. Economic factors doubtless lay at the heart of this transformation and had always been a potential problem. Early in the century, cotton became the staple crop in most of Alabama, Mississippi, and central Tennessee; the remainder of the region had a much more diversified economy, and Kentucky could be said to have six or more distinct economic subregions. By the 1840s, even upland Alabama and Mississippi had given way to King Cotton. A comparison of demographic characteristics from the census of 1850 reflects this agricultural pattern. Slaves in Alabama constituted 44.4 percent of the population in 1850; in Mississippi they formed a majority. In sharp contrast, slaves accounted for only 20 percent of the total population of Kentucky and Tennessee. The size of the plantations, the necessity of strict slave discipline, and the fear among whites of slave uprisings compounded the differences in life in Mississippi and Alabama.[35]

In politics, the two sections of the Old Southwest had begun to develop different characteristics as well. In Kentucky and Tennessee, vigorous party squabbles continued through the 1840s and 1850s. In Tennessee, a cohesive Whig party existed until 1858, when it changed its name to the Constitutional Union party.[36] Some Republican sentiment developed in Kentucky just before the Civil War.[37] In each state, the different needs and desires of the upland region contrasted with the interests of the central plains. In the lower Southwest, however, these distinctions had blurred by the mid-1840s. By then it was impossible to detect a two-party system in Alabama, and party activity in Mississippi had deteriorated into concentration on personalities rather than issues. Few debates over substantive matters could emerge in states where harmony of interests prevailed.[38]

Perhaps Frederick Law Olmsted's observations help explain part of the difference. In Mississippi he noticed the "immoral, vulgar and ignorant new rich," whereas in Kentucky he praised the "stalwart propositions" of the inhabitants.[39] Olmstead overstated the difference, but in general the upper Southwest was relatively secure, settled, and tradition-bound by the mid-1840s. It was also troubled by a myriad of internal divisions such as usually characterize a highly developed society. The lower Southwest, by contract, still retained some of the characteristics of a frontier.[40]

In the absence of any events that would force the potential differences in the culture of the Southwest to impinge upon the work of these ministers, they could behave as though such differ-

35. *The Seventh Census of the United States, 1850* (Washington, 1853), p. xxxiii.
36. Abernethy, *From Frontier to Plantation*, pp. 335-336.
37. Davenport, *Antebellum Kentucky*, p. 184.
38. See Percy Rainwater, *Mississippi* (Baton Rouge, 1938); Thomas P. Abernethy, "The Basis of Alabama's Two Party System," *Alabama Review* 19 (1966):243-276; Thornton, *Politics and Power in a Slave Society.*
39. Frederick Law Olmsted, *A Journey in the Back Country* (1860; reprint, New York, 1970), pp. 27, 20.
40. See, for example, Joseph G. Baldwin, *The Flush Times of Alabama and Mississippi* (1853; reprint New York, 1957).

ences did not exist or at least did not matter. But the church divisions brought tensions within the fourth-generation clergy. The least significant subregion in the overall development of southwestern evangelical thought was clearly the eastern upland and mountain section of Tennessee. Without a major urban center, an important college, or a significant periodical, this part of the Southwest remained peripheral to the evangelical enterprise, and its support for New School Presbyterians and antislavery agitation further isolated the subregion.

The crucial distinction that began to emerge by the late 1830s was that ministers from Mississippi and Alabama tended to react to the issues in the national churches with a great deal more aggressiveness than that exhibited in Kentucky and much of Tennessee. Almost every demand for recognition of the importance of slavery, from James Smylie's manifesto of the early 1830s to the Alabama State Baptist Convention's resolutions of the mid-1840s, emerged from the southernmost points of the region. Most, although by no means all, of the calls for caution and compromise, for balance and restraint, came from ministers in the small towns of the Kentucky bluegrass or preachers in Nashville and Louisville. In this sense, the divisions of the 1830s and 1840s represented the beginning of the end of one phase in the development of American religion. Although there was no significant support for abolitionism among southwestern ministers, there were important stylistic differences in their responses to the national divisions. The moderation and caution of ministers from Kentucky and Tennessee and the contentiousness and vigor of clergymen further south did not immediately come into conflict. Instead, these subtle stylistic differences served as a warning that future divisions were inevitable.

Coming of the Civil War

The divisions among southwestern clergy which had remained beneath the surface during the controversies of the 1830s and 1840s began to emerge as full-blown factionalism by the 1850s. The decades of development, in which generation after generation of ministers created a regional religion, finally gave way in the 1850s to an inevitable process of fragmentation, such as had happened in New England in the eighteenth century. The 1850s and 1860s, therefore, mark the beginning of a different story in the history of American religion and its relation to race.

Development of a Proslavery Argument

Preachers in Mississippi and Alabama began in the 1850s to perfect a proslavery argument. Before the liberating division of the national churches, virtually no fully developed proslavery analysis came from southwestern ministers. In the wake of these fissures, however, Richard River, C. T. Sturgis, and Fred Ross of Alabama, T. W. Randle of Tennessee, and Samuel Baldwin of Mississippi all wrote proslavery tracts. Of these, the most bizarre was Baldwin's *Dominion*. Adam's fall, this extremist argued, negated all natural human rights. God occasionally chose to return a few of these rights, but He withheld some as a curse on certain men and their descendants. Baldwin insisted that God cursed Ham and his offspring to eternal servitude: "The question of Hamitic or negro right...can be finally decided only by reference to the written law in correlation with its providential interpretation. All that pertains to man, in the present, the future, and the past, is interwoven with the decision of this question. It is not an American question, but a problem of the world. . . . It lies between the Bible and Providence—between man and his maker." Baldwin concluded that black bondage was, as a consequence, in no way a problem, but instead an important feature of God's plan. It would eventually extend to all parts of the world. Moreover, he argued that blacks naturally understood their status and typically showed great satisfaction with their lot in life: "While mobs and insurrections and nullification have been of constant occurrence among the white race, the negro has given but very few examples of dissatisfaction since the organization of the confederacy, and those examples were never general." Emancipation was clearly against God's will; fortunately, practical considerations would prevent successful and sinful manumission. "The abolition of Hamitic slavery is an impossibility," Baldwin declared. He then continued with a chilling suggestion: "unless it be abolition by extermination."[1]

In the less radical proslavery arguments of the other deep southwestern ministers, several ideas recurred. The inescapable issue was the degree to which the Bible could be seen to agree with their analysis. Biblical passages abounded, especially from the Old Testament, which discussed slavery and gave little indication that God was an abolitionist. Not only had the Pentateuch given apparent sanction to the South's peculiar institution, the Apostle Paul had sent a slave back to his master. These proslavery ministers argued that "the relation of master to slave is not sin, but sanctioned of God."[2] Abolitionists contended that in the New Testament Christ suggested a repudiation of slavery. The proslavery writers considered this idea virtually sacrilegious. As one pointed out, "We maintain that God's law is always right, and that whatever God established is right, not because he established it, but we maintain that God established it because he saw it was right."[3] Although Southwestern ministers had seldom needed to

1. Samuel Baldwin, *Dominion* . . . (Nashville, 1857), pp. 12, 101, 453.
2. Fred Ross, *Slavery Ordained of God* (New York, 1859).
3. Richard H. Rivers, *Elements of Moral Philosophy* (Nashville, 1859), p. 331.

call upon such biblical literalism in the early development of religion in the region, the proslavery ministers used their exegetical skills in a manner that presaged the southwestern variant of fundamentalism. The abolitionist argument would fail, one minister argued, "as long as the Bible is taken as authority and is interpreted according to the established laws of interpretation."[4]

One crucial consequence of God's sanction of slavery was His special protection of the slave-master relationship. It was sacred, analogous to the husband-wife and parent-child relations. Of course, the master was the crucial figure in the relationship. "The position of the master is a very responsible one," Richard Rivers argued. "Providence has placed under his control human beings whose destiny is to a great extent determined by his influence."[5] Yet it should not be concluded that God had sanctioned the master to be an unfeeling dictator. One writer stressed that "a man's servants will not, generally, long continue to be his, unless he is willing, in some sense, to belong also to them."[6] That meant that masters would have to abandon their emphasis upon legal and financial aspects of the relationship. One minister condemned the tendency of masters to view their slaves as little more than an investment, for such an attitude produced "selfishness, injustice, cruelty and utter disregard of humanity and the law of God."[7] God created the institution, these ministers argued, for the moral betterment of all participants in slavery.

These proslavery analyses had to address the antislavery accusations that the peculiar institution served as a haven for sadists and degenerates. Indeed, William Buck declared that "we wish our readers distinctly to understand that the institution of slavery, through the cupidity and rapaciousness of wicked men, has been awfully perverted and abused."[8] Southwestern proslavery writers chose not to dismiss such assertions, but rather to advocate reforms that would take away this issue from abolitionists. The

4. *Duties of Masters to Servants: Three Premium Essays* (Charleston, 1851), Holmes essay, p. 59; see also *Alabama Baptist Advocate* 2 (1850):112.

5. Rivers, *Elements of Moral Philosophy*, p. 370.

6. *Duties of Masters to Servants*, Holmes essay, pp. 65-66.

7. William C. Buck, *The Slavery Question* (Louisville, 1849), pp. 17.

8. Ibid., p. 12; see also *Christian Advocate* 14 (1850):45.

duties of masters should be multifaceted. These ministers called for well-maintained cabins, free time for recreation, good clothing and bedding, leisurely meals, and good medical care. Punishment, they argued, should usually take the form of withheld privileges rather than physical discipline.[9] If they could promote the regular observation of such practices, they felt confident that the Christian nature of the peculiar institution could be protected, and attacks from the North would lose much of their power.

Of course, one component of the master's duty to his slaves was to provide for their moral education. "The slavery of the Scriptures," declared one writer, "was conceived in divine benevolence, and intended, mainly, to secure the happiness of the slave—to preserve life—to afford protection and to furnish the means of moral culture, to those who would otherwise be destitute of one or all of these great blessings."[10] Slaves would delight in this mission to protect their souls because of "that feeling of childlike dependence and leaning upon their master, which is well-known as one of the elements in their nature."[11] Properly channeled, this childlike attitude toward life would allow the slaves to become excellent Christians. For the proper instruction of slaves, Christian masters should hold regular religious services, "stopping them in their work to hear gospel." Marriage must be sanctified, and proper Christian manners and morals must be cultivated.[12]

Of course, underlying all of these analyses was a set of assumptions about black inferiority. For the most part, however, there was little expression of a sense that slaves were dangerous. Instead, these proslavery thinkers tended to assume that blacks were naturally foolish, thoughtless, improvident, and slothful. The slave community had no culture worthy of the name. Their

9. Proceedings of the Alabama Baptist State Convention, pp. 5, 7, 18-19; *Christian Advocate* 11 (1847):113; *Proceedings Convention of the Baptist Denomination of the State of Mississippi*, pp. 17, 22, 28; Kendall, *History of the Tennessee Baptist Convention*, pp. 81-82; *Duties of Masters to Servants*, Holmes essay, passim.

10. Buck, *Slavery Question*, p. 10.

11. *Duties of Masters to Servants*, Holmes essay, pp. 95-96; Proceedings of the Alabama State Convention, p. 21; Proceedings, Convention of the Baptist Denomination in the State of Mississippi, pp. 28-29.

12. *Christian Advocate* 18 (1854):29.

generalizations about blacks usually took the form of either amusement or contempt. These southwestern ministers, then, had little of the harshness of George Fitzhugh or other secular advocates of the institution. Instead, they served as exemplars of the paternalistic defense of slavery.

Reemerging Antislavery Thought

A number of ministers from Kentucky and Tennessee began to drift back toward active participation in the antislavery movement by the 1850s. Although such men cannot be seen as altogether representative of clerical attitudes in their part of the Southwest, the moderate antislavery ministers included some of the most important figures in their respective denominations. In this sense, they provided a prominent voice for gradualist antislavery in the region.

Old School Presbyterian ministers in Kentucky were by far the most activist antislavery advocates in the Southwest during the fifteen years before the Civil War, and the major figure within this group was Robert J. Breckinridge. Breckinridge had been a colonizationist and gradual emancipationist virtually from the beginning of his career. After he developed his reputation as a minister in Maryland and college president in Pennsylvania, Breckinridge returned to his home state to take over the pulpit at the First Presbyterian Church of Lexington. The governor promptly appointed him superintendent of public education, and he quickly returned to his role as a leading figure in the intellectual and political life of Kentucky. He began to promote his gradualist plans for ending slavery in Kentucky, which would include the emancipation of all slaves at age twenty-five and their eventual transportation to Liberia. In 1848 and 1849, Breckinridge campaigned tirelessly for his scheme and for the reintroduction of a law prohibiting the importation of slaves into Kentucky.

Breckinridge, John Young, Stuart Robinson, and other gradual emancipation advocates within the Old School Presbyterian leadership of Kentucky led the organization of a state emancipation party in 1849. This movement culminated in the convening of a state emancipationist convention in Frankfort, in which 13 of the 150 members were Presbyterian ministers. The convention ultimately called for a constitutional amendment banning the importation of slaves into the state. Members then focused their attention upon the August 1849 election of delegates to the state constitutional convention, to which they hoped to elect Breckinridge and other representatives of the gradualist position. The disastrous results at the polls only dimmed the political ambitions of the Presbyterians; many continued to campaign for an end to slavery throughout the 1850s.[13]

John Graves and James Pendleton, two young and energetic leaders of the southwestern Baptist church, exhibited numerous reservations about the morality of the peculiar institution. Of the two, Graves was by far the most impressive. Alexander Campbell once commented, "I have known a few men in my life who have made themselves simpletons, in attempting to act as knaves. Mr. Graves certainly had kept bad company, else he does himself great injustice."[14] Born in Chester, Vermont, in 1830, Graves began to preach in his late teens, and he became the principal of the Kingsville Academy in Ohio when he was just nineteen. In 1841 he came to Kentucky and in 1845 moved to Nashville to set up the Vine Street Classical Academy. The next year he became assistant editor of the *Baptist*; two years later he took over control of the journal.[15] Pendleton had a much less exalted career. Rising to the position of minister in the Bowling Green Baptist Church after almost no formal training, he enjoyed writing for the various

13. Victor B. Howard, "Robert J. Breckinridge and the Slavery Controversy in Kentucky in 1849," *Filson Club History Quarterly* 53 (1979):328-343; Victor B. Howard, "The Kentucky Presbyterians in 1849: Slavery and the Kentucky Constitution," *Register of the Kentucky Historical Society* 76 (1975); 217-240; Cassius M. Clay, *The Life of Cassius Marcellus Clay: Memoirs, Writings, Speeches, Showing His Conduct in the Overthrow of American Slavery* ... (1886; reprint, New York, 1969), pp. 219-220; David Smiley, *The Lion of White Hall: The Life of Cassium M. Clay* (Madison, 1962), pp. 133-134.

14. Elliott, *History of the Great Secession*, p. 385; see also A. H. Redford, *History of the Organization of the Methodist Episcopal Church, South* (Nashville, 1875), pp. 416-420.

15. *Baptist Banner* 12 (1845):73; see also Proceedings, Convention of the Baptist Denomination in the State of Mississippi (1845).

denominational journals and soon became a reasonably well-known young controversialist. The two joined forces in the early 1850s when, after a visit from Graves, Pendleton wrote a controversial pamphlet entitled *Three Reasons Why I am a Baptist*.[16] Graves campaigned throughout the Southwest against cooperation among the denominations, and in 1851 he drafted the Cotton Grove resolutions, which called upon Baptists to repudiate all connections with non-Baptists. The two young ministers soon focused their attention upon the evil of Methodism, especially in Pendleton's pamphlet *An Old Landmark Reset*, and Graves' book-length treatise *The Great Iron Wheel*. By 1854 the *Tennessee Baptist* included a column entitled "Controversy" simply to handle all the difficulties Graves and his allies had caused.[17]

Graves was uncharacteristically cautious in his treatment of the peculiar institution. Indeed, one of the few accounts of his views came from one of the enemies he made in his career, John Waller, who stated that Graves "avowed his intention to leave Kentucky on account of slavery."[18] Pendleton, however, showed no such caution. He wrote twenty antislavery articles for the Louisville emancipationist periodical *The Examiner*, calling himself "A Southern Emancipationist." He soon decided that his position on the peculiar institution mandated that he resign his position as pastor in Bowling Green, but his congregation refused to accept his decision. Increasingly publicizing his views Pendleton wrote the *Baptist Banner* a ringing statement of his position: "I am not a slave-holder. I would rather utter this declaration than sit on a Monarch's throne and wear a Monarch's crown.[19]

16. McAnnally, *Statement of Facts*, p. 44; Will F. Steeley, "The Established Churches and Slavery," *Register of the Kentucky Historical Society* 58 (1957):99.

17. O. L. Hailey, *J. R. Graves: Life, Times and Teachings* (Nashville, 1929), pp. 12-23; Kendall, *History of the Tennessee Baptist Convention*, pp. 106-108; Pendleton, *Reminiscences*, p. 105; J. R. Graves, *The Great Iron Wheel* . . . (Nashville, 1855), p. 35; *Tennessee Baptist* 5 (1849):169.

18. *Alabama Baptist Advocate* 10 (May 13, 1858).

19. *Baptist Banner* 16 (September 12, 1849). A few other Kentucky Baptists joined these young turks in advocating antislavery action. For example, William W. Everts, one of the most prominent figures among Louisville Baptists, opposed slavery from his pulpit in the Walnut Street Church. See Steeley, "Established Churches and Slavery," p. 99.

No Methodist opponents of slavery took public stands as did Pendleton and Breckinridge. Two leading Kentucky Methodists did speak within their denominational meetings to protest the proslavery ideology that was increasingly appearing within the church. One of these men, John C. Harrison, was born in North Carolina, the son of a Methodist preacher. When the family moved west, Harrison underwent a conversion in a Kentucky camp meeting. Soon he began to preach, and his career described an ascending arc as he moved from major pulpit to major pulpit in the cities of Kentucky. Although no record remains of his specific views on slavery, he appears to have been the leader of the faction within Kentucky Methodism which opposed Bascom and called for compromise on the issue of slavery and slaveholding clergy. He voted against the creation of a southern church, although he finally decided to stay with his brethren in Kentucky.[20]

Drummond Welburn took a clearer stance against the erosion of the antislavery heritage within the southern church. Welburn's parents were active in the Methodist church as laymen, and he therefore had a strong sense of its tradition. As a young man he taught school in Philadelphia, and at age twenty moved to Lexington, where he became a Methodist preacher. An active member of the Kentucky Converence, Welburn convinced his fellow preachers to begin publishing the minutes of the annual meeting. He was a typical energetic fourth-generation clergyman. In 1858, he alone among Kentucky Methodist preachers refused to agree to the abrogation of the general rule on slavery within the church, South. He also insisted that the permanent record of the meeting specified his protest against this violation of Methodist tradition.[21]

These antislavery ministers lacked anything approaching a carefully articulated gradual abolitionist doctrine. Both Pendleton and Breckinridge carefully analyzed what they considered the short-comings of the peculiar institution. Breckinridge provided one of the harshest condemnations of slavery in forty years of southwestern religion. It was "robbery" of slave labor; it encouraged the

20. Redford, *Western Cavaliers*, pp. 520-527; Ray Short, *Methodism in Kentucky* (Rutland, 1879), p. 13.

21. Redford, *Western Cavaliers*, pp. 436-438; Short, *Methodism in Kentucky*, p. 21.

"universal prostitution" of female slaves; it violated the moral training of blacks; it interrupted the ordinary workings of the family.[22] Pendleton added his condemnation of the economic inefficiency of slavery, which "brings labor into disrepute, and thereby promotes idleness."[23] Both men enthusiastically promoted gradual abolition of slavery through manumission and eventual transportation of free blacks to Liberia. Other Kentucky and Tennessee opponents of slavery left no record of a coherent policy; their opposition, indeed, was mixed with ecclesiastical and national worries, which appear to have had higher priority in their concerns.

These specific clerical condemnations of slavery did not, therefore, constitute a full-fledged antislavery movement in Kentucky and Tennessee. Instead, they represented the possibility of open discussion of the issue in the upper half of the Old Southwest. It was precisely that possibility, and the variety of thought which it allowed, that most clearly distinguished one half of the region from the other.

Intraregional Conflict

The more the two halves of the Old Southwest evolved into subregions by the 1850s, the more the churches of the area found factionalism over the issue of slavery inescapable. The first open conflict developed within the Baptist church, as deep South preachers began to express their outrage at the open antislavery positions taken by Pendleton and the mostly covert support given to him by Graves. Which of the many controversial actions of the two leaders of "Landmarkism" set off the attack was never clear, but in 1855 the *Alabama Baptist* began a series of articles condemning the two men as abolitionists. The editor, Dr. Dawson, was particularly outraged that a fellow editor would be soft on antislavery. He therefore condemned "the opposition of Elder J. R. Graves, editor

22. Howard, "Robert J. Breckinridge," p. 332.
23. Victor B. Howard, "James Madison Pendleton: A Southern Crusader against Slavery," *Register of the Kentucky Historical Society* 74 (1973):194-196.

of the *Tennessee Baptist*, to the southern Institution of slavery."[24] Although the journal found little evidence of Graves's antislavery pronouncements, it continued to ask, "Will Baptists at the South, true Southern Baptists, stand by a man who had been an abolitionist as a leader? Never!"[25] Pendleton was fairer game, and the *Alabama Baptist* demanded that he cease teaching because antislavery men had nothing to say to the youth of the South.[26]

Although the internecine struggles of the Baptist denomination helped emphasize the differences between the upper and lower halves of the Southwest, they did not result in any broader confrontation. Such a confrontation, however, was the fate of the southwestern Methodists and Presbyterians. John Bruce and J. R. Eads joined Drummond Welburn and John C. Harrison as Methodist supporters of the Union in Kentucky. A majority of members of the Kentucky Conference followed the lead of these men in seceding from the Methodist Episcopal church, South, and eventually rejoining the northern church.[27] Presbyterians in Kentucky faced an even more clearly defined issue. When the Old School church divided into northern and southern branches, Robert J. Breckinridge led the pro-Union, antislavery ministers of the Kentucky Synod into the northern branch. Stuart Robinson held a cadre of Kentucky Presbyterians for the South, and the church remained hopelessly divided for decades thereafter.[28]

By the end of the Civil War, then, the troubling signs of a disintegrating regional church which had begun to emerge in the divisions of the 1830s and 1840s had turned into reality. Three interrelated conclusions can be drawn from the state of the southwestern churches by the time of the Civil War. The developments of the 1850s ended the process of denominational development in the southwestern clergy. Not only had ministers in the upper and lower halves of the Southwest taken a markedly different set of stances on the peculiar institution, they gradually had

24. Pendleton, *Reminiscences*, pp. 93-97.

25. *Alabama Baptist* 10 (1855):9.

26. Ibid., 12 (1858):18.

27. William W. Sweet, *Methodism in American History* (New York, 1933), p. 281.

28. Thompson, *Presbyterians in the South*, 2:156-175.

begun to move away from one another in institutional ways as well. The unique intersection of intellectual generations, regional culture, and the problem of slavery ended at the same time that each element changed or, as was the case with slavery, ceased to exist. Inevitably, ministers in what were once the states of the Old Southwest would form into cohorts over the issue of Reconstruction or, most dramatically, over modernism, and the background of early nineteenth-century clerical development would provide a context in which to see current issues. But the development of a fifth or sixth southwestern clerical generation would forever be foreclosed as the region itself disappeared as a coherent framework.

As the movement from generation to generation ended for ministers by the time of the Civil War, a second message to be read from this phase of southwestern religion is the constant danger churches must face as they strive to work within secular America. Sidney Mead, in his seminal essay "Denominationalism: The Shape of Protestantism in America," describes the dilemma American churches faced when they discovered that the cost of religious freedom was the loss of coercive power. Forced to embrace what Mead terms "voluntaryism," American denominations found themselves struggling against one another not just for members but for influence and a place in American culture. For southwestern ministers, this struggle had meant a certain amount of compromise, especially on the issue of slavery. By the 1850s, it led to a breakup of southwestern religion itself. Forced by their multilayered relationships with society to follow more than shape the developments within the region and the nation, ministers of the fourth generation found their aspirations for an exalted role in American life turning into ashes before their eyes. In this story, more than most in the chronicles of American religion, the fate of the churches had touch of pathos.[29]

There was a third, and perhaps happier, result of the developments in the 1850s and 1860s. The divisions within the southwestern clergy and the gradual disintegration of the region in which ministers had devoted their careers brought with them a touch of liberation. Proslavery, and later race-baiting, ministers, could ex-

29. Sidney E. Mead, *The Lively Experiment* (New York, 1963), pp. 113-115.

press their views without worry about whom they might offend. Kentucky ministers could chart out a moderate course, free in the knowledge that no southwestern unity on the issue of race had to be maintained. Graves and Pendleton could issue into their often intemperate "Landmarkism" because the fourth-generation commitment to a united benevolence movement no longer had a chance of survival. Perhaps most revealing was the almost casual way in which most ministers viewed the exodus of blacks from their churches after the war. Ministers saw their churches virtually gutted, yet they reacted with a sense of relief, almost of liberation. As they bade the slaves farewell, the ministers of what was left of the Old Southwest watched decades of compromise, ill feeling, and not a few troubled consciences leave them.[30]

30. See, for example, Minutes, Severns Valley Baptist Church (1866-67), HCSBC; see also William W. Barnes, *The Southern Baptist Convention, 1845-1953* (Nashville, 1954), pp. 59-61. For a summary of the black sources on the exodus, see Leon F. Litwack, *Been in the Storm So Long* (New York, 1979), pp. 219-226.

Data on Ministers

The statistical descriptions of each cohort of ministers in the introduction to each section of this book are based upon material gathered from the following sources:

Baptists
    J. H. Spencer, *A History of Kentucky Baptists*
    J. J. Burnett, *Sketches of Tennessee's Baptist Preachers*
    L. S. Foster, *Mississippi Baptist Preachers*
Presbyterians
    Alfred Nevin, *Encyclopedia of the Presbyterian Church in the United States of America*
    Robert Davidson, *History of the Presbyterian Church in the State of Kentucky*
Methodists
    A. H. Redford, *The History of Methodism in Kentucky*
    John McFerrin, *History of Methodism in Tennessee*
    Anson West, *History of Methodism in Alabama*
Disciples of Christ
    Frederick Power, *Sketches of Our Pioneers*
Cumberland Presbyterians
    Richard Bond, *Brief Biographical Sketches of Some of the Early Ministers of the Cumberland Presbyterian Church*
Multiple denominations
    William Sprague, *Annals of the American Pulpit*

These sources provide basic data: birthdate, birthplace, date of conversion, date the man became a minister, migration patterns, changes in denomination, education, and date of death. In addi-

261

tion they infrequently mention mariages, children, property ownership, and other information that cannot be reliably quantified because of the number of missing cases and variations among sources. A study of probate records or manuscript censuses might yield a wider range of materials but would require a complicated sampling technique which, given the complexity of this culture, might not prove to be representative.

The statistics are based upon the following sample sizes:

Cohort 1	Cohort 2	Cohort 3	Cohort 4
204	264	329	458

It is impossible to determine the precise size of the clergy over this period. Nevertheless, the absolute sizes of these figures would be sufficient for most modern statistical tests. If the sources are biased, they are biased consistently over time to the better-educated, more prestigious, longer-lived ministers, and therefore, although the general picture they give reflects these biases, if the data are used to compare ministers over time, the biases are less pernicious.

Bibliographical Note

Much of my understanding of the subject of this book has come from a close reading of primary sources. Nevertheless, many works by historians are valuable for a full understanding of religion, slavery, and the culture of the Old Southwest. The books specifically on the religious history of the region are legion. I found particularly useful a number of nineteenth-century studies of denominations in specific states. By far the best, most helpful, and most comprehensive is J. H. Spencer, *A History of Kentucky Baptists* (Cincinnati, 1885). Also on the Baptists, a somewhat less comprehensive but nevertheless good and personal account is Hosea Holcombe, *A History of the Rise and Progress of the Baptists in Alabama* (Philadelphia, 1840). Two state studies of Presbyterians match the Holcombe work as mines of information: Robert Davidson, *History of the Presbyterian Church in the State of Kentucky* (New York, 1847), and Robert Bishop, *An Outline of the History of the Church in the State of Kentucky...* (Lexington, 1824). The Bishop work is, I think, somewhat more valuable as a moderate's attempt to make sense of the turmoil caused by the Great Revival. The best state study of the Methodists in John McFerrin's *History of Methodism in Tennessee* (Nashville, 1888). James B. Finley's anecdotal and amusing *Sketches of Western Methodism* (Cincinnati, 1854), gives the best flavor of the Methodist denomination in the region.

Twentieth-century historians have been able to avoid the basic problem of the nineteenth-century works, a tendency to present a rosy picture of each denomination. This fault occurred, of course, because these were histories written for the denominations and not for a general public. One must start any study of religion in the Old Southwest with the works of Walter Posey, in particular *The Presbyterian Church in the Old Southwest, 1778-1838* (Richmond, 1952).

The literature on slavery seems to grow daily. Four studies of the intellectual history of white thought on slavery helped me understand to some extent the complicated psychology of proslavery sentiment. These are Winthrop Jordan, *White over Black* (Chapel Hill, 1967), David Brion Davis, *The Problem of Slavery in Western Culture* (Ithaca, 1965), Davis, *The Problem of Slavery in the Age of Revolution* (Ithaca, 1975), and William Jenkins, *Proslavery Thought in the Old South* (Chapel Hill, 1935). Jenkins is particularly helpful in providing a background to antebellum proslavery, although his work is somewhat outdated. Kenneth Stampp's *The Peculiar Institution: Slavery in the Antebellum South* (New York, 1956), remains indispensable for its full understanding of the internal workings of the institution. Several recent studies have expanded on Stampp's study in a variety of directions. I found the most useful of these to be John Blassingame, *The Slave Community* (New York, 1972), Albert Raboteau, *Slave Religion* (New York, 1978), and Lawrence Levine *Black Culture and Black Consciousness* (New York, 1977). Although I have some reservations about his techniques, Eugene Genovese's *Roll, Jordan, Roll: The World the Slaveholders Made* (New York, 1974), is helpful in giving a coherent picture of the experience of slaves. *Roll, Jordan, Roll* does, however, go significantly beyond its sources and misses, I think, much of the struggle and pain endemic to slavery.

Five states studies of slavery gave insight into the differences within the institution. The best of these is James Sellers, *Slavery in Alabama* (Birmingham, 1950). The others include Chase Mooney, *Slavery in Tennessee* (Bloomington, 1957), Charles Sydnor, *Slavery in Mississippi* (New York, 1933), Caleb Patterson, *The Negro in Tennessee* (Austin, 1922), and John Coleman, *Slavery Times in Kentucky* (Chapel Hill, 1940).

Several studies of antislavery and reform in the Southwest and South give some perspective to this study. Niels Sonne, *Liberal Kentucky* (New York, 1939), is the best work of intellectual history written about this region, with subtle and persuasive analysis of the rise and decline of the intellectual elite in Lexington. The one reservation I have regarding Sonne's work is that he fails to place his elite into the context of the frontier experience well enough, leaving the unwary reader with the sense of an Arden south of the Ohio. Asa Martin, *The Antislavery Movement in Kentucky prior to 1850* (Louisville, 1919), is the only detailed study of abolitionism in the region, but pieces of the story also appear in Carl Degler, *The Other South* (New York, 1974). I also found helpful Clement Eaton, *The Freedom-of-Thought Struggle in the Old South* (reprint, New York, 1964), which for years was the only important proof that the antebellum South had a complex intellectual history.

Several histories of the broader antislavery and reform movements helped focus my understanding of the events in the Southwest. Gilbert Barnes, *The Antislavery Impulse* (New York, 1931), remains the key work for understanding the movement, while Aileen Kraditer, *Means and Ends in American Abolition* New York, 1969) and Lewis Perry, *Radical Abolitionism: Anarchy and the Government of God in Antislavery Thought* (Ithaca, 1973), brilliantly rebut Barnes's attack on the anarchist strain. Clifford Griffin, *Their Brothers' Keepers: Stewardship in the United States, 1800-1865* (New Brunswick, 1960), gives the best picture of the general scope of the "benevolent empire," whereas Bertram Wyatt-Brown, *Lewis Tappan and the Evangelical War against Slavery* (Cleveland, 1969), fills in the human dimension of the movement. Also related to the northern reform movement, Whitney Cross, *The Burned-Over District* (Ithaca, 1950), influenced my study in many ways. Cross explains both the development of a regional culture and the nature of the reform spirit in the great tinderbox of antebellum American life. Finally, two books that give a clear analysis of the problem of slavery for American religion are Donald Mathews, *Slavery and Methodism* (Princeton, 1965), and T. E. Drake, *Quakers and Slavery in America* (New Haven, 1950).

A large number of books depict life in the Old Southwest. Thomas D. Clark's many works provide insight into the day-to-day life of the frontier, although his writings tend to stress anecdote over analysis. His most useful and entertaining work is probably *The Rampaging Frontier* (reprint, Bloomington, 1964). Clark's work should be read in tandem with Arthur K. Moore, *The Frontier Mind* (Lexington, 1951), which provides less richness of detail but much more analysis. Several state political studies are necessary reading for a full understanding of the unique position of this region. Two books by Thomas Abernethy are dated but have a great feel for the political atmosphere of the region: *The Formative Period in Alabama* (Tuscaloosa, 1965), and the *From Frontier to Plantation in Tennessee* (reprint, Tuscaloosa, 1967). Theodore Jack, *Sectionalism and Party Politics in Alabama, 1819-1842* (Menasha, Wis. 1919), gives a thorough presentation of the complexities of Alabama political life; a similar close analysis of Mississippi politics is Edwin Miles, *Jacksonian Democracy in Mississippi* (Chapel Hill, 1960).

Four categories of primary sources are necessary reading for any understanding of religion and its relation to slavery in this region. The first and most important is church records. These include individual church and circuit minutes, which are available for the Baptists and Presbyterians in great quantities and very scarce for the Methodists. Often equally useful are local and state organizational reports, including association, presbytery, synod, and convention records, which give a broader view of the needs and interests of the churches. A second category is biographical information, coming from individual papers in archives (such as the invaluable Phillip Fall papers), memoirs, and diaries. Unfortunately, overemphasis of the few surviving records in this category can distort accounts of southwestern churches, stressing such well-documented figures as Basil Manley, Jr., for example, at the expense of equally important figures for whom few papers have survived. Third, controversial literature abounds in this region, and I have used it, in this study, less for its own sake then as a means of understanding the attitudes of the clergy. A number of very interesting theological studies might well arise from this literature, however, especially from the struggle between radicals and conservatives in the Second Great Awakening. A final and critical body of source material is the denominational journals, which provide fascinating insight into the interests of the editors and, to a great extent, the needs and desires of the clergy and laity. Unfortunately, the great body of denominational journals in the Southwest arose in the 1820s and 1830s and give little information on the important formative years of religion in the Old Southwest.

Selected Bibliography

Abbreviations

BHS   Baptist Historical Society, Rochester, New York.
HCSBC   Historical Commission of the Southern Baptist Church, Nashville, Tennessee.
HFPC   Historical Foundation of the Presbyterian Church, Montreat, North Carolina.

Primary Sources

MANUSCRIPTS

Bagwell, James E. "James Hall." HFPC.

Barrow, David. "Diary." Southern Baptist Theological Seminary, Louisville, Kentucky.

Blythe, James. Papers. Presbyterian Historical Society, Philadelphia, Pennsylvania.

Coffin, Charles. "Tennessee Journal." 1800-1822. Presbyterian Historical Society, Philadelphia, Pennsylvania.

Fall, Phillip S. Collection (microfilm). Disciples of Christ Historical Society, Nashville, Tennessee.

Hall, John. Letter about Gideon Blackburne, HFPC.

Hickman, William. "A Short Account of My Life and Travels," Southern Baptist Theological Seminary, Louisville Kentucky.

Howe, Joseph. Papers. Presbyterian Historical Society, Philadelphia, Pennsylvania.

Littlejohn, John. "Journal." Methodist Historical Society, Lake Junaluska, North Carolina.

Logan, James. Papers. Presbyterian Historical Society, Philadelphia, Pennsylvania.

Lyle, John. "Diary and Journal of a Missionary Tour within the Bounds of the Cumberland Presbytery Performed in the Year 1805." HFPC.

Manley, Basil. "Diary" (microfilm). BHS.

Marshall, Robert. Papers. Presbyterian Historical Society, Philadelphia, Pennsylvania.

McAnnally, David Rice. "Diary," Methodist Historical Society, Lake Junaluska, North Carolina.

McChord, James. Papers. Presbyterian Historical Society, Philadelphia, Pennsylvania.

Norton, Herman. "Life Story of Phillip Fall." Disciples of Christ Historical Society, Nashville, Tennessee.

Rankin, John. "Autobiography. HFPC.

Ray, John. "Memoirs." Methodist Historical Society, Lake Junaluska, North Carolina.

Rice, David. "Will." Presbyterian Historical Society, Philadelphia, Pennsylvania.

INDIVIDUAL CHURCH RECORDS

Alabama

Antioch Baptist Church (1833-60) (microfilm). HCSBC.

Bethsalem Presbyterian Church (1835-60). HFPC.

Carmel Presbyterian Church (1838-60). HFPC.

Centre Ridge Presbyterian Church (1844-60). HFPC.

Concord Presbyterian Church (1822-60). HFPC.

Elizabeth Presbyterian Church (1844-60). HFPC.

Hickory Grove Baptist Church (1844-56). (microfilm). HCSBC.

Mesopotamia Presbyterian Church (1848-57). HFPC.

Mount Moriah Baptist Church (1827-44) (microfilm). HCSBC.

Oakgrove Presbyterian Church (1837-60). HFPC.

Philadelphia Presbyterian Church (1841-60). HFPC.

Springhill Baptist Church (1833-60) (microfilm). HCSBC.

Kentucky

Bardstown First Presbyterian Church (1812-60) (microfilm). University of Kentucky, Lexington.

Bethel Presbyterian Church (1823-60) (microfilm). University of Kentucky, Lexington.

Bethlehem Baptist Church (1805-59) (microfilm). HCSBC.

Clear Creek Presbyterian Church (1828-60) (microfilm). University of Kentucky, Lexington.

Concord Presbyterian Church (1822-60) (microfilm). University of Kentucky, Lexington.

Dandridge Baptist Church (1786-1842) (microfilm). HCSBC.

Davis Presbyterian Church (1820-40). HFPC.

Greenup Union Presbyterian Church (1817-60). HFPC.

Louisville First Christian Church (Baptist) (1830-40) (microfilm). HCSBC.

Louisville First Presbyterian Church (1817-60). HFPC.

Mt. Zion Presbyterian Church (1823-60). HFPC.

New Concord Presbyterian Church (1813-43). HFPC.

New Providence Presbyterian Church (1812-43). HFPC.

Old Salem Baptist Church (1805-60) (microfilm). HCSBC.

Pisgah Baptist Church (1828-60). HFPC.

Salem Presbyterian Church (1819-60). HFPC.

Sand Run Baptist Church (1819-60) (microfilm). HCSBC.

Severns Valley Baptist Church (1788-1880) (microfilm). HCSBC.

Walnut Hill Presbyterian Church (1818-60). HFPC.

West Fork Meeting House (1803-22) (microfilm). HCSBC.

Yelvington Baptist Church (1813-33) (microfilm). HCSBC.

Mississippi

Bethany Presbyterian Church (1818-60). HFPC.

Bethel Presbyterian Church (1829-40). HFPC.

Errata Presbyterian Church (1839-60). HFPC.

Fellowship Baptist Church (1838-60) (microfilm). HCSBC.

Good Hope Presbyterian Church (1839-60). HFPC.

Hopewell Presbyterian Church (1846-60). HFPC.

Louisville First Baptist Church (1835-53) (microfilm). HCSBC.

Monroe Presbyterian Church (1826-60). HFPC.

Philadelphus Presbyterian Church (1821-52). HFPC.

Pisgah Presbyterian Church (1823-60). HFPC.

Salem Baptist Church (1815-34) (microfilm). HCSBC.

Unity Presbyterian Church (1832-60). HFPC.

Tennessee

Dumplin Creek Baptist Church (1797-1860) (microfilm). HCSBC.

Ebenezer Presbyterian Church (1823-60). HFPC.

Franklin Presbyterian Church (1810-48). HFPC.

Knoxville First Presbyterian Church (1816-37) (microfilm). Tennessee Historical Society, Nashville.

Knoxville Second Presbyterian Church (1841-60) (microfilm). Tennessee Historical Society, Nashville.

Murfreesboro Presbyterian Church (1812-60). HFPC.

Nashville First Baptist Church (1820-60) (microfilm). HCSBC.

Nashville Old School Baptist Church (1839-60) (microfilm). HCSBC.

Ponds Creek Baptist Church (1824-60) (microfilm). HCSBC.

Red River Baptist Church (1791-1826) (microfilm). HCSBC.

Sinking Creek Baptist Church (1803-60) (microfilm). HCSBC.

Slate Creek Baptist Church (1812-60) (microfilm). Tennessee Historical Society, Nashville.

Turnbull Primitive Baptist Church (1806-60) (microfilm). Tennessee Historical Society, Nashville.

Wilson Creek Primitive Baptist Church (1804-60) (microfilm). HCSBC.

Virginia

Caskey's Fork Meeting House (1818-56). BHS.

Denominational Records

Baptists

Alabama State Convention, *Proceedings*, N.p., 1844.

Anderson Association (1842-60). BHS.

Boone's Creek Association (1822-62). BHS.

Bracken Association (1803-60). BHS.

Campbell County Baptist Association (1830-53). BHS.

Concord Association (1831-60). BHS.

Cumberland River Association (1815-60). BHS.

Elkhorn Association (1785-1860). BHS.

Franklin Association (1815-56). BHS.

Freedom Association (1845-46). BHS.

Gasper River Association (1812-58). BHS.

Goshen Association (1818-59). BHS.

Green River Association (1800-59). BHS.

Greenup Association (1845-58). BHS.

Laurel River Association (1843-59). BHS.

Liberty Association (1840-59). BHS.

Licking Association (1814-59). BHS.
Licking-Locust Association (1807). BHS.
Little Bethel Association (1836-49). BHS.
Little River Association (1829-59). BHS.
Long Run Association (1802-59). BHS.
Middle District Association (1838-58). BHS.
Mississippi Baptist Association, *A Republication of the Minutes of the Mississippi Baptist Association, From Its Organization in 1806 to the Present Time.* New Orleans: Hinton & Co., (1849).
Mt. Olivet Association (1848-59). BHS.
Nelson Association (1848-59). BHS.
Russell Creek Association (1804-59). BHS.
Salem Association (1802-59). BHS.
South Concord Association (1825-59). BHS.
South District Association (1807-57). BHS.
Sulphur Fork Association (1826). BHS.
Tates Creek Association (1824-59). BHS.
Ten Mile Association (1831-59). BHS.
Union Association (1840-59). BHS.
West Union Association (1834-57). BHS.

Methodists

Alabama Conference (1852-60), Liberty of Congress, Washington, D.C.
Holston Conference (1824-60), Liberty of Congress, Washington, D.C.
Minutes of the Annual Conferences of the Methodist Episcopal Church (1784-1860). 4 vols. New York: T. Mason and J. Lane, (1840-56).
Western Conference, *Rise of Methodism in the West, Being the Journal of the Western Conference,* ed. William Sweet. New York: Methodist Book Concern (1920).

Presbyterians

Alabama Presbytery (1821-27). HFPC.
Alabama Synod (1837-49, 1857-60). HFPC.
East Alabama Presbytery (1842-60). HFPC.
East Mississippi Presbytery (1855-59). HFPC.
Ebenezer Presbytery (1820-42). Presbyterian Historical Society, Philadelphia.
Kentucky Presbytery (1802-59). Presbyterian Theological Seminary, Louisville.
Kentucky Synod (1802-60). Presbyterian Theological Seminary, Louisville.
Louisville Presbytery (1815-60). HFPC.

Memphis Synod (1847-57). HFPC.

Mississippi Synod, *Extracts from the Records.* New Orleans: D. Davies & Son, 1849.

Mississippi Synod, Minutes. Jackson, Miss., 1855.

Mississippi Synod (1857-60). HFPC.

Mississippi and South Alabama Synod, *Extracts from the Records.* Jackson: Clarion Steam, 1880.

Nashville Synod (1851-60). HFPC.

North Alabama Presbytery (1825-44). HFPC.

"Original" Cumberland Presbytery, Minutes, Louisville, 1906.

Transylvania Presbytery (1786-1855). HFPC.

Tuscumbia Presbytery (1849-60). HFPC.

West Lexington Presbytery (1799-1860). HFPC.

BOOKS

American Baptist Register. New York, 1856.

Ashworth, Henry. *A Tour in the United States, Cuba and Canada.* London: A. W. Bennett, 1861.

Baird, Robert. *View of the Valley of the Mississippi, or, The Emigrant's and Traveller's Guide to the West.* Philadelphia: H. S. Tanner, 1832.

Baldwin, Samuel Davies. *Dominion, or the Unity and Trinity of the Human Race, with the Divine Political Constitution of the World, and the Divine Rights of Shem, Ham and Japheth.* Nashville: E. Stevenson and F. A. Owen, 1857.

Bascom, Henry B. *Methodism and Slavery.* Frankfort, Ky.: Hodges, Todd & Pruett, 1845.

Benedict, David. *The General History of the Baptist Denomination in America and Other Parts of the World.* Boston, 1813.

Bibb, Henry. *Life in Slavery.* N.p., 1849.

Bishop, Robert. *An Apology for Calvinism.* Lexington: Daniel Bradford, 1804.

——. *A Discourse Occasioned by the Death of Rev'd James McChord.* Lexington: Thomas T. Skillman, 1821.

——. *A Legacy to Vacant Congregations.* Lexington: Daniel Bradford, 1804.

Blanchard, J., and N. R. Rice. *A Debate on Slavery, Held on the First, Second, Third and Sixth Days of Oct., 1845, in the City of Cincinnati.* Cincinnati: William H. Moore, 1846.

Blythe, James. *A Portrait of the Times.* Lexington: Thomas T. Skillman, 1814.

Booty, James. *Three Months in Canada and the United States*. London: By the Author, 1862.

Buck, William C. *The Slavery Question*. Louisville: Harney, Hughes & Hughes, 1849.

——. *Theology: The Philosophy of Religion*. Nashville: South-Western Publishing House, 1857.

Cameron, Archibald. *An Appeal to the Scriptures for Their Decision Relative to the Design, Extent and Effect of the Propitiation Made by Jesus Christ*. Frankfort: Johnston & Pleasants, 1811.

——. *A Defence of the Doctrines of Grace, in a Series of Letters to Judge Davidge*. Shelbyville, Ky.: Cox & Ballard, 1816.

Campbell, John P. *The Doctrine of Justification by Imputed Righteousness Considered, in Letters to a Friend*. Danville: Ogilsby & Demaree, 1805.

——. *The Pelagian Detected; or A Review of Mr. Craighead's Letters, Addressed to the Public and the Author*. Lexington: Thomas T. Skillman, 1811.

——. *A Sermon . . . in Which Christian Baptism, in Its Primitive Mode of Administration and as It Respects Both Infant and Adult Subjects, Is Largely Treated*. Lexington: Thomas Skillman, 1811.

——. *Strictures on Two Letters*. Lexington: Daniel Bradford, 1805.

——. *Vindex, or the Doctrines of the Scriptures Vindicated, against the Reply of Mr. Stone*. Lexington: Daniel Bradford, 1806.

Capers, Bishop. *Short Sermons, and True Tales*. Nashville: Southern Methodist Publishing House, 1885.

Cartwright, Peter. *Autobiography*. New York: Carlton & Parter, 1856.

Case of Maccalla against Blythe, Tried before the Synod of Kentucky, in September, 1814. Chillicothe, Ohio: James Barnes, 1814.

Clark, Christopher. *A Shock to Shakerism; or a Serious Refutation of the Idolatrous Divinity of Ann Lee*. Richmond, Ky.: T. W. Ruble & Son, 1812.

Clark, Elmer T., ed. *The Journal and Letters of Francis Asbury*, 3 vols. Nashville: Abington Press, 1958.

Craig, Elijah. *A Few Remarks on the Errors That Are Maintained in the Christian Churches of the Present Day*. Lexington: James H. Stewart, 1801.

Craig, James. *Address Delivered on the Occasion of Laying the Cornerstone of Christ Church, Lexington, Kentucky*. Lexington: Scrugham & Dunlop, 1847.

Cuming, Fortescue. *Sketches of a Tour to the Western Country, through the States of Ohio and Kentucky*. Pittsburgh: Cramer, Spear & Eichboum, 1810.

Selected Bibliography

Dagg, John L. *Autobiography*. Rome, Ga.: J. F. Shamklin, 1886.

Doak, John *A Farewell Sermon*. Jonesborough, Tenn.: George Wilson, 1803.

Drake, Daniel. *Pioneer Life in Kentucky*. Cincinnati: R. Clarke, 1870.

Duties of Masters to Servants: Three Premium Essays. Charleston: Southern Baptist Publishing House, 1851.

Ewing, Fenis. *A Series of Lectures, on the Most Important Subjects in Divnity*. Fayetteville, Tenn.: E. & J. B. Hill, 1827.

Faux, William. *Memorable Days in America*. London, 1823.

Fishback, James. *A Defence of the Elkhorn Association and the Terms of General Union among the Baptists*. Lexington: Thomas Skillman, 1822.

——. *An Oration Delivered in the First Presbyterian Church in the Town of Lexington, Kentucky on the 4th Day of July, 1816*. Lexington: Thomas Skillman, 1816.

Flint, James. *Letters from America*. Edinburgh: W. & C. Tait, 1822.

Flint, William. *Memorable Days in America: Being a Journal of a Tour through the United States*. London: W. Simpkin & R. Marshall, 1823.

Flower, Richard, *Letters from Lexington and Illinois*. London: C. Trulon, 1819.

Gano, Hohn. *Biographical Memoirs*. New York: Southwich & Hardcastle, 1806.

Gospel News, or a Brief Account of the Revival of Religion in Kentucky, and Several Other Parts of the United States. Baltimore, 1801.

Graves, J. R. *The Great Iron Wheel, or, Republicanism Backwards and Christianity Reversed*. Nashville: Graves, Marks & Rutland, 1855.

Hall, James. *A Brief History of the Mississippi Territory*. Salisbury: Francis Coupee, 1801.

Head, Jesse. *A Reply to the Arguments Advanced by the Rev. Thomas Cleland*. Lexington: Joseph Charless, 1805.

Hutchison, J. R. *Reminiscences, Sketches and Addresses*. Houston: E. H. Cushing, 1874.

Journal of the Faithful Servant of the Christ Charles Osborne. Cincinnati: Achilles Pugh, 1854.

Journal of the First Constitutional Convention of Kentucky. Lexington: State Bar Association of Kentucky, 1942.

Kentucky Synod. *A Serious Address to the Churches under Their Care*. Lexington: Daniel Bradford, 1804.

Marshall, Robert, and John Thompson. *A Brief Historical Account of Sundry Things in the Doctrines and State of the Christian, or as It Is Commonly Called, the Newlight Church*. Cincinnati: J. Carpenter, 1811.

McAnnally, David Rice. *A Statement of Facts in Regard to the Official Acts of the Methodist Episcopal Church, on the Subject of Slavery.* St. Louis: Methodist Book Depository, 1856.

McChord, James. *The Body of Christ.* Lexington: Thomas T. Skillman, 1814.

———. *The Morning Star, or Precurser of the Millennium, a Sermon Delivered in the Presbyterian Church of Lexington, the 17th of July, 1813.* Lexington: S. Penn, 1813.

———. *National Safety: A Sermon Delivered in the Legislative Hall, before the Honors the Legislature of Kentucky (in pursuance of their appointment) on Thursday, the 12th Jan. 1815 Observed by Them as a Day of National Fasting.* Lexington: Thomas T. Skillman, 1815.

M'Henry, Barnabas. *Remarks on Some Passages in a Periodical Work, Printed in Lexington, K., Entitled "The Evangelical Record and Western Review."* Lexington: Smith, 1813.

McNemar, Richard. *The Kentucky Revival.* Cincinnat: John W. Broune, 1807.

McTyeire, H. N. *Duties of Christian Masters.* Nashville: Southern Methodist Publishing House, 1859.

Michaux, F. A. *Travels to the West of the Allegheny Mountains in the States of Ohio, Kentucky and Tennessee.* London: B. Crosby, 1805.

Mills, Samuel. *Missionary Tour through That Part of the United States Which Lies West of the Allegheny Mountains.* Andover: Flagg & Gould, 1815.

Morris, Thomas Asbury. *Miscellany: Consisting of Essays, Biographical Sketches and Notes of Travel.* Cincinnati: L. Swormstedt & J. H. Power, 1852.

Ogden, George W. *Letters from the West.* New Bedford: Melcher & Rogers, 1823.

Olmsted, Frederick Law. *A Journey in the Back Country.* 1860; reprint, New York: Schocken Press, 1970.

Pendleton, J. M. *Reminiscences of a Long Life.* Louisville: Baptist Book Concern, 1891.

Presbytery of Springfield. *An Apology for Renouncing the Jurisdiction of the Synod of Kentucky.* Lexington: Joseph Charless, 1804.

Rankin, Adam. *Review of the Noted Revival in Kentucky.* N.p., 1803.

Rice, David. *An Epistle to the Citizens of Kentucky, Professing Christianity.* Lexington: Daniel Bradford, 1805.

———. *An Essay on Baptism.* Baltimore: William Goddard, 1789.

———. *A Sermon on the Present Revival of Religion, etc. in the Country.* Lexington: Joseph Charless, 1803.

———. *Slavery Inconsistent with Justice and Good Policy.* Philadelphia: Parry Hall, 1792.

Rivers, Richard H. *Elements of Moral Philosophy.* Nashville: Southern Methodist Publishing House, 1859.

Rogers, George. *Memoranda of the Experience, Labors and Travels of a Universalist Preacher.* Cincinnati: John A. Gurley, 1845.

Royall, Anne. *Letters from Alabama on Various Subjects.* Washington, 1839.

Shapiro, Henry D., and Zane L. Miller, eds. *Physician to the West: Selected Writings of Daniel Drake on Science and Society.* Lexington: University of Kentucky Press, 1970.

Smith, James. *Remarkable Occurrences, Lately Discovered among the People Called Shakers; of a Treasonous and Barbarous Nature, or Shakerism Developed.* Paris, Ky.: Joel R. Lyle, 1810.

——. *Shakerism Detected: Their Erroneous and Treasonous Proceedings and False Publications, Contained in Different Newspapers, Exposed to Public View by the Depositions of Ten Different Persons Living in Various Parts of the States of Kentucky and Ohio.* Paris, Ky.: Joel R. Lyle, 1810.

Smylie, James. *A Review of a Letter from the Presbytery of Chillicothe to the Presbytery of Mississippi on the Subject of Slavery.* Woodville, Miss.: William A. Morris, 1836.

Stone, Barton W. *Atonement.* Lexington: Joseph Charless, 1805.

——. *A Reply to John P. Campbell's Strictures on Atonement.* Lexington: Joseph Charless, 1805.

Tarrant, Carter. *The Substance of a Discourse Delivered in the Town of Versailles, Woodford County, State of Kentucky, April 20, 1806.* Lexington: Daniel Bradford, 1806.

Taylor, John. *A History of Ten Baptist Churches, of Which the Author Has Been Alternatively a Member.* Frankfort: J. H. Holeman, 1823.

——. *Thoughts on Missions.* Franklin County, Ky.: N.p., 1820.

Thomas, David. *The Observer Trying the Great Reformation.* Lexington: John Bradford, 1802.

Travis, Joseph. *Autobiography.* Nashville: E. Stevenson & F. A. Owen, 1856.

Welby, Adlard. *A Visit to North America and English Settlements in Illinois.* London: J. Drury, 1821.

Secondary Sources

CHURCH AND DENOMINATIONAL HISTORIES; BIOGRAPHIES OF MINISTERS

Acorns to Oaks: The Story of Nashville Baptist Association and Its Affiliated Churches. N.p., n.d.

Alexander, J. E. *A Brief History of the Synod of Tennessee, from 1817–1850.* Philadelphia: MacCalla, 1890.

Andrews, Edward D. *The People Called Shakers: A Search for the Perfect Society.* New York: Oxford University Press, 1953.

Arnold, W. E. *A History of Methodism in Kentucky.* N.p.: Herald Press, 1935.

Baim, Frank. "The Contribution of John R. Howard to the Reformation of the Nineteenth Century." Ph.D. dissertation, Butler University, 1948.

Baird, Samuel. *A History of the New School and of the Questions Involved in the Disruption of the Presbyterian Church in 1838.* Philadelphia: Claxton, Remsen & Haffelfinger, 1868.

Bassett, Ancel. *A Concise History of the Methodist Protestant Church.* Pittsburgh: William McCracken, 1877.

Baxter, William. *Life of Elder William Scott.* Nashville: Gospel Advocate Co., n.d.

Bishop, Robert. *An Outline of the History of the Church in the State of Kentucky, during a Period of Forty Years; Containing the Memoirs of Rev. David Rice.* Lexington: Thomas T. Skillman, 1824.

Boles, John. *The Great Revival in the South.* Lexington: University of Kentucky Press, 1972.

Bond, John. *History of the Baptist Concord Association of Middle Tennessee and North Alabama.* Nashville: Graves, Marks, 1860.

Bond, Richard. *Brief Biographical Sketches of Some of the Early Ministers of the Cumberland Presbyterian Church.* Nashville: Southern Methodist Publishing House, 1867.

Boyd, Jesse. *A Popular History of the Baptists in Mississippi.* Jackson: Baptist Press, 1930.

A Brief Account of the Life of the Rev. Francis Hamilton Porter, Late a Member of the Presbytery of Tuscaloosa. N.p., 1845.

Broadley, Sidney. *The Life of Bishop Richard Whatcoat.* Louisville Pentecostal Publishing Co., 1869.

Broadus, John. *Memoir of James Petigru Boyce.* Louisville: Baptist Book Concern, 1893.

Brooks, John. *The Life and Times of the Rev. John Brooks.* Nashville: Christian Advocate Office, 1848.

Brown, John Thomas, ed. *Churches of Christ.* Louisville: John Morton, 1904.

Browning, D. P. *One Hundred Years of Church History.* N.p., 1922.

Burnett, J. J. *Sketches of Tennessee's Pioneer Baptist Preachers.* Nashville: Press of Marshall and Bruce Co., 1919.

Burroughs, P. E. *The Spiritual Conquest of the Second Frontier: The Biography of an Achieving Church, 1820-1942*. Nashville: Broadman Press, 1942.

Calico, Forrest. *History of Garrard County, Kentucky, and Its Churches*. New York: Hobson Book Press, 1947.

Cleveland, Catherine. *The Great Revival in the West*. Chicago: University of Chicago Press, 1916.

Clifford, Cecil. "The Role of Basil Manley, 1798-1868, in the Establishment of Furman University and the Southern Baptist Theological Seminary." Ph.D. dissertation, Furman University, 1962.

Conkwright, S. J. *History of the Churches of Boone's Creek Baptist Association of Kentucky*. Winchester, Ky., 1923.

Crimson, Leo, ed. *Baptists in Kentucky, 1776-1976*. Middletown, Ky.: Kentucky Baptist Convention, 1977.

Crook Roger. "The Ethical Emphases of the Editors of Baptist Journals Published in the Southwestern Region of the United States up to 1865." Ph.D. dissertation, Southern Baptist Theological Seminary, 1947.

Crow, Mattie Lou Teague. *Ashville Baptist Church and Its Beginnings*. Birmingham: Banner Press, 1965.

Cummings. A. W. *The Early Schools of Methodism*. New York: Phillips & Hume, 1886.

Darnell, Ermina Jett. *Forks of Elkhorn Church*. Louisville: Standard Printing Co., 1946.

Davidson, Robert. *History of the Presbyterian Church in the State of Kentucky*. New York: Robert Carter, 1847.

Diamond Jubilee of the General Association of Colored Baptists in Kentucky. Louisville: American Baptist, 1943.

Donan, P. *Memoir of Jacob Creath, Jr., to Which Is Appended the Biography of Elder Jacob Creath, Sr.* Cincinnati: Chase & Hale, 1877.

Durham, John, and John Ramond, eds. *Baptist Builders in Louisiana*. Shreveport: Durham-Ramond, 1934.

Elliott, Charles. *History of the Great Secession from the Methodist Episcopal Church in the Year 1845, Eventuating in the Organization of the New School, Entitled the "Methodist Episcopal Church, South."* Cincinnati: Swormstedt & Poe, 1855.

Ewell, John. *Life of Rev. William Keele*. Noah, Tenn.: W. J. Stephenson, 1884.

Fife, Robert. "Alexander Campbell and the Christian Church in the Slavery Controversy." Ph.D. dissertation, Indiana University, 1960.

Finley, James B. *Sketches of Western Methodism: Biographical, Historical and Miscellaneous; Illustrative of Pioneer Life*. Edited by W. P. Strictland. Cincinnati: Methodist Book Concern, 1854.

Fortune, Alonzo Willard. *The Disciples in Kentucky*. Published by the Convention of the Christian Churches in Kentucky, 1932.

Foster, L. S. *Mississippi Baptist Preachers*. St. Louis: National Baptist Publishing Co., 1895.

Garrett, Lewis. *Recollections of the West*. 2 vols. Nashville: W. Cameron, 1834.

Garrison, Wilfred, and Alfred De Groot. *The Disciples of Christ, a History*. St. Louis: Christian Board of Publication, 1948.

Grime, J. N. *History of Middle Tennessee Baptists*. Nashville: Baptist and Reflector, 1902.

Hailey, O. L. *J. R. Graves: Life, Times and Teachings*. Nashville, 1929.

Harmon, M. T. *A History of the Christian Churches (Disciples of Christ) in Mississippi*. Aberdeen, Miss., 1929.

Henkle, Moses. *The Life of Henry Bidleman Bascom*. Nashville: Publishing House of the Methodist Episcopal Church, South, 1894.

History and True Position of the Church of Christ in Nashville. Nashville: Cameron & Fall, 1854.

Holcombe, Hosea. *A History of the Rise and Progress of the Baptists in Alabama*. Philadelphia: King & Baird, 1840.

Horne, Linwood. "A Study of the Life and Work of R. B. C. Howell." Ph.D. dissertation, Southern Baptist Theological Seminary, 1958.

Howe, George. *History of the Presbyterian Church in South Carolina*. Columbia: W. J. Duffie, 1883.

Huey, Thomas. *Ruchama, the Story of a Church 1819–1945*. Birmingham: Birmingham Printing Co., 1946.

Humphrey, Edward. *Memoirs of the Rev. Thomas Cleland, D.D., Compiled from His Private Papers*. Cincinnati: Moore, Wilstack, Keys, 1859.

Irby, Henry Clay. *History of the First Baptist Church, Jackson, Tennessee, 1837-1912*. Jackson: McCowat-Mercer, n.d.

James, Richard. "The Disciples of Christ in Alabama, 1830-60." Ph.D. Dissertation, University of Chicago, 1937.

Jones, John. *A Complete History of Methodism as Connected with the Mississippi Conference of the Methodist Episcopal Church, South*. Nashville: Publishing House of the Methodist Episcopal Church, South, 1908.

Jones, Labon. *A Brief Memoir of the Rev. Samuel Ayres Noel, Minister of the Gospel of the Cumberland Presbyterian Church; with Sermons of Important Practical Subjects*. Louisville: C. C. Hull & Bros., 1846.

Keller, Charles R. *The Second Great Awakening in Connecticut*. New Haven: Yale University Press, 1943.

Kendall, William Frederick. *A History of the Tennessee Baptist Convention*.

Brentwood, Tenn.: Executive Board of the Tennessee Baptist Convention, 1974.

Knott, W. T. *History of the Presbyterian Church in What Is Now Marion County and the City of Lebanon, Kentucky.* N.p., n.d.

Lawrence, Matthew. *John Mason Peck, the Pioneer Missionary.* New York: Fortuny's, 1940.

Lawrence, Spencer. "David Rice, 1733-1816: A Biographical Study in Religious and Social Reform." Master's thesis, Southern Illinois University, August 1966.

Lazenby, Marion E. *History of Methodism in Alabama and West Florida.* Published by the North Alabama Conference and Alabama–West Florida Conference of the Methodist Church, 1960.

Leavell, Z. T., and T. J. Bailey. *A Complete History of Mississippi Baptists from the Earliest Times.* 2 vols. Jackson: Mississippi Baptist Publishing Co., 1904.

Lee, Jesse. *A Short History of the Methodists in the United States of America; Beginning in 1766, and Continued till 1809.* Baltimore: Magill & Clime, 1810.

Lowry, David. *Life and Labors of the Late Rev. Robert Donnell, of Alabama, Minister of the Gospel in the Cumberland Presbyterian Church.* Alton, Ill.: S. V. Crossman, 1867.

Masters, Frank. *A History of Baptists in Kentucky.* Louisville: Kentucky Baptist Historical Society, 1953.

Masters, Lois W. *The Gospel Trail in Kentucky.* Louisville: Baptist State Board of Missions, n.d.

Mathews, Donald. *Religion in the Old South.* Chicago: University of Chicago Press, 1977.

——. *Slavery and Methodism.* Princeton: Princeton University Press, 1965.

Matlack, Lucius C. *The History of American Slavery and Methodism, from 1780 to 1849; and History of the Wesleyan Methodist Connection of America.* New York, 1849.

May, Henry F. *The Enlightenment in America.* New York: Oxford University Press, 1976.

May, Lynn. *The First Baptist Church of Nashville, Tennessee, 1820-1970.* Nashville, 1970.

McAnnally, D. R. *Life and Times of Rev. William Patton, and Annals of the Missouri Conference.* St. Louis: Methodist Book Depository, 1858.

McClintoch, John, ed. *Sketches of Eminent Methodist Ministers.* New York: Carlton & Phillips, 1854.

McFerrin, John. *History of Methodism in Tennessee*. 3 vols. Nashville: Publishing House of the Methodist Episcopal Church, South, 1869-73.

McTeer, Will A. *History of New Providence Presbyterian Church, Maryville, Tennessee, 1786-1921*. Maryville: New Providence Church, 1921.

McTyeire, Holland. *A History of Methodism*. Nashville: Southern Methodist Publishing House, 1884.

Miller, Gene R. *A History of North Mississippi Methodism, 1820-1900*. Nashville: Parthenon Press, 1966.

Moore, W. T., ed. *The Living Pulpit of the Christian Church: A Series of Discourses, Doctrinal and Practical, from Representative Men among the Disciples of Christ*. Cincinnati: R. W. Carroll, 1868.

Mullins, Chaplain G. G., ed. *Caskey's Book: Lectures on Great Subjects, Selected from the Numerous Efforts of That Powerful Orator and Noble Veteran of the Cross, Thomas W. Caskey*. St. Louis: Christian Publishing Co., 1891.

Northcott, H. C. *Biography of Rev. Benjamin Northcott*. Cincinnati: Western Methodist Book Concern, 1875.

Norton, Herman. *Tennessee Christians: A History of the Christian Church (Disciples of Christ) in Tennessee*. Nashville: Reed, 1971.

Nowlin, William D. *Kentucky Baptist History, 1770–1922*. N.p.: Baptist Book Concern, 1922.

Paine, Robert. *Life and Times of William M'Kendree, Bishop of the Methodist Episcopal Church*. 2 vols. Nashville: Southern Methodist Publishing House, 1869–70.

Paris, John. *History of the Methodist Protestant Church*. Baltimore: Sherwood, 1849.

Phillips, Joseph W. "Jedidiah Morse: an Intellectual Biography." Ph.D. dissertation, University of California, Berkeley, 1978.

Posey, Walter B. "The Development of Methodism in the Old Southwest, 1783-1824." Ph.D. dissertation, Vanderbilt University, 1933.

———. *The Presbyterian Church in the Old Southwest, 1778-1838*. Richmond, Va.: John Knox Press, 1952.

———. *Religious Strife on the Southern Frontier*. Baton Rouge: Louisiana State University Press, 1965.

Purviance, Levi. *The Biography of Elder David Purviance*. Dayton: For the Author by B. F. and G. W. Ells, 1848.

Ranck, George W. *The Travelling Church: An Account of the Baptist Exodus from Virginia to Kentucky in 1781 under the Leadership of Rev. Lewis Craig and Capt. William Ellis*. Louisville: Press of the Baptist book Concern, 1891.

Selected Bibliography

Redford, A. H. *The History of Methodism in Kentucky.* 3 vols. Nashville: Southern Methodist Publishing House, 1868-70.

——. *History of the Organization of the Methodist Episcopal Church, South.* Nashville: A. H. Redford, 1875.

——. *Western Cavaliers: Embracing the History of the Methodist Episcopal Church in Kentucky from 1832 to 1844.* Nashville: Southern Methodist Publishing House, 1876.

Reid, Avery Hamilton. *Baptists in Alabama: Their Organization and Witness.* Montgomery, Ala.: Paragon Press, 1967.

Riley, B. F. *History of the Baptists of Alabama.* Birmingham: Roberts & Son, 1895.

Rivers, Robert. "The Early Life, Ministry, and Denominational Contributions of Basil Manley, Sr., 1798-1837." Ph.D. dissertation, Southeast Baptist Theological Seminary, 1959.

Rogers, John, ed. *The Biography of Barton W. Stone.* Cincinnati, 1847.

Rone, Wendell. *A History of the Daviess-McLean Baptist Association in Kentucky.* N.p., n.d.

Rothert, Otto, *A History of Unity Baptist Church, Muhlenberg County, Kentucky.* Louisville: John P. Morton, 1914.

Sanders, Robert Stuart. *Presbyterianism in Paris and Bourbon County, Kentucky, 1786-1961.* Louisville: Dunne Press, 1961.

Shakelford, Josephus. *History of the Muscle Shoals Baptist Association.* Trinity, Ala., 1891.

Simpson, Addison. *Life and Service of Reverend John Springer.* N.p., n.d.

Spender, J. H. *A History of Kentucky Baptists,* 2 vols. Cincinnati, 1885.

Summers, Thomas, ed. *Biographical Sketches of Eminent Itinerant Ministers Distinguished for the Most Part, as Pioneers of Methodism within the Bounds of the Methodist Episcopal Church, South.* Nashville: Southern Methodist Publishing House, 1859.

Taylor, O. W. *Early Tennessee Baptists, 1769-1832.* Nashville: Tennessee Baptist Convention, 1957.

Watson, George, and Mildred B. Watson. *History of the Christian Churches in the Alabama Area.* St. Louis: Bethany Press, 1965.

Weaver, Mary. *One Hundred Years—A Story of the First Baptist Church, Clinton, Tennessee.* Clinton, 1940.

Wilburn, James. *The Hazard of the Die: Tolbert Fanning and the Restoration Movement.* Austin, Tex.: Sweet Publishing Co., 1969.

Williams, John Augustus. *Life of Elder John Smith: With Some Account of the Rise and Progress of the Current Reformation.* St. Louis: Christian Board of Publication, 1879.

Selected Bibliography

GENERAL BOOKS

Abernethy, Thomas P. *The Formative Period in Alabama, 1815-1828.* Tuscaloosa: University of Alabama Press, 1965.
——. *From Frontier to Plantation in Tennessee.* 1932; reprint, Tuscaloosa: University of Alabama Press, 1967.
Adams, Alice. *The Neglected Period in American Antislavery.* 1908; reprint, Gloucester, Mass.: Peter Smith, 1964.
Barnes, Gilbert. *The Antislavery Impulse.* 1938; reprint, New York: Harcourt, Brace, 1964.
Birney, William. *James G. Birney and His Times.* New York: D. Appleton, 1890.
Bogart, William H. *Daniel Boone and the Hunters of Kentucky.* Auburn, N.Y.: Miller, Orton & Mulligan, 1854.
Butler, Mann. *A History of the Commonwealth of Kentucky.* Cincinnati: J. A. James, 1836.
Casseday, Ben. *The History of Louisville from Its Earliest Settlement till the Year 1852.* Louisville: Hull & Bros., 1852.
Chinn, George Morgan. *Kentucky Settlement and Statehood, 1750-1800.* Frankfort: Kentucky Historical Society, 1875.
Clark, Thomas D. *The Rampaging Frontier.* 1939; reprint, Bloomington: Indiana University Press, 1964.
——. *Three American Frontiers.* Lexington: University of Kentucky Press, 1968.
Clark, Willis G. *History of Education in Alabama, 1762-1889.* Contributions to American Educational History No. 8. Washington, D.C.: U.S. Government Printing Office, 1889.
Clayton, W. W. *History of Davidson County, Tennessee, with Illustrations and Biographical Sketches of Its Prominent Men and Pioneers.* Nashville: Charles Elder, 1971.
Coleman, J. Winston *Slavery Times in Kentucky.* Chapel Hill: University of North Carolina Press, 1940.
Davenport, F. Garvin. *Antebellum Kentucky.* Oxford, Ohio: Mississippi Valley Press, 1943.
Finley, Alexander. *The History of Russellville and Logan County, Kentucky, Which Is To Some Extent a History of Western Kentucky.* Russellville: O. C. Rhea, 1878.
Fladeland, Betty. *James Gillespie Birney, Slaveholder to Abolitionist.* Ithaca: Cornell University Press, 1955.
Flint, Timothy. *Biographical Memoir of Daniel Boone.* Cincinnati: G. Conclin, 1846.

——. *The History and Geography of the Mississippi Valley.* Cincinnati: E. H. Flint and L. R. Lincoln, 1832.

Gray, Lewis Cecil. *History of Agriculture in the Southern United States to 1860.* Washington, D.C.: Carnegie Institution, 1933.

Griffin, Clifford S. *Their Brothers' Keepers: Moral Stewardship in the United States, 1800-1865.* New Brunswick: Rutgers University Press, 1960.

Hall, James. *Sketches of the History, Life and Manners in the West.* Philadelphia: Harrison Hall, 1835.

Harrison, Lowell. *John Breckinridge, Jeffersonian Republican.* Louisville: Filson Club, 1969.

Hedrick, Charles, *Social and Economic Aspects of Slavery in the Transmontane prior to 1850.* Nashville: George Peabody College for Teachers, 1927.

History of the Ohio Falls Cities and Their Counties. Cleveland: L. A. Williams, 1882.

Hurd, John Codman. *The Law of Freedom and Bondage in the United States.* New York: D. Van Nostrand, 1862.

Jack, Theodore. *Sectionalism and Party Politics in Alabama, 1819-1842.* Menasha, Wisc.: George Banta, 1919.

Jenkins, William Sumner. *Pro-Slavery Thought in the Old South.* Chapel Hill: University of North Carolina Press, 1935.

Johnston, J. Stoddard, ed. *Memorial History of Louisville from Its Settlement to the Year 1896.* 2 vols. Chicago: American Biographical Publishing Co., 1896.

Jordan, Winthrop. *White over Black.* Chapel Hill: University of North Carolina Press, 1967.

Kincaid, Robert L. *The Wilderness Road.* New York: Bobbs-Merrill, 1947.

Little, John. *History of Butler County, Alabama.* Greenville, Ala.: J. G. Little, Jr., 1971.

Martin, Asa. *The Antislavery Movement in Kentucky prior to 1850.* Louisville: Filson Club, 1919.

McCormick, Richard R. *The Second American Party System.* Chapel Hill: University of North Carolina Press, 1966.

Miles, Edwin. *Jacksonian Democracy in Mississippi.* Chapel Hill: University of North Carolina Press, 1960.

Miller, Perry. *The Life of the Mind in America.* New York: Harcourt, Brace & World, 1965.

Mooney, Chase. *Slavery in Tennessee.* Bloomington: Indiana University Press, 1957.

Moore, Arthur K. *The Frontier Mind.* Lexington: University of Kentucky Press, 1957.

Moore, John Hebron. *Agriculture in Antebellum Mississippi.* New York: Bookman Associates, 1958.

Patterson, Caleb. *The Negro in Tennessee.* Austin: University of Texas Bulletin, 1922.

Perry, Lewis. *Radical Abolitionism: Anarchy and the Government of God in Antislavery Thought.* Ithaca: Cornell University Press, 1973.

Raboteau, Albert. *Slave Religion: The "Invisible Institution" in the Antebellum South.* New York: Oxford University Press, 1978.

Railey, William E. *History of Woodford County, Kentucky.* Baltimore: Regional Publishing Co., 1838.

Ranck, George W. *History of Lexington, Kentucky.* Cincinnati: Robert Clarke, 1972

Rothbard, Murray N. *The Panic of 1819.* New York: Columbia University Press, 1962.

Sellers, James Benson. *Slavery in Alabama.* Birmingham: University of Alabama Press, 1950.

Sillers, Florence W., comp. *History of Bolivar County, Mississippi.* Spartanburg, S.C.: Reprint Co., 1976. 1948; reprint,

Smith, Henry Clay. *Outline History of the Wilderness of Kentucky and Religious Movements of the Early Settlers of Our Country and the Church History of the North Middletown Community.* Paris, Ky.: Frank Remington, Printer, [1923].

Smith, Zachariah F. *The History of Kentucky from Its Earliest Discovery and Settlement to the Present Date.* Louisville: Prentice Press, 1895.

Sonne, Niels. *Liberal Kentucky.* New York: Columbia University Press, 1939.

Spraker, Hazel. *The Boone Family.* Rutland, Vt.: Tuttle, 1922.

Staudenraus, P. J. *The African Colonization Movement.* New York: Columbia University Press, 1961.

Sydnor, Charles. *Slavery in Mississippi.* New York: D. Appleton-Century, 1933.

Talbert, Charles G. *Benjamin Logan, Kentucky Frontiersman.* Lexington: University of Kentucky Press, 1962.

Townsend, John W. *Kentucky in American Letters.* Cedar Rapids: Torch Press, 1913.

——, ed. *O Rare Tom Johnson, Kentucky's First Poet.* Lexington: Bluegrass Bookshop, 1949.

Truett Randle B. *Trade and Travel around the Southern Appalachians before 1830.* Chapel Hill: University of North Carolina Press, 1935.

Tyler, Alice Felt. *Freedom's Ferment.* 1942; reprint New York: Harper & Row, 1962.

ARTICLES

Alexander, Thomas, et al. "The Basis of Alabama's Two-Party System." *Alabama Review* 19 (1966):243-276.

Allen, Jeffrey Brooke. "Were Southern White Critics of Slavery Racists? Kentucky and the Upper South, 1791-1824." *Journal of Southern History* 44 (1978):169-190.

"Biographical Sketch of David Rice." *Danville Quarterly Review* 4 (1864).

Martin, Asa. "The Antislavery Societies of Tennessee." *Tennessee Historical Magazine* 1 (1915):261-281.

Meyer, Leland. "The Great Crossings Church Records." *Register of the Kentucky State Historical Society* 34 (1936):15-28, 58-70.

Moody, V. Alton. "Early Religious Efforts in the Lower Mississippi Valley." *Mississippi Valley Historical Review* 22 (1935):161-176.

Moore, Margaret DesChamps. "Protestantism in the Mississippi Territory." *Journal of Mississippi History* 29 (1967): 358-370.

Morrow, Ralph. "The Great Revival, the West, and the Crisis of the Church." In *The Frontier Reexamined*, edited by John McDermot, pp. 65-78. Chicago: University of Chicago Press, 1967.

Opie, John. "James McGready: Theologian of Frontier Revivalism." *Church History* 34 (1965):445-456.

Owsley, Frank . "The Pattern of Migration and Settlement on the Southern Frontier." *Journal of Southern History* 11 (1945):147-176.

Posey, Walter. "Baptist Watch-Care in Early Kentucky." *Register of the Kentucky State Historical Society* 34 (1936):311-317.

Russell, C. Allyn. "The Rise and Decline of the Shakers." *New York History* 49 (1968):29-55.

Wyatt-Brown, Bertram. "The Antimission Movement in the Jacksonian South." *Journal of Southern History* 36 (1970):501-530.

Index

Index

Library of Congress Cataloging in Publication Data

Bailey, David T.
  Shadow on the church.

  Bibliography: p.
  Includes index.
  1. Slavery and the church. 2. Slavery—Southwest, Old—History.
  3. Southwest, Old—History.   I. Title
E441.B3   1985   261.8'34567   84-45795
ISBN 0-8014-1763-5 (alk. paper)